International and Development Education

The *International and Development Education Series* focuses on the complementary areas of comparative, international, and development education. Books emphasize a number of topics ranging from key international education issues, trends, and reforms to examinations of national education systems, social theories, and development education initiatives. Local, national, regional, and global volumes (single authored and edited collections) constitute the breadth of the series and offer potential contributors a great deal of latitude based on interests and cutting edge research. The series is supported by a strong network of international scholars and development professionals who serve on the International and Development Education Advisory Board and participate in the selection and review process for manuscript development.

SERIES EDITORS
John N. Hawkins
Professor Emeritus, University of California, Los Angeles
Senior Consultant, IFE 2020 East West Center

W. James Jacob
Assistant Professor, University of Pittsburgh
Director, Institute for International Studies in Education

PRODUCTION EDITOR
Heejin Park
Project Associate, Institute for International Studies in Education

INTERNATIONAL EDITORIAL ADVISORY BOARD
Clementina Acedo, *UNESCO's International Bureau of Education, Switzerland*
Philip G. Altbach, *Boston University, USA*
Carlos E. Blanco, *Universidad Central de Venezuela*
Sheng Yao Cheng, *National Chung Cheng University, Taiwan*
Ruth Hayhoe, *University of Toronto, Canada*
Wanhua Ma, *Peking University, China*
Ka-Ho Mok, *University of Hong Kong, China*
Christine Musselin, *Sciences Po, France*
Yusuf K. Nsubuga, *Ministry of Education and Sports, Uganda*
Namgi Park, *Gwangju National University of Education, Republic of Korea*
Val D. Rust, *University of California, Los Angeles, USA*
Suparno, *State University of Malang, Indonesia*
John C. Weidman, *University of Pittsburgh, USA*
Husam Zaman, *Taibah University, Saudi Arabia*

Institute for International Studies in Education
School of Education, University of Pittsburgh
5714 Wesley W. Posvar Hall, Pittsburgh, PA 15260 USA

Center for International and Development Education
Graduate School of Education & Information Studies, University of California, Los Angeles
Box 951521, Moore Hall, Los Angeles, CA 90095 USA

Titles:

Higher Education in Asia/Pacific: Quality and the Public Good
Edited by Terance W. Bigalke and Deane E. Neubauer

Affirmative Action in China and the U.S.: A Dialogue on Inequality and Minority Education
Edited by Minglang Zhou and Ann Maxwell Hill

Critical Approaches to Comparative Education: Vertical Case Studies from Africa, Europe, the Middle East, and the Americas
Edited by Frances Vavrus and Lesley Bartlett

Curriculum Studies in South Africa: Intellectual Histories & Present Circumstances
Edited by William F. Pinar

Higher Education, Policy, and the Global Competition Phenomenon
Edited by Laura M. Portnoi, Val D. Rust, and Sylvia S. Bagley

The Search for New Governance of Higher Education in Asia
Edited by Ka-Ho Mok

International Students and Global Mobility in Higher Education: National Trends and New Directions
Edited by Rajika Bhandari and Peggy Blumenthal

Curriculum Studies in Brazil: Intellectual Histories, Present Circumstances
Edited by William F. Pinar

Access, Equity, and Capacity in Asia Pacific Higher Education
Edited by Deane Neubauer and Yoshiro Tanaka

Policy Debates in Comparative, International, and Development Education
Edited by John N. Hawkins and W. James Jacob

Increasing Effectiveness of the Community College Financial Model: A Global Perspective for the Global Economy
Edited by Stewart E. Sutin, Daniel Derrico, Rosalind Latiner Raby, and Edward J. Valeau

Curriculum Studies in Mexico: Intellectual Histories, Present Circumstances
William F. Pinar

Internationalization of East Asian Higher Education: Globalization's Impact
John D. Palmer

Taiwan Education at the Crossroad: When Globalization Meets Localization
Chuing Prudence Chou and Gregory S. Ching

Mobility and Migration in Asian Pacific Higher Education
Edited by Deane E. Neubauer and Kazuo Kuroda

Mobility and Migration in Asian Pacific Higher Education

Edited by
Deane E. Neubauer and
Kazuo Kuroda

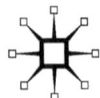

MOBILITY AND MIGRATION IN ASIAN PACIFIC HIGHER EDUCATION
Copyright © Deane E. Neubauer and Kazuo Kuroda, 2012.
Softcover reprint of the hardcover 1st edition 2012 978-0-230-11818-8

All rights reserved.

First published in 2012 by
PALGRAVE MACMILLAN®
in the United States—a division of St. Martin's Press LLC,
175 Fifth Avenue, New York, NY 10010.

Where this book is distributed in the UK, Europe and the rest of the world, this is by Palgrave Macmillan, a division of Macmillan Publishers Limited, registered in England, company number 785998, of Houndmills, Basingstoke, Hampshire RG21 6XS.

Palgrave Macmillan is the global academic imprint of the above companies and has companies and representatives throughout the world.

Palgrave® and Macmillan® are registered trademarks in the United States, the United Kingdom, Europe and other countries.

ISBN 978-1-349-29815-0   ISBN 978-1-137-01508-2 (eBook)
DOI 10.1057/9781137015082

Library of Congress Cataloging-in-Publication Data is available from the Library of Congress.

A catalogue record of the book is available from the British Library.

Design by Newgen Imaging Systems (P) Ltd., Chennai, India.

First edition: June 2012

Contents

List of Illustrations   vii

Editor's preface   ix

Acknowledgments   xi

1   Introduction: Giving Dimension and Direction to Mobility and Migration in Asian Pacific Higher Education   1
Deane E. Neubauer

Part 1   National and Regional Transformations on Mobility and Migration in Asian Pacific Higher Education

2   Mobility, Markets, and Equity in Higher Education: Match or Mismatch?   21
Peter D. Hershock

3   Learning the Hard Way: Lessons from Australia's Decade of Innovation in Student Migration Policy   39
Christopher Ziguras

4   "Shared Space" in Global Higher Education: A Southeast Asian Perspective   53
Morshidi Sirat

5   International Mobility of Faculty and Its Impacts on Korean Higher Education   65
Jung-Cheol Shin

6   The Changing Structure of Japanese Higher Education: Globalization, Mobility, and Massification   83
Reiko Yamada

Part 2 Institutional Responses to Mobility and Migration in Asian Pacific Higher Education

7 The Rhetoric and Reality of Mobility and Migration in Higher Education: The Case of the University of California, Los Angeles   105
John N. Hawkins

8 Internationalization Strategies and Academic Mobility in Europe: Sciences Po and the London School of Economics   125
Marie Scot

9 International Student Mobility for East Asian Integration   143
Kazuo Kuroda

10 Constructing a "Global University Centered in Asia": Globalizing Strategies and Experiences at the National University of Singapore   157
Francis Leo Collins and Ho Kong Chong

11 Contributions of Foreign Experts to Chinese Academic Development: A Case Study of Peking University   175
Ma Wanhua

12 International Accreditation and Its Impact on Student Mobility in Taiwan Universities—A Case Study of School of Management of Fu Jen Catholic University   191
Yung-chi Hou (Angela)

Part 3 Conclusion

13 Conclusion: Ways Forward for Migration and Mobility in Asia-Pacific Higher Education   211
Deane E. Neubauer and Kazuo Kuroda

Contributors   225

Index   231

Illustrations

Figures

6.1	The Proportion of Students Who Take Remedial Classes	95
6.2	Non-Articulation Model and Articulation Model between Secondary School and Higher Education in Japan	99
9.1	Growing Number of Students Move from Asia to Asia	145
12.1	International Students in Taiwan Universities	195
12.2	Rate by Different Elements of Internationalization	199

Tables

3.1	International Students in Higher Education: Completions, Permanent Residency (PR) Visas Issued and Enrollment Growth	42
3.2	Indian Students in Australian Tertiary Education	45
5.1	Distribution of Sample by County of PhD Earned	68
5.2	Faculty Perception, Performance, and Culture	71
6.1	Learning Experiences of Japanese and American Students	92
6.2	Student Self-Evaluation of Learning Outcomes: USA and Japan	93
6.3	Proportion of Integration of First-Year Seminars in the Curriculum in Japanese Higher Education	97
9.1	Inbound Mobile Students to Three Western Countries	144

9.2	Inbound Mobile Students to Three Asian Countries	144
10.1	Reasons Given by NUS International Students for Studying in Singapore	162
10.2	Country Attributes and Its Influence on NUS International Students' Education Choice	162
10.3	Satisfaction with Student Experience in NUS	164
10.4	Social Life On and Off Campus	164
12.1	Proportion and Number of International Students in Top 5 Universities in Taiwan	195
12.2	Different Type of Respondents 'Attitude Toward Level of Impact on International Accreditation	200

Editor's Preface

We are pleased to welcome the newest volume in the International Forum on Education 2020 series (IFE 2020). IFE 2020 was launched in 2004 under the sponsorship and leadership of the East West Center in Honolulu Hawaii. These volumes are the result of annual senior seminars offered by the East West Center in cooperation with counterpart institutions in the Asia/Pacific region. The seminars began in 2006 and since that time have involved a cohort of key scholars and policy analysts from throughout the Asia/Pacific region. The seminars have focused on critical issues in higher education transformation such as access and equity, the knowledge society, public good and commodification, quality assurance and higher education, and now mobility and migration. The participants constitute a forum for continuing debate and discussion interacting at both academic and policy levels.

The chapters in this volume cover a wide range of topics but all address the focal issue of what mobility and migration mean in the context of higher education and what impact this phenomenon has on the transformation of higher education in the region. On the one hand, there can be found a general enthusiasm for the range and scope of these movements or circuits of exchange as Neubauer suggests. We hear a lot about brains on the move, the brain race, the brain drain, the brain train, and so on, and the case can be made that this is an accelerating social movement that will have profound implications for higher education. Several case examples of this point of view are provided in the volume. On the other hand, the case can also be made that in light of the immense expansion of higher education in the region, proportionately; diversification as a result of mobility and migration remains a small share. This point of view appears in at least three chapters. The volume is concerned not only with the movement of people, but also of ideas and institutional forms. Higher education institutions are inherently conservative and nationally focused so it is of interest as to the degree that mobility and migration can impact the core of university life. The volume engages this debate in a lively manner leaving it to the reader to reach their own conclusions, and for on-going research on this topic. We believe this study will add significantly to the growing literature on this topic, and provide rich material for a continuing discussion.

Acknowledgments

The editors and the East-West Center wish to acknowledge the extraordinary support provided by President Satoh of J. F. Orbrin University of Tokyo, and the entire staff in cosponsoring the Senior Seminar event that produced the original version of these chapters.

The editors also wish to thank the East-West Center for its continuing support of the International Forum for Education 2020, which is the overall structure through which this collection of chapters was developed. The Global Institute for Asian Regional Integration (GIARI) of Waseda University supported Kazuo Kuroda's travel to Hawaii and provided support for manuscript editing, for which both editors are grateful.

Additional thanks is due our series editors, John N. Hawkins and William James Jacob for their encouragement and contributions.

Two final notes of thanks are extended to our editor, Burke Gerstenschlager and assistant editor Kaylan Connally of Palgrave Macmillan, and Ellen Waldrop who prepared our index.

Chapter 1

Introduction: Giving Dimension and Direction to Mobility and Migration in Asian Pacific Higher Education

Deane E. Neubauer

Introduction

As complex organizations, higher education institutions (HEIs) comprise a highly interactive set of structures, activities, and currencies. Despite the extant effect of historical experiences and national particularities, it is useful to view HEIs as consisting of familiar structural components (e.g., divisions into undergraduate and graduate education, students, faculties, staffs, disciplines, schools, etc.); governance components (e.g., internal administrative structures, governing boards, linkages to external constituencies including governments, networking with other HEIs either within or between nations, engaging professional societies, etc.); activities (e.g., teaching, research, community engagements); and currencies (e.g., publishing, exchanging personnel, creating, validating and exchanging credentials [including grades, credits, and degrees], quality markets [such as program and institutional accreditation], and intellectual/knowledge content).

With increasing national integration and global engagement, the processes by which exchange takes place across these elements grow more complex and the volume of exchanges increases. This chapter explores the nature of these circuits of exchange, creates some differentiation among them, and initiates a process of identifying and measuring some of the content that flows within them. In moving in this direction, the core conceptual focus will be on migration and mobility—viewing the increasing globalization of higher education as a process within which migration of all these elements is both promoted and legitimized and through which greater mobility of these institutional attributes, capacities, and capabilities is accomplished. A question to be considered would be the extent to which these exchanges, however extensive they are, have any substantive impact on the institutions involved.

I begin by setting context. As an individual who has interacted with this increasingly globalized world over the past five decades, I find that I have created for myself a kind of controlled schizophrenia of knowledge about that world. In one part of my consciousness I appear to be actively aware of many of the changes that are taking place directly as a result of increased globalization, interaction, and dependency. Yet in another part of my consciousness (or more precisely, in various other parts of my consciousness) other processes are at work: the "pictures inside my head" (as Daniel Boorstin once put it–1962) about what the "world is" are constantly shifting, bit by bit, as information filters in (and as it happens, the amounts of information are constantly increasing, in some cases exponentially). Typically, one event in the world will trigger an inflection of consciousness and I will begin to work with it only to realize with a start that the more I "look at" that bit of the conscious world, I no longer recognize it. Parts of it are familiar, but other parts are not. The picture inside my head no longer has effective currency.[1]

The changes that are making obsolete these views of the world are of many orders. I want to suggest just four. First is the change that results from authentic innovation. New knowledge, new technology, new production, and consumption practices can and do change the world in both previously unexperienced, and often unanticipated kinds of ways. Such technologies move through diffusion cycles and at some point reach a level of density and frequency that as observers, consumers, producers, regulators, and so on, we are moved to acknowledge that the world has changed in this regard, and often, to take action accordingly. We have noted and observed this process throughout the "digital revolution" and in many respects accept it and regard it as no longer in very many ways exceptional (Mahajan, Muller, and Bass 1990). The Internet is constantly cited as a primary example of such innovation, but within the entire range of digital technology, instances abound and are emerging with extraordinary rapidity and regularity. Yet we must also be cognizant in the area of technology of the many "divides" that exist, and various spatial limits (who populates areas of the globe that do not participate as others do in these new technologies).

The second kind of change is what we might see as less truly innovative, but nevertheless profound and transforming. These can range from those that take place when the activities of a group, institution, or society undergo what we think of as "fundamental change," as when an institution undergoes mission change, or basic social institutions change. In these situations it is sometimes useful to note that even though structural change is occurring, many social practices, cultural routines, and even roles remain essentially unchanged. We would note this kind of change for example when normal schools become graduate institutions and are further transformed into research-oriented doctoral institutions.

A third kind of change we might term *normal* or *conventional* change, in which some aspects of behaviors are altered, but structures and practices tend to remain relatively unaffected. These constitute many of the change dynamics of our lives, and with a tinge of irony lead to our individual and collective senses that often change is "more apparent than real" or *"le plus de change, le plus de meme chose."* It is also a kind of change that one sees and hears referred to commonly especially in media coverage of globalization in which the changes of globalization are often interpreted as superficial, or as an overlay of what exists—especially if that involves some appreciation of "the local."

A fourth kind of change appears to be persistent within the current dynamics of contemporary globalization and suggests how many aspects of migration and mobility operate within global higher education settings.[2] This version of change is often illustrated by pointing to the relationship of how interval scales relate to dichotomous categorization. Given my own age group and gender, it can pointedly be illustrated by the transition of a man who is balding into one who is bald: at what point (we were asked as graduate students in a methodology class) does the man stop being balding and become bald?

The relationship, of course, applies to the progression of any incremental process past the point at which another nominal category is "entered." Thus, given our purposes here (and as clearly exemplified by Hawkins's chapter 7 of this volume) at what point does a university undergoing incremental transitions toward increased internationalization or globalization become such—that is: internationalized, or globalized? Part of any answer, of course, will depend on the kinds of definitions, conceptual and operational, that are assigned to the category (for example, we could—if desired—clearly "map" the head of any balding individual, count the hairs, and so on, and have an empirical "measure" of the degree of balding). While such simple notions are clearly understood and widely applied in many areas of endeavor, these distinctions tend to be elusive in our conversations about globalization and increased interdependence in higher education. I want to suggest, however, that it is most often this kind of change that is taking place in our institutions and that stand critically in the center of our efforts to understand how mobility and migration function in higher education contexts. Or to put the point more simply, and to refer again to Hawkins: numbers alone do not mean that fundamental institutional behaviors are changing.

Often in the everyday practice of institutions the resolution of these thorny conceptual issues is brilliantly simple. One resolves the issue of categorical assignment by stipulation. The observer simply develops a given level of categorical achievement and stipulates that when such a level is reached, the institution is deserving of the categorical assignment—in this case numbers are taken as equal to "category movement" or behavior change. I think this happens all too frequently with notions of whether institutions are becoming internationalized or globalized. When the number of international students reaches a given level, or the number of faculty having had international assignments reaches a given level, the institution is then held to have become internationalized. This practice is certainly understandable, but as Hawkins points out, it does little to advance the study of the degree to which institutional character is being altered by internationalization or globalization. It is for this reason in part that I am suggesting the approach of conceptualizing and then measuring institutional change through the metaphor of circuits of exchange.

Circuits of Exchange

Saskia Sassen has developed sophisticated and complex analyses of how contemporary globalization is constituting and reconstituting global cities. She has sought to examine such changes through various sociological and anthropological perspectives. "For me this has meant going all the way from the top levels to the bottom levels in an effort to capture the variety of work processes, work cultures, infrastructures, and so on, that are part of the global control capacity concentrated in cities, a capacity that is one of the features of the global economic system." She views these structures through the lens of highly specialized crossborder circuits or circuits of exchange. Each such, whether they be located in financial subsectors, such as accounting, legal, advertising, and so on, has—Sassen holds—its own specific geography of networks, even if they overlap with others (Sassen in Steger 2010, 91).

I wish to argue that higher education constitutes another circuit of exchange within globalization and is itself made up of many other sub-circuits, all of which can be usefully analyzed through this methodology. We can go one step farther and suggest that much of "what we are talking about" when we discuss migration and mobility can be usefully conceptualized with the circuit metaphor and that adopting this conceptual focus in and of itself enriches our understandings of the process, in part by alerting us to the multiple dimensions of change that are involved. Should we do so, I contend, we invite our everyday consciousness of institutional realities to develop expanded perspectives toward internationalization and globalization—to "see more with the same glance"—as it were.

Having presented this approach, we can return to examining higher education exchange circuits from the standpoint of the kinds of change outlined above. My contention is twofold: one, higher education mobility and migration are "underconceptualized" to the extent that they are not viewed as an increasingly regularized circuit of exchange, and second, the extent to which existing institutions are being transformed by these processes—the subject of many of the chapters in this volume—might also need to be reconceptualized.

Higher Education Mobility and Migration as a Circuit of Exchange

The idea of a circuit of exchange is simple.[3] To make it interesting one should want to know where the circuit initiates and to where it goes, what is exchanged within the circuit, who has access to it, who contributes contents, who extracts contents, who establishes and maintains it, and its "state:" is it growing (in size, volume, complexity, etc.), declining, steady state, and so on? After Sassen, we would also want to know whether such a circuit has subcircuits or whether it interacts with others in either regular or episodic ways.

Were we to conceptualize Asia-Pacific higher education in some of these ways, how would we characterize it as a circuit of exchange? One opportunity might be to examine elements that are plentiful in the literature, for example, through the agendas of meetings of higher education administrators, or the articulations of public policy. These elements can be seen as aspects of the architecture or geography of circuits. When we have them worked out in some manner, to gain a sense of the impacts that are being created by and within the circuit, it is then necessary to seek some kind of quantitative measure of the activity associated with a given circuit.

In effect we need to find ways to place one or more meters across the circuit in order to measure the degree of traffic or exchange within it. Where such measurement becomes conceptually sensible and admits to effective measurement, one has then reached the point hypothesized above at which the ability to characterize the kinds and degrees taking place within an institution or between an institution is ultimately based on some form of measurement that allows one to have base points, describable increments, and comparative outcomes over time.

Creating the Task

To achieve comparative coherency, it is useful to establish some parameters within which an examination of migration and mobility will be conducted. In doing so one can suggest fruitful avenues of inquiry rather than to mandate them, since some of the suggestions offered here may suit one country context better than another. Yet what should knit all these inquiries together is the effort to further our understanding of how these circuits of exchange operate and how they are impacting any given institution. Examples of such exchanges might involve *directions of movements* (what are the primary directions of movement? From Asia to "the West;" from "the West" to Asia; within Asia?); *persons* (students, faculty, talent and components of human capital, patterns of degree seeking); *ideas* (how education should be conducted, how curricula should be modified [e.g., by expanding "general education" requirements], the place of research); and *structures* (as in the development of branch campuses from outside sources, or the creation of multicampus systems within countries, the transformation of individual campuses as a result of such exchanges, or the creation of international consortia). Some of these aspects of higher education endeavor fit within the commonly accepted notion of crossborder or transborder exchange, whereas others require refining the category or extending it beyond what is customarily dealt with by these terms.

Directions of Movement

For the past three decades our observations of movement have been largely unidirectional: students moved overwhelmingly from "Asia" (however defined) to the West for education, training, and degree acquisition. To a lesser degree this was probably true of faculty as well: those without terminal degrees moved outside Asia for degree acquisition; those with terminal degrees did so for postdoctoral training. We suggest two kinds of inquiry could be fruitful here. First, are these still the dominant patterns of mobility, or have they begun to change? If the latter, is the emergent pattern of exchange within Asia (e.g., Chinese students/faculty to Japan, or visa versa), or in the opposite direction(s) (e.g., bringing Chinese philosophy and notions of Confucian education into Western settings, or sending Japanese, Korean, or Chinese scholars to lecture and conduct research in Western settings)? The second direction of inquiry is to assess the *impact or consequences* of such mobility. How prevalent is it within the institution? Has it changed some aspect of the institution? If so, which aspect? How well distributed are such changes? (e.g., are such activities concentrated mainly in the sciences, or throughout various faculties?)

Persons

People are the most obvious objects of attention in investigating mobility and migration in higher education. We note immediately that over the past several decades higher education migration seen in these terms is but a special case of vast migrations that have taken place throughout the world, but particularly throughout Asia, as literally hundreds of millions of people have left the countryside for urban areas and move throughout the world in search of employment. Dominant patterns also include the crowded pathways of temporary employment (often lasting for years into decades) that characterize much interregional movement, both documented and undocumented. Of particular import are large numbers of persons who have studied outside their own countries and have returned, remained in the receiving country after acquiring their degrees, or migrated to yet a third country. This latter category is very much the "stuff" of cross- and transborder higher education research and should inform our discussions, which are, however, meant to take a somewhat different form. There is already a considerable literature on the scope of such exchanges (Knight 2006).

In examining the migration and mobility of persons in higher education we are interested in observing the effects on and consequences for both receiving and sending institutions. Some examples indicate the kind of step we suggest this research and inquiry take. In a first exemplary case, it has been common over the past several decades for both students and serving faculty of HEIs to engage in external degree seeking and experiences as postgraduate, postdoctoral, and visiting scholars. What happens to such persons when engaged in the degree-seeking process and what happens as a result? In cases where existing faculty return to positions with advanced degrees, what impact do they have on the curriculum, research, and ongoing processes of their institutions? Do they in effect return as change agents, or might they return as faculty whose interests and professional engagements may have been elevated in kind and quality, but are essentially directed toward external (read: international) audiences? Are their personal careers enhanced as a result of such international experiences or is there a cost to bear? Are they "carriers" of "other cultural material" and if so do they act to diffuse such materials within their host and home institutions, or are they most likely mainly to "export" these materials back to external environments? To what degree does this cultural material get changed in the transmission process and how is it indigenized? Indeed, are these sensible questions to ask? What might we make of the answers we receive? At the heart of the inquiry is a desire to gauge the effect of external degree acquisitions on sending and subsequent returning institutions. Many (most) HEIs of international or global pretense devote significant resources to promoting this kind of student and faculty mobility. Our question is: what difference (ultimately) does it make?

Ideas

The notion of tracking the migration of ideas throughout Asia-Pacific higher education is both fascinating and daunting. If there is more than mere heuristic value to the notions of circuits of exchange, then identifying and tracking the kind, quality, and impact of key ideas would seem to be a central task. Certainly there are many places to look such as the annual or biennial congregations of university presidents that take place within the region, or in regional conferences of educational ministers, or in developing an inventory of journals proliferating in the region and their content. Within this general category of interests we are most interested in the migration and mobility of "ways of doing higher education," which could include curriculum innovation and change—especially with regard to shifts in emphasis and investment within curricula, changes in pedagogic emphasis, or indeed proliferation of ways to examine quality and "do" quality assurance. For example, much is made on the policy side of higher education of the increasing and seemingly boundless pressures to emphasize the vocational relevance of higher education—to ensure employment of graduates; to create a basis of support for continued public funding; to justify increased user fees; to promote innovation, technology transfer, and economic development; and so on. In short, growing attention is paid to what has been called the "alignment issue" throughout the world. What are the practical and pragmatic effects of these policy environment changes on actual curricula? Are vocational subjects being advanced? And if so, is it at the expense of other elements of the curricula, for example, philosophy and other parts of the humanities? Further, how do institutions know the effects of such changes? Are surveys routinely done that track the employment of graduates and if so what are they telling us?

Pedagogy constitutes another example. Much is made of the importance of "teaching for the values of the workplace"—again, to ensure that graduates not only find jobs, but that employers regard them as well prepared. Increasingly, HEIs are urged to ensure that students have various critical skills and are equipped to function well in problem-oriented environments, that they understand working in teams and cooperatively, and that they possess requisite technological literacies and skills. Can one identify sets of pedagogical similarities that are traveling though these circuits of exchange and moving not only within a country's HEIs but also across borders and throughout the region? If so, then again: to what effect? (see, for example, Australia-Korea Teacher Exchange Program 2007.)

Assessment is another such element that has migrated rapidly and extensively throughout the region, sufficiently so that viewing the 1990s as the decade of quality assurance came to be a commonplace designation. However, to what extent have the overall structures and processes of quality assurance affected what institutions do, and through these processes how much better do we understand aspects of institutional performance such as the nature and quality of research, or the quality and effect of teaching and student learning? Again, what are the impacts of the migration of these ideas as they are processed within discrete and specific institutional contexts? In a larger context, how have the dynamics of globalization come to affect what has developed as quality assurance writ on a global stage and how do these dynamics affect what institutions seek to "do" across the range of their policy activities and decisions (GUNI 2007; Wolff 2009; Neubauer 2010; Woodhouse 2010)? Finally, larger ideas such as the notion of "world-class universities" have captured the attention of many first tier universities in the region. Where did this idea come from and how did it get so thoroughly engrained in the thinking of higher education policymakers (Mok 2005)?

Structures

For much of the past century the basic structures of higher education have been largely the same, organized with strong verticality of departments and colleges (or faculties), and easily identified as either public (often national) or private institutions. The past decade and a half shows evidence of much transition in these structures as the rise of new disciplines (e.g., in computing and bio sciences) has brought new "faculties" into institutional play, and as the press of new technologies and problematics has resulted in the creation of crossdisciplinary and multidisciplinary organization (e.g., climate change, global studies, etc.). Indeed, the European model of seeking to develop a commonality of interests and identities in degrees and degree programs (the Bologna process) has stimulated similar interests within some Asian universities to explore reorganization of existing structures. As we have emphasized in other contexts, the degree of institutional and structural innovation that has occurred with respect to governance, funding, and administration is sufficient to challenge the very utility of continued use of the terms "public" or "private" to characterize many higher education institutions (Bigalke-Neubauer 2009, see especially Chapter 3). In some ways, rapid change in various higher education environments such as that of the United States has prompted thinking in the direction of an emergent "new ecology of learning" within higher education with novel institutional structures continually being established. Whether these structural forms are unique to the particularities of the US system of higher education, or an early forerunner of other manifestations throughout Asia is a matter of both interest and concern (Neubauer 2011).

In another direction, as "top" universities throughout Asia grapple with pressures to render them more globally competitive, some have sought to learn from, model, or adopt curricular and/or organizational changes intended to add value to a particular activity. Thus, one can observe experiments with various forms of remodeled "general education," with problem-based learning, with first-year and senior-year seminars based on small interactive classes that feature critical thinking, capstone courses to integrate learning experiences, and so on. We are interested in tracking some of the structural/organizational innovations that are moving throughout the circuits of higher education exchange in the Asia-Pacific region to look to their origin and how and if they have gained traction in specific institutional cases.

Yet another example of the mobility of structures is evident in numerous instances of physical reorganization that have occurred in institutions across the region. This takes the form of either consolidation of existing institutions into more focused, concentrated institutions, or the expansion of existing institutions into multicampus entities, often organized as systems, such as those characterizing many US state university systems, or De La Salle in the Philippines.

Many additional examples might be given in each of these four large categories detailed above. In all cases, however, what is of most interest to us here is the degree to which these kinds of mobility and migration have impacted and transformed individual higher education institutions, and if not, why not.

Initiating the Task

How might we initiate the task of developing these observations into a coherent body of data from which to extract a more complete framework for the study of migration and mobility? Step one would be the enumeration and clarification of the elements within the circuits of exchange. This step should have two components. One is "theoretical" in the sense that the element is defined and delineated in a way that allows for an explicit appreciation of the nature of the element involved. In some cases this is obvious and relatively uninteresting (or at least apparently so) as it seems clear what students are and what their role is within such a circuit. But maybe not. As we move beyond simple enumeration of bodies, we may wish to explore aspects of related elements that affect how and where students move, for example, visa requirements, financial aid, standardization of admission criteria, and even quotas. All of this leads to a consideration of a second element, which is the operational nature of the definition or measure, which focuses on what we seek (or choose) to measure and how we do so within any data-gathering enterprise.

These issues are common, of course, to any effort to build a complex, composite measure such as an index. (See, for example, the ambitious efforts of A. T. Kearney to develop and employ an index of globalization [A. T. Kearney 2011]). Doing so always invites and involves making compromises on what should and can be measured (and at what expense). For an initial effort to develop effective indicators on which to construct such an enterprise, it is probably most useful to raise questions at the most basic methodological level, namely seeking to be clear about "what" we are choosing to discuss (measure) and our rationales for believing that our measures have sensible dimensions.

Were such an outcome to be pursued, the benefits, I think, would be gained across several fronts. One would be the advantage to scholarship itself. We could come to know much more about the extent and degree of migration and mobility across the region. A second would be to the policy process, as policymakers could have a clearer view of both the outcomes and "payoffs" of given policy choices with system systems. Do given policies, such as student exchange, "work" (in the sense that they provide the expected outcomes)? Is, as Hawkins asks, an institution changed in some desired way by a given policy step? Do policymakers have effective data on which to make choices, or to assess the effect of significant investments, such as the "globalization" investments of various countries, such as projects 211 and 985 in China, the five-year Fifty Billion program of Taiwan, Brain 21 in Korea, or the 21 COE program in Japan? A third would be to create a comparative data base that on various dimensions could admit to measurement for purposes that could well serve the internal needs of institutions, but do so outside the context of the International and/or Global rankings game. League tables tend to succeed because people desire this kind of comparative data, but also because of the purported value of the ranking itself and the notion that the higher up the table one is, the better one is. A comparative index/project such as this could provide such measures for mobility and migration without developing some of the more invidious aspects of league tables.

Developing Variables and Indicators

An initial set of "variables" can be seen to make up the primary dimensions of the circuit of exchange for higher education mobility and migration.

Movement of Faculty, Students, and Administrators for Various Purposes

Initially one needs to differentiate between the kinds of movements within the three major categories, the purposes that define them, and the relative numbers of exchanges involved. In the most conventional way, it is necessary to differentiate students who move for the purposes of degree study and those for less than degree study; undergraduate students from graduate and postgraduate (to use the American usage); whether supported externally or not; whether within permissive or restrictive visa categories; whether within permissive or restrictive acceptance categories; the direction of their flow (destinations); and, perhaps most importantly, their distribution across other distinctions such as field of study. Within these inquiries, as among others, their value as research findings is largely predicated on time-series data to demonstrate trends.

Circulation of Ideas

As suggested above, rightfully this is probably less a "category" than the name of an approach. Labeling it as such draws attention to the fact that a key element exchanged within the circuit is ideas—of all kinds. Some stick and catch on; many are transitory and disappear. But, the essential "movements" within higher education in one or another meaningful sense (including that represented by the current "movement" toward university rankings) are occasioned by sets of ideas for which one could hypothesize a "market" and note that some ideas certainly have greater currency than others. To take perhaps the most notable example from the past two decades, neoliberalism is an idea, or more appropriately a set of ideas, that have normative content (they say the way things *should be* for various presumed reasons), descriptive content (neoliberalism singles out a set of human behaviors that are important for normative reasons and then seeks to define these behaviors in specific kinds of ways), and analytical pretensions (they see the world in terms of the *kinds* of analyses that should be done to support neoliberal views, e.g., array public and private outcomes within selective definitions of those outcomes). Overall, neoliberalism has become an ideology, a way of seeing the world, a set of policy prescriptions, and a set of organizing tools for social institutions, including those of higher education (Harvey 2005; Steger and Roy 2010). Much of what has occurred within Japan, Korea, Taiwan, Indonesia, Thailand, Hong Kong, and China higher education over the past 20 years has, in one way or another and despite its being cast in various other local policy languages, been of a neoliberal cast (Mok 2011). From the perspective being suggested here, it is a set of ideas that has migrated widely and powerfully throughout the region and with considerable effect.

Within the constructs of a proposal for migration and mobility research one could examine such things as the growth and development (and diversification) of faculty participation in various research endeavors. (E.g., what were the modal categories of faculty research ten years ago? Fifteen years ago?) Indeed, the *idea* of faculty research as a conventional requirement of holding university positions has itself been one of *the* transforming ideas in the region as many HEIs that saw their role primarily through the lens of teaching have come to adopt active and continuous faculty research as a requirement of holding such positions.

Another variable of interest is the growth and development of outlets for scholarly "product" of all kinds, new journals including web journals, book publishers, other legitimated web publications, and so on. Indeed, a measure of change throughout the region, much employed by the league tables, is the frequency of faculty publication and its means, represented as a measure usually through citation indexes that themselves are in a constant state of change to reflect the growth of legitimacy of new scholarly publications.

Yet another set of ideas of considerable interest involves efforts to change pedagogy, ranging from efforts to shift the emphasis from "teaching" to "learning" and to modalities of learning such as "problem-based learning" that is prevalent throughout the curriculum from engineering to medicine to language instruction. As such ideas develop and spread from one context to another, as they are exchanged throughout the circuit of higher education, they encounter resistance and are absorbed and transformed by the forces of institutional conservatism that constitute so much of higher education into derivations and in some cases parodies of themselves. For the research endeavor, this means that one needs to "burrow down" into the nature of the circuits of exchange to see how education at all levels is or is not really affected by the movement, migration, and spread of such ideas. (Sassen has done just this analysis, in global cities, where she has identified multiple layers for the institutionalization of global capital from the "very top," where capital markets have created a new class of actors with extraordinary wealth and reach, to the movements of labor in and out of capital cities, bringing, for example, entire new classes of people into urban areas to do routine jobs such as building, cleaning, and other janitorial services, which in turn leads to changing patterns of neighborhood living, commerce, etc. [Sassen in Steger 2010].)

Another "bundle" of ideas that constitutes a significant quanta of exchanges involves the development, growth, and spread of "institutional standards," that range from notions of what constitutes quality and how it is to be measured, to governance issues, financial modalities, and ideas of accountability. Issues of institutional standards are transmitted through a variety of subcircuits including those of global and international scholarly and executive/leadership meetings, and by organized efforts to create uniformity or at the very least coherence of behavior in certain realms. This can be one way to view the Bologna endeavor as well as the recent agreement between Japan, Korea, and China to create a credit recognition union (the Agreement from the Third Japan-China-Korea Committee for Promoting Exchange and Cooperation among Universities).

Finally, it can also be useful in this regard to examine the growth and development of various public policy discourses that stand aside from macropolicy texts such as neoliberalism. One of these has come to be the alignment issue within public policy. Whereas virtually every country in the region has experienced or is experiencing a version of the alignment tension, its recognition and resolution differs country by country. It is useful, I suggest, to see it as a policy discourse sub text that is deserving of analysis as a separate constituent element within the circuit of exchange (Hershock 2011).

Circulation of Structures

I separate this set of ideas from others, perhaps for no good reason other than that they suggest how institutions of higher education may be structured to achieve various outcomes. Under closer examination some of these outcomes seem to emerge from broader discursive patterns such as neoliberalism, but many are particularistic to the kinds of HEI structures that have developed within a given national setting, but that are now giving way in one form or another to international or global forces or initiatives (Sugimura 2009).[4]

Within this category I include transformative ideas in the nature of the professorial role (linking it more directly to "global standards"), ideas about how internal structures should be located within institutions (e.g., liberal arts, general studies, general education, etc.), how admissions should be conducted (by the university as a whole or through individual faculties), where students are "located" within the institution (who "owns" them for budgetary and accounting purposes), transformations in traditional institutional roles such as president and dean, institutionalization of new forms of internal audit, and externally, the aggregation of units within a national system into multicampus systems with linked governance and financial structures. I also include in this set of variables the emergence of "new" institutions performing educational functions outside existing structures of higher education both public and private.

Linkages

The final category I propose for inclusion at this time I have termed "linkages" and mean by this ways in which institutions are coming to be linked to others throughout international and global settings across an entire continuum of formal to informal linkages. Within this frame, it is useful to include such things as branch campuses across national borders, allowing for both the import and export of these. Another subcategory consists of consortia linkages of all kinds from informal agreements to cooperate to formal agreements that create a consortia entity with defined and supported purposes, such as an aggregation of universities that produces a secretariat, with a dedicated budget, defined product, and so on. A less formalized version of this can be membership organizations whose purposes include quality improvement, research, pedagogy, standards, and so on. To these I would add both conventional and unconventional efforts to expand institutional capacity by linking one institution to another through shared campuses, twinning relationships, or formal projects for instruction, research, technology development, and so on.

Conclusion

I have suggested above that "change" can admit of at least four differentiations, each of which develops different consequences for those who hold to or embrace a given way of "seeing change." Accepting this, the changes that are taking place as a result of increased migration and mobility within the Asia-Pacific region can be calculated and measured to gauge their overall effect. To do so requires some form of disciplined research and data gathering that can eventuate a kind of comparative coherence that allows us to be specific about both the nature of the things—symbolic and material—that flow through the circuits of higher education exchange and the consequences that are progressively wrought from these exchanges. The goal of such a project is to encourage an empirically based scholarship of Asia-Pacific higher education that both enhances our knowledge of what is and promotes informed speculation about what is possible.

Notes

1. In a way not much different perhaps from the trope employed by Thomas Friedman in his enormously popular book about globalization *The World is Flat,* in which he entitles the first chapter "While I Was Sleeping," and argues that bit by bit the world changed around him to the point that he finally had an experience that "put the whole thing" together for him, at which point he remarked to his wife, "Honey, I think the world is flat." In retrospect, it was as if the whole world transformed itself as he was sleeping. Others have used the expression of seeing the world "through a new set of lenses," etc. (Friedman 2007).
2. Differences in the kinds of changes occasioned by contemporary globalization have probably been most acutely studied by David Harvey. His pathbreaking study of the *Post Modern Condition* in 1989 signaled a range of technological and cultural shifts already identifiable within globalization. Subsequent works in the 1990s and after the turn of the century, most particularly his work on the history of neoliberalism in which he continues to speculate on how the nature of change itself may be changing under this regime of globalization, contribute much to an appreciation of the overall subtlety of these processes. See also Harvey 1996.
3. The idea of a circuit of exchange is similar to that of "international or global flows" that have been explored by Marginson and Sawir at some length, situating them (as does Sassen) within an extended globalization framework. For example, they write "Globalization in higher education entails 'action at a distance,'" to use Giddens's (1990) phrase. Global flows involve universities and academic leaders as subjects and objects in a never finished circulation and oscillation of effects. Changes in university templates, organizational practices, and academic behaviors pass across the world with accelerating speed, and the changes are often similar. But while tendencies to convergence are obvious, when we look more closely for difference as well as similarity we find the global

transformations are not identical by time and place. Rather, they are constituted in each place by an amalgam of global, national, and local factors in complex ways" (Marginson and Sawir 2011, 289).
4. The circulation of students into international flows is perhaps the best studied of all these variables, including 20 years of work by UNESCO. Sugimura reviews the most salient data here.

References

Australia-Korea Teacher Exchange Program. 2007. Now called Australia-Korea Teacher Bridge Project Available at: http://www.dfat.gov.au/akf/program_activities/bridge_program.htm (accessed February 2, 2012).
Bigalke, Terance W. and Deane E. Neubauer, eds. 2009. *Higher Education in Asia/Pacific: Quality and the Public Good.* New York: Palgrave Macmillan.
Boorstin, Daniel J. 1962. *The Image: A Guide to Pseudoevents in America.* New York: Harpers.
Friedman, Thomas L. 2007. *The World is Flat: A Brief History of the Twenty-First Century. (Further Updated and Expanded).* New York: Picador/ Farrar, Straus and Giroux.
Giddens, Anthony. 1990. *The Consequences of Modernity.* Stanford: Stanford University Press.
Global University Network for Innovation. 2007. *Higher Education in the World 2007: Accreditation for Quality Assurance: What is at Stake?.* New York: Palgrave Macmillan.
Harvey, David. 1989. *The Condition of Postmodernity.* Oxford: Oxford University Press
———. 1996. *Justice, Nature and the Geography of Difference.* Malden, MA: Blackwell Publishing.
———. 2005. *A Brief History of Neoliberalism.* Oxford: Oxford University Press.
Hershock, Peter. 2011. "Information and Innovation in a Global Knowledge Society: Implications for Higher Education," in *The Emergent Knowledge Society and the Future of Higher Education: Asian Perspectives,* ed. D. Neubauer. Oxford: Routledge.
Kearney, A. T. 2011. *Globalization Index.* Available at: http://www.atkearney.com/index.php/Publications/globalization-index.html (accessed February 2, 2012).
Knight, Jane. 2006. *Higher Education Crossing Borders. A Guide to the General Implications of the General Agreement on Trade in Services (GATS) for Cross-Border Education.* Education Resources Information Center, Vancouver: Commonwealth of Learning.
Mahajan, Vijay, Eitan Muller, and Frank M. Bass. 1990. "Product Diffusion Models in Marketing: A Review and Directions for Research." *Journal of Marketing* 54(January, 1990): 1–26.
Marginson, S. and E. Sawir. 2011. "Interrogating Global Flows in Higher Education." *Globalization, Societies and Education* 3(3): 281–310.

Mok, K. H. 2005. "The Quest for World Class University: Quality Assurance and International Benchmarking in Hong Kong." *Quality Assurance in Education* 13(4): 227–304.

———. 2011. "When Neoliberalism Colonizes Higher Education in Asia: Bringing the 'Public' Back to the Contemporary University," in *Knowledge Matters: The Public Mission of the Research University*, ed. D. Rhoten. New York: Columbia University Press, 195–230.

Neubauer, Deane. 2010. "Ten Globalization Challenges to Higher Education Quality and Quality Assurance." *Evaluation in Higher Education* 4(1): 13–37.

———. 2011. "Accountability and Student Learning Outcomes in Higher Education: The Search for New Perspectives," Keynote address to 2011 HEACT International Conference, *Internationalization of Standards in Higher Education: Accountability, Student Learning Outcomes and Collaborations in Quality Assurance Agencies*. Taipei, Taiwan: Howard International House, June 3.

Steger, Manfred, ed. 2010. *Globalization: the Greatest Hits: A Global Studies Reader*. Boulder: Paradigm Publishers.

Steger, Manfred, and Ravi K. Roy. 2010. Neoliberalism—A Very Brief Introduction. Oxford: Oxford University Press.

Sugimura, Miki. 2009. "Higher Education Strategies and International Student Flows in Asian Countries," Working Paper 2008-E-18, Global Institute for Asian Regional Integration. Tokyo, Japan: Waseda University Global COE Program.

Wolff, Ralph A. 2009. "Future Directions for U.S. Higher Education Accreditation," in *Higher Education in Asia Pacific: Quality and the Public Good*, ed. T. Bigalke and D. E. Neubauer. New York: Palgrave Macmillan.

Woodhouse, David. 2010. "The Pursuit of International Standards." *Evaluation in Higher Education* 4 (2): 1–20.

Part 1

National and Regional Transformations on Mobility and Migration in Asian Pacific Higher Education

Chapter 2

Mobility, Markets, and Equity in Higher Education: Match or Mismatch?

Peter D. Hershock

Transformations are now under way that are radically affecting both the provision and purposes of higher education. Like the larger-scale globalization processes that constitute their historical environment, these transformations are characterized by both integrating and fragmenting dynamics, by expanding commodification and privatization, by accelerating flows of goods and services, and by heightened personal and institutional mobility. And, while these transformations are commonly identified with "internationalization" and the increasing importance of "cross-border" educational activity, neither term does justice to the complexity of the changes taking place in higher education.

"Internationalization" suggests that nation-to-nation interactions are crucial to the changes occurring in contemporary higher education. But while such interactions are important—as in the governmentally orchestrated Bologna process—they do not seem to be central, and nation-states have tended to be followers rather than leaders in global trends toward regionalization (Scott 1998; Capannelli 2009). Indeed, in relation to the transformations taking place in higher education, the term "cross-border" seems best understood as a metaphor—a way of gaining critical purchase on phenomena that do not fit into existing conceptual frames. Yet the metaphor of crossing borders directs us toward seeing higher education mobility as leaving both borders and those moving across them essentially intact, bringing higher educational systems into new, but essentially *external* relationships. In fact, beyond certain thresholds, the quantitative expansion of "cross-border" exchanges begins bringing about the qualitatively distinct kinds of *internal* relations—the emergence of truly complex, multidomain systems within and among which interdependence also entails interpenetration. Previously distinct institutions and systems of higher education are interacting—with varying degrees of resolution at subnational, national, regional, and global scales—in ways that are no longer essentially contingent, but rather constitutive.

The dominant narrative—encouraged by understanding twenty-first-century higher education mobility and migration in terms of internationalization and cross-border exchanges—is that the ongoing transformation of higher education is inevitable, that our efforts should be directed to effectively and efficiently managing it, and that the competitive dynamics of a soon-to-materialize global higher education market will foster both accelerated epistemic innovation and tightening alignment of higher education outputs and market needs. For reasons rooted in the complex nature of contemporary globalization and modernization processes, I want to complicate this story. On its present heading, the arc of higher education change may ironically be one of ever-expanding educational access and options while at the same time compromising epistemic diversity and exacerbating global educational inequity.

From External to Internal Relations: Going Beyond the Border-Crossing Metaphor

Metaphors serve as conceptual bridges cantilevered out from the familiar into the unknown. When they work, metaphors open navigable access to domains for which we otherwise would lack any useful point of entry; when they do not, they encourage leaping to at times dangerously inappropriate sets of assumptions and expectations. In the context of contemporary globalization processes, the educational metaphor of crossing borders is misleading in a number of ways. Boundaries separate two known entities. These can be two countries, the lands owned by two neighbors, or the administration and faculty in a college or university. To cross a boundary is to move from one place to another—a position changing movement that we tend to understand as linear, as reversible, as quantifiable in terms of velocities and distances, and as having no substantial effect on either the boundary itself or whatever is traversing it. Border crossing does not change either geographies or identities.

Higher education has, since its beginnings, been characterized by border crossing in this sense. The earliest Western institutions of what we now call higher education, like the University of Bologna (founded in 1088), attracted students from across Europe. In Asia, from the sixth to ninth centuries, the Buddhist university at Nalanda (founded in 450) was a learning community of more than ten thousand students and two thousand faculty members drawn from across Eurasia. Continental and intercontinental student and faculty mobility is nothing new.

The boundaries crossed for educational (or trade) purposes in the premodern world, however, were not borders in the modern sense. The movement of students and teachers was in contemporary terms virtually unregulated, and borderlands between political and cultural domains—like those lying between distinct ecosystems—were fluid and diversity-rich interfaces. Rather than serving to restrict movement, borderlands functioned as complexly dynamic zones within which exchange, interaction, and mobility were at once expanded and intensified (Power and Standen 1999). It was with the birth of the modern nation-state as a geographically defined political entity that borders came to function principally as barriers. In the modern sense, border crossings *control access*.

Although statistical data is both scarce and spotty, evidence suggests that in late medieval and early modern European universities foreign students would typically have accounted for roughly 10 percent of total enrollments. And, from the mid-nineteenth century, as higher education came to be explicitly aligned with scientific research, industrialization, building national identity, and securing international stature, international enrollments in Germany, Britain, France, and the United States—the global academic leaders of the day—averaged between 6 and 15 percent.[1] It was in the aftermath of the World War II that a significant break took place from the historical pattern of predominantly one-way flows of students from regions lacking high quality (and in some cases, any) tertiary education institutions to leading centers of higher education in Europe and (to a lesser extent) the United States. International student and faculty exchanges began to be aggressively pursued as important dimensions of national foreign relations policy—in effect, soft diplomatic means to consolidating and expanding spheres of influence. "Internationalism" in higher education came to be regarded, not as a simple matter of fact, but rather as something to be instrumentally and intensively valorized. With the fall of the Berlin Wall in 1989 and the end of the Cold War in 1991, the prevailing *national geopolitical logic* of international exchange began giving way to an aggressively neoliberal *global economic logic* in which the valorization of internationalism nevertheless remained quite powerful.

Over this period, however, higher education worldwide underwent phenomenal growth, with total gross enrollments rising from 2.1 percent in 1955 to 7.7 percent in 1965, 10.7 percent in 1975, 12.9 percent in 1985,

16.2 percent in 1995, 19 percent in 2000, and 26 percent in 2007 (Scott 1998; Gürüz 2008; Altbach et al. 2010). In Trow's (1972) terms, whereas prior to the World War II, higher education was conducted as an "elite" phenomenon (gross enrollments under 15 percent), over the past 50 years gross enrollments in the majority of industrialized countries rose to "universal" levels (over 50 percent), and "mass" levels (from 15 to 50 percent) have been reached in a majority of developing countries. As a result of this dramatic overall growth, the number of students studying in foreign countries decreased proportionally from the historical average of 10 percent to just over 2 percent.

This proportional decline is, of course, misleading. Global student enrollments rose from 6.3 million in 1950 to 28 million in 1970, and to 43.4 million in 1997 (Gürüz 2008, 21). Just ten years later, in 2007, there were an astonishing 150 million students enrolled in higher education worldwide (Altbach et al. 2010). This unprecedented explosion of access to higher education dwarfs the flow of students traveling outside of their own countries for higher education. Nevertheless, the volume of internationally mobile students is structurally formidable. In 1950, global foreign student enrollment was approximately 110,000 students. Fifty years later, in 2000, it had increased more than 16 fold to 1.8 million; by 2007, in spite of greatly tightened visa restrictions in the United States and in the European Union, it had risen to 2.8 million (Altbach et al. 2010). In the next decade, global foreign student enrollment is variously projected to reach between 5 and 8 million (Gürüz 2008, 162–163).

Granted the relative stability of national borders, the approximate 30-fold increase of foreign student enrollments over the last 60 years demonstrates that these borders have become vastly more porous. If both the increasing mobility of university faculty members and administrators—now valorized as a key factor in global higher education rankings—and the mobility of academic programs and institutions in the form of branch campuses are taken into account, the metaphor of *border crossing* seems much less apt for understanding the ongoing global transformation of higher education than that of *border erosion*.

Borderless Higher Education? Or, Borders of a Different Kind?

From the early 1990s, there has been widespread and deepening appreciation that contemporary globalization processes are bringing about increasing social, economic, political, and cultural interdependence and interpenetration—a qualitative shift from predominantly external to increasingly internal relations. In light of this shift, many have been encouraged to envision a world without nation-states and hence without borders in the modern sense (Ohmae 1995; Guéhenno 2000).

The vision of a borderless world resonates well with modern valorizations of universality and equality, and the global imaginary of geography-liberated freedoms of choice. And it is a vision given substantial experiential support by the striking, planetwide erasure of spatial and temporal limits to communication brought about by the computing and telecommunications revolutions of the last quarter century. Indeed, in light of the global triumph of free market ideology since the demise of the Soviet Union and Chinese economic liberalization, it is easy to conclude that if borders control access, and if free market growth is pegged to everexpanding consumer options through unrestricted flows of goods, services, people, and capital, then the world's free market future will of necessity be borderless.

The reality, however, is very much more complicated. One of the unsettling features of contemporary globalization processes is that while they are bringing about greater homogeneity, uniformity, and integration, they are at the same time bringing about increasing heterogeneity, variety, and fragmentation. Hence, while late twentieth and early twenty-first-century globalization processes have undeniably brought about an accelerating *erosion* of borders and their regulatory and control functions, this is not resulting in a total *dissolution* of borders. Contemporary scales and scopes of globalization processes have been inseparable from the advent of increasingly "uneven geographies of development" (Harvey 1996)—a multiplication and magnification of differences that has had the effect of recursively reconfiguring boundaries both within and across scales, from the local to the national, regional, and global.

This reconfiguring of global topographies of advantage and opportunity has been nothing short of astonishing. At a global level, for example, the benefits of globalization have been redistributed in such a way that over the past 30 years there has been a doubling of the income gap between the richest and poorest 20 percent of the planet's population. So uneven is the geography of globalization benefits that, as of 2008, the top 2 percent of the world's population owned more than 50 percent of global wealth while the bottom 50 percent could claim less than 1 percent. In spite of steadily increasing global GDP, estimated in 2009 at $70 trillion, 45 percent of the planet's 6.8 billion people live on less than $2/day Purchasing Power Parity (PPP). This deepening divide between what is now commonly referred to as the global North and South is found, of course, not only among societies, but also within them. In short, although expanding circuits of exchange and accelerating flows of goods, services, people, and information have *not* brought about the complete erasure of geopolitical boundaries, their volume and velocity *have* been sufficient to bring about a highly contingent and yet value-driven disintegration and reconfiguration of not only geographical landscapes, but also social, economic, political, and cultural topographies.

Given how the expansion and transformation of higher education over especially the last 50 years has been closely entrained with unprecedentedly rapid and sustained global economic growth over the same period, we are forced into the unsettling position of needing at least to consider the possibility that contemporary higher education has been historically complicit in this reconfiguration of global boundaries. Perhaps even more unsettling is the prospect of such complicity deepening as the provision and purposes of higher education come to be more thoroughly aligned with market needs and, by extension, with apparently growing inequalities and inequities with respect to wealth, opportunity, and life outcomes.

This is not to impugn the good intentions of those who have dedicated their lives to higher education. The possibility that higher education might be deeply implicated in the appearance of increasingly uneven and inequitable geographies of global development is not one that presumes ill intentions on the part of those directly involved in higher education, whether as learners, teachers, administrators, or policymakers. Rather it is a structural possibility.

The university as we know it is a key institutional embodiment of such central modern values of universality, equality, sovereignty, autonomy, precision, competition, and control (Toulmin 1990). As such, it has played crucial roles in the many positive and liberating achievements of modernization as a force for "progressive" change. Yet, one of the key structural effects associated with modernization has been the "emancipatory" disintegration of traditional *communities* that are sustained through concrete and ongoing rehearsals of shared meaning and their replacement, first, by abstract and yet relatively stable, interest-based *collectives* of individuals (especially from roughly 1750 to 1950), and then increasingly by highly fluid and electively defined affinity groups. Sustained by an ongoing technological revolution that has vastly expanded human capacities for control (Beniger 1986; Hershock 1999), however, these "emancipatory" processes have been shadowed from the outset by the evolution of new constellations of power and the production of new kinds of populations suited to the recursively amplifying and disciplining dynamics of nationalization, marketization, and industrialization (Foucault 1995)—dynamics in which higher education has been integrally involved since at least the middle of the nineteenth century (Scott 1998; Hershock 2007).

The "inconvenient truth," then, is that from its beginnings, modern higher education has been infused with values that have structurally implicated it in the "creative destruction" of human relational ecologies. Moreover, the "emancipatory" goals of higher education notwithstanding, what we now know of the wider ecological and climatic effects of modern industrialization, makes it hard to avoid concluding that higher education has also been structurally implicated in the potentially catastrophic degradation of natural ecologies and the systematic attenuation of natural, cultural, and epistemic diversity.[2]

Networks, Complexity, Volatility, and Values

As a means to productive critical engagement with these troubling possibilities, it is useful to bring into somewhat greater focus the global processes that constitute the historical environment higher education transformation.

Networks

Among the most significant results of the Cold War was a technologically impelled transition, over the 1960s and 1970s, from the predominance of the military-industrial complex to that of the military-industrial-communications complex. As connectivity-amplifying advances in transportation, computing, and telecommunications technologies were practically and commercially embraced, there resulted a gradual and yet ultimately radical reconfiguration of social, economic, political, and cultural playing fields. With considerable analytic force, this reconfiguration can be understood in terms of the emergence of "network society" and "global informational capitalism" (Castells 1996, 1997, 1998)—the birth of a world in which social structures and activities are organized around and through electronically mediated flows of information.

The term "network" is being used here in the technical sense of a connectivity-rich, dynamically distinctive, nonhierarchic organizational structure. Among the key features of network organization is that membership value is functionally linked to both the *quantity* of nodes comprised in a network and the *quality* of their informational input. Unlike grids, networks do not grow by simple and externally controlled extension. Rather, network growth is spurred and shaped by negative (relation-stabilizing) and positive (interaction-accelerating and difference-amplifying) feedback. That is, network growth is internally generated as a complex function of recursively structured flows of information, both within the network and between the network and its various environments.[3]

A second key feature of the global networks emerging with practically instantaneous and ubiquitous global telecommunications is an erosion of the constraints imposed by both biological and logical time—the advent of a "space of flows" in which all places are effectively contiguous. The "space-time compression" characteristic of industrial modernization and globalization (Harvey 1989) is giving way to immersion in an unbounded space-time singularity that—like the core processes of modernization—can be seen as at once emancipatory and disciplinary. Freedoms to access virtually any information or agent on the planet at any moment has been correlated with an increasing identification of the optimal with the optional, but also with significant "reflection compression" as we are structurally disciplined into ever more quickly exercising continuously expanding experiential and communicative freedom of choice.

Complex Interdependence

Importantly, beyond certain scales and scopes of interactivity and recursivity, the dynamics of global networks foster the emergence of complex adaptive systems—that is, systems that are both self-organizing and novelty generating. Distinctively, complex systems change in ways that are in principle *impossible to anticipate*. While the negative feedback informing the growth of complex networks *stabilizes relations*, ongoing positive feedback both *accelerates differentiation* and *accentuates uncertainty*. Thus, while global dynamics over the past half-century have been inflected toward increasing interdependence, they have not only been marked by increasing *coherence*, but also by increasing, internally generated *volatility*.

Complex dynamics, however, are not random. As illustrated by the financial market meltdown that began in the United States in the summer of 2008 and then quickly spread around the world, while complex systems are prone to exhibiting significantly nonlinear dynamics, these dynamics are both responsive and historically cogent. This is because network growth is not simply a function of quantities or densities of interaction, but also qualities of interactive content. To make use of Hedley Bull's (2002) distinction between systems and societies, while increased interaction may suffice to form a *network system*, the emergence of *network society* correlates with the advent of shared norms and practices. That is, the network dynamics of complex emergence are an expression of *values-infused adaptation*.

Reflexive Modernization

As made evident by the financial market collapse of 2008 and subsequent global recession, it is not the case that there is a single global network society. Neither is it the case that network adaptations are equally benign with respect to all who are affected by them. The past half-century has seen both the proliferation and interpenetration of variously attuned networks, and hence the increasing importance of differences in—and, indeed, conflicts over—basic norms and values. As already noted, industrial modernization and marketization have brought about increasingly disparate fortunes for globalization "winners" and "losers" in terms of wealth and opportunity distribution. But in addition, the emergence of complexly networked circuits of exchange has brought about increasing disparities of risk—a transformation that has been usefully theorized as the advent of "reflexive modernization" (Beck et al. 1994) and "world risk society" (Beck 1992, 1999; Wynne et al. 1996).

Reflexive modernization occurs when the scale and scope of global interdependencies reach the point beyond which it is impossible to externalize the costs of further growth and development. From this point, further expansions of instrumental rationality and technological control result in the amplifying production of unpredictable risks, hazards, and threats in the face of which responsible decisions nevertheless have to be made. If earlier phases of modernization were characterized by *public goods* discourses addressing conflicts over how best to distribute the benefits of progress, reflexive modernity is characterized by intensifying considerations of and conflicts over how to distribute such *public bads* as pollution, poverty, environmental degradation, and the effects of climate change that are unplanned, ironic consequences of continued industrialization and globalization.

Importantly, the risks, threats, and hazards that are produced in pursuit of continued economic growth are *not* a function of the failure of current systems of expertise or their practical application. On the contrary, they are a result of the *successes* of these systems. Differently stated, the challenges posed by reflexive modernization are not *problems* that can be solved simply by developing new strategies and techniques for furthering existing patterns of aims and interests. Rather, these challenges confront us with *predicaments* that can only be successfully addressed by resolving intensifying conflicts among our own values, aims, and interests. Global warming and climate volatility, for example, do not present us with a geophysical problem that can be solved by astute planetary engineering. Instead, they force confrontation with conflicts among our social, economic, political, technological, and cultural values, and can only be addressed through greater resolution—greater clarity and commitment—regarding the means-to and meanings-of "good" and "healthy" environments, and human-with-planetary flourishing.[4]

Rethinking the Trajectory of Higher Educational Change

In light of the global interplay among networks, complexity, and the problem-to-predicament transition, several observations seem warranted about the course of higher education change. First and foremost, if we are warranted in predicting anything about the trajectory of higher education change, it is that it will be "other than expected." We are in the midst of a *nonlinear* transformation in which causal explanations have only very local predicative value and in which—contrary to what is suggested by dependency theory or by the educational adaptation of the "flying geese" model of economic development (Kuroda and Passarelli 2009)—change is neither being imposed (globally) from above nor percolating up (locally) from below. Rather, it is being continuously effected/affected at/from all educational scales and positions as an emergent function of cascading, unpredictable, and yet nonrandom movements in the direction of heightening interactivity, accelerating differentiation, and reduced organizational hierarchy. While we can anticipate strengthening global governance to be part of the trajectory of twenty-first-century higher education change, it is likely to be a "mobius-strip" form of governance that "neither begins nor culminates at any level or any point of time" (Rosenau 2002, 81).

In light of the presence of both integrating and fragmenting dynamics in contemporary globalization processes, we would also seem warranted in anticipating higher education change to make evident and accentuate tensions between, for example, increasing structural uniformity and standardization on one hand, and increasing variation and flexibility on the other. In other words, we can expect higher education to assume forms that are ambiguously modern and postmodern, public and private, pure and applied, operationally demonstrating a shift from an either/or logic to a both/and logic of systemic, institutional, and programmatic development.

In connection with this, as the density and quality of network interactions cross crucial thresholds, we are likely to witness a shift from predominantly contingent, instrumentally established external relations in which the essential integrity of relational partners remains unchallenged toward increasingly constitutive, thematically improvised internal relations. That is, we can expect first, the advent of global higher education *systems* built cooperatively around *common practices,* and then the emergence of global higher education *societies* coordinated dynamically around *shared norms and values.* The global *system-building* dimension of higher education change is already abundantly evident, for example, in the construction of everexpanding frameworks for credit transfer and articulation, in the building of branch campuses, and in the spread of "twinning" programs resulting in joint or dual degrees. And intimations of the strengthening coalescence of *society-realizing* dynamics can be found in the form of deepening engagement with issues of institutional/systemic compatibility, comparability, and transparency, and in increasingly concerted efforts to develop coordinated approaches to assessing higher education qualifications and quality.

Finally, the problem-to-predicament transition associated with the rise of reflexive modernity and world risk society would seem to warrant expectations of an epistemic revolution involving the displacement of individual "bodies of knowledge" by "knowledge ecologies" and a progressive reembedding of the technical within the ethical, a healing of the modern severance of knowledge (knowing-that and knowing-how), and wisdom (knowing-to) (Hershock 2011). Because higher education has played an intimate role in creating the expert systems that have informed modernization, marketization, and industrialization processes, and their ironic production of expanding risks, hazards, and threats to ecological and social well being, this is likely to be a highly contested revolution.

These are, I think, reasonably defensible expectations regarding the arc of higher education change in broad structural terms. But granted the profound embeddedness of higher education within the plural social, economic, political, technological, and cultural relations that are constitutive of contemporary societies, there are also things that we are *not* warranted in expecting, some of which are quite worrying.

To begin with, we cannot reasonably expect the trajectory of higher education change to be either continuous or globally uniform. Like the dynamics of global informational capitalism with which they have become ever more deeply entrained in the course of broader neoliberal reforms, the dynamics of higher education provision are likely to exhibit considerable volatility and unevenness. As Per Bak (1996) has noted, once a network becomes truly complex, unpredictable fluctuations and catastrophes are inevitable because such events serve to redistribute stresses internal to the network. And in ways that have been made painfully apparent since the onset of the "Great Recession" in 2008, the prospects of market fluctuations profoundly disrupting higher education provision and forcing its purposes to be called into question cannot reasonably be expected to lessen.[5] In addition, the ways in which these stresses are redistributed—both in society and within higher education—are likely to become increasingly uneven as the costs of further growth are "exported" to those least able to protest, adapt to, or bear them.

All other things remaining equal, increased marketization, commodification, and competition within higher education are likely to reproduce therein the same kinds of disparities found in other markets where, in Ivan

Illich's memorable terms, the commodification of basic needs has translated into the institutionalization of entirely new classes of the poor. As higher education comes to be less and less fully supported and provided as a public good and delivered instead as a marketable commodity, vast populations are likely to find themselves disciplined into a compulsory, lifelong consumption of educational goods and services that will reinforce rather than eliminate poverty (Hershock 2007). And, at a more systemic level, the commodification of higher education will render it subject to market failures in the form, for example, of sudden and unpredicted devaluations of certain degrees or a long-term collapses of employment prospects for graduates overall. In short, the marketization of higher education cannot be expected to be without the fickle and fractious potentials associated with other forms of capitalist "creative destruction."

From a more philosophical perspective, we would not be warranted in assuming that actualizing the common practices and shared values needed to bring about global higher education systems and societies will inexorably result in greater, worldwide educational diversity and equity. As is to be expected in the context of global network society, issues of gender, cultural, cognitive, and institutional difference are already well recognized, and responding to them has become a core value of global higher education. But in and of itself, this is sufficient only to guarantee increasing *variety* with respect to, for example, student populations, program offerings, and types of institutions and partnerships among them. As an emergent relational quality indexing the extent to which differences are activated as the basis of meaningful contribution to sustainably shared flourishing, *diversity* cannot be either mandated or expected to happen simply as a matter of course.

Likewise, while the network-driven differentiation and expansion of higher education portends globally increasing gross enrollments and perhaps the eventual achievement of universal access worldwide, this alone cannot guarantee global educational equity. At present, equity is predominantly conceived as an essentially quantitative measure of comparative equality of opportunity. This conception of equity is a product of modern liberalism, and is of increasingly limited critical value in the context of globalization-driven multiplications and magnifications of differences, and the complexity-driven pairing of interdependence with interpenetration. Yet, even in this limited sense, the unprecedented expansions of global wealth and economic activity over the last 60 years have not been accompanied by greater equity. The conditions of equality of opportunity chartered by the 1949 UN Declaration of Universal Human Rights and the more recent Millennium Development Goals remain unrealized. And granted the current dominance of policies aimed at bringing higher education into ever more precise and effective alignment with market values that have historically resulted in exacerbating developmental inequalities, greater equity cannot be assumed to be a natural result of the present transformation of higher education.

Alternatively, if equity is more aptly understood as a distinctive *relational quality* that emerges with strengthening clarity—about and commitments—to acting in one's own self interest in ways that are deemed valuable by others, then realizing the conditions for greater equity will depend on realizing those needed for enhanced diversity. Given the current inflection of higher education toward the breakdown of higher education *communities* in favor of increasingly varied, individualized, elective, and instrumentally effective *delivery systems*, the relationship between the current orientation of higher education change and increasing equity in this more robust sense are even more tenuous. Unlike variety, which can be instantaneously realized, diversity emerges in an educational context—if at all—only over time as the facts about *how much* we *differ— from* each another are subsumed within valuing *how well* we are able to *differ— for* one another. The extent and depth of interaction needed to produce and sustain conditions ripe for the emergence of diversity are very unlikely to be realized in context of retrenching disciplinary silos, expanding short-term programs, and the normalization of the wholly elective and limited relational bandwidth that is tacitly imposed by distance education. Increased connectivity in higher education cannot be expected, by itself, to enhance educational diversity, whether in epistemic, social, cultural, or political terms.

Finally, to return to concerns raised earlier about the complicity of higher education in the increasingly uneven geographies of development that have materialized along with the phenomenal market-driven economic growth and wealth generation of the last 30 years, it is *not* reasonable to expect higher education to function as a force for greater equity outside of the education sector. Universities and colleges are exceptionally dense relational nexuses. And as such, they have a unique potential for contributing to the articulation and functioning of global networks by greatly expanding their constitutive kinds and quantities of connectivity. Yet, as is true for any node in a network, the value of the connections that a particular university or college brings to a network is a function not only of the sheer number of connections made possible, but also the quality of their informational input. To the degree that the provision and purposes higher education are more closely aligned with market needs—that is, the degree to which the common practices and shared values crucial to the emergence of global higher education systems and societies are aligned with such market practices and values as competition, choice, convenience, and control—the *less* likely it is that higher education will contribute significantly to realizing more equitably oriented patterns of globalization and economic activity.

Conclusions

Placing the trend toward increasing higher education mobility in the context of the historically recent emergence of global networks, complex interdependence, and reflexive modernization raises considerable worries about capitulating to the purported inevitability both of this trend generally and its more specific orientation toward a "free market" higher education future. If the boundaries between the practices and values of higher education and those of the market erode sufficiently, higher education runs the risk of being subject not only to both the emancipatory and disciplinary dimensions of globalization, but also to the recapitulation in education of the pattern of stalled development and uneven attainments that have resulted historically as the "bad Samaritan" promises of a free market future have been embraced at face value (Chang 2007).

Contrary to the view epitomized by Francis Fukuyama's announcement of a victoriously neoliberal "end of history," I do not think that the mobilization of higher education to serve the needs of global informational capitalism is already a "done deal." Globally, we are still in positions to place higher education mobility into more critical perspective and to work toward aligning twenty-first-century higher education change processes with deepening emphases on the values of diversity and equity as a global relations commons and global public good—a commons and public good crucial to the activation of especially cognitive and cultural differences as the basis of articulating viable means-to and meanings-of truly shared global flourishing.

In concrete terms, we might turn to currently heterodox insights into the history of neoliberal free markets and consider the merits of "protectionist" policies in higher education—working, for example, to ensure that the frictionless flows of both learners and providers, and of knowledge and information, are conducive to conserving, and indeed more fully appreciating, the distinctive contributions to be made by indigenous and local epistemologies. We might also entertain delinking higher education mobility from the metaphorical and practical implications of internationalization and cross-border engagements as deliberate efforts "to cope with the influences and challenges of globalization at various levels" (Kuroda and Passarelli 2009, 7), and instead to align mobility with fueling critical efforts to build global networks disposed toward redirecting the dynamics of globalization.

As a crucial node within a complexly networked global higher education society, the university might then serve as a nexus of extraordinarily rich and free of flows of people and knowledge—flows coordinated in such a way as to counter, rather than aid and abet, the erosion of diversity both within and among global relational ecologies, and to equitably resolve the predicaments emerging as the dangerous and perhaps still opportune legacy of globalization as we have come to know it.

Notes

1. For a summary of the history of higher education in the context of globalization, see Guruz (2008), Chapter 5, especially pp. 117–138.
2. I am using the term "diversity" here in a technical sense in contrast with mere variety. In brief, diversity is a qualitative relational dynamic that emerges as a function of complex interdependence and consists in mutually reinforcing contributions to sustainably shared flourishing. In contrast, variety is a quantitative index of multiplicity that entails nothing more than either simple or complicated patterns of coexistence. For a more involved discussion of this conceptual contrast in an educational context, see Hershock (2010).
3. On the contrast of grids and networks and a useful, multidisciplinary approach to complexity and social change, see Taylor (2001).
4. For an expanded, but still succinct discussion of distinction between problems and predicaments, see Hershock (2007, 123–125).
5. Importantly, Bak also draws attention to the fact that while we are tempted to try to control circumstances to prevent or minimize such fluctuations, interfering with a complex system to prevent a cascade only serves to relocate the point of stress reduction, leading to a different cascade on different terrain, but a cascade nonetheless (Bak 1996, 191).

References

Altbach, Philip G., Liz Reisberg, and Laura Rumbley. 2010. "Tracking a Global Academic Revolution," *Change* March/April 2010. Available at: http://www.changemag.org/Archives/Back%20Issues/March-April%202010/tracking-global-full.html (accessed June 27, 2011).
Bak, Per. 1996. *How Nature Works: The Science of Self-Organized Criticality*. New York: Copernicus Press.
Beck, Ulrich. 1992. *Risk Society: Towards a New Modernity*. London: Sage Publications.
———. 1999. *World Risk Society*. London: Polity Press.

Beck, Ulrich, with Anthony Giddens, and Scott Lash. 1994. *Reflexive Modernization: Politics, Tradition and Aesthetics in the Modern Social Order.* Stanford: Stanford University Press.

Beniger, James. 1986. *The Control Revolution: Technological and Economic Origins of the Information Age.* Cambridge, MA: Harvard University Press.

Bull, Hedley. 2002. *The Anarchical Society: A Study of Order in World Politics,* 3rd edition. New York: Columbia University Press.

Capannelli, G. 2009. "Asian Regionalism: How Does It Compare to Europe's?" *East Asia Forum* post on April 21, 2009. Available at: http://www.eastasiaforum.org/2009/04/21/asian-regionalism-how-does-it-compare-to-europes/. (accessed June 28, 2011).

Castells, Manuel. 1996. *The Rise of the Network Society, The Information Age: Economy, Society and Culture,* Vol. I. Cambridge, MA: Blackwell.

———. 1997. *The Power of Identity, The Information Age: Economy, Society and Culture,* Vol. II. Cambridge, MA: Blackwell.

———. 1998. *End of Millennium, The Information Age: Economy, Society and Culture,* Vol. III. Cambridge, MA: Blackwell.

Chang, Ha-Joon. 2007. *Bad Samaritans: The Myth of Free Trade and the Secret History of Capitalism.* New York: Bloomsbury Press.

Foucault, Michel. 1995. *Discipline and Punish: The Birth of the Prison,* trans. Alan Sheridan. New York: Vintage Books.

Guéhenno, Jean-Marie. 2000. *The End of the Nation-State,* trans. Victoria Elliot. Minneapolis, MN: The University of Minnesota Press.

Gürüz, Kemal. 2008. *Higher Education and International Student Mobility in the Global Knowledge Economy.* Albany, NY: State University of New York Press.

Harvey, David. 1989. *The Condition of Postmodernity.* Oxford: Oxford University Press.

———. 1996. *Justice, Nature and the Geography of Difference.* Malden, MA: Blackwell Publishing.

Hershock, Peter D. 1999. *Reinventing the Wheel: A Buddhist Response to the Information Age.* Albany: State University of New York Press.

———. 2007. "Education and Alleviating Poverty: Educating for Equity and Diversity," in *Changing Education: Leadership, Innovation and Development in a Globalizing Asia Pacific,* ed. Peter D. Hershock, Mark Mason, and John N. Hawkins. Hong Kong: Springer.

———. 2010. "Higher Education, Globalization and the Critical Emergence of Diversity," *Paideusis* 19 (1): 29–42.

———. 2011. "Information and Innovation in a Global Knowledge Society: Implications for Higher Education," in *The Emergent Knowledge Society and the Future of Higher Education: Asian Perspectives.* London: Routledge

Kuroda, Kazuo, and David Passarelli. 2009. "Modeling TNE Directions in Asia." *The Observatory on Borderless Higher Education,* December 2009, p. 7. Available at: http://www.obhe.ac.uk/documents/view_details?id=787 (accessed February 2, 2012).

Ohmae, Kenichi. 1995. *The End of the Nation-State: The Rise of Regional Economies.* New York: Simon and Schuster.

Power, Daniel, and Naomi Standen, eds. 1999. *Frontiers in Question: Eurasian Borderlands, 700–1700*. New York: St. Martin's Press.
Rosenau, James N. 2002. "Governance in a New Global Order," in *Governing Globalization: Power, Authority, and Global Governance*, ed. David Held and Anthony C. McGrew. Cambridge: Polity Press.
Scott, Peter. 1998. "Massification, Internationalization and Globalization," in *The Globalization of Higher Education*, ed. Peter Scott. Philadelphia, PA: The Society for Research into Higher Education and Open University Press.
Taylor, Mark C. 2001. *The Moment of Complexity: Emerging Network Culture*. Chicago: University of Chicago Press.
Toulmin, Stephen. 1990. *Cosmopolis: The Hidden Agenda of Modernity*. Chicago: University of Chicago Press.
Trow, Martin. 1972. "The Expansion and Transformation of Higher Education." *International Review of Education* 18(1): 61–83.
Wynne, Brian, with Scott Lash, and Bronislaw Szersynski, eds. 1996. *Risk, Environment and Modernity: Towards a New Ecology*. London: Sage Publications.

Chapter 3

Learning the Hard Way: Lessons from Australia's Decade of Innovation in Student Migration Policy

Christopher Ziguras

Australia has been a destination for large-scale immigration for 200 years and over that period has attracted successive waves of migrants. A large part of the contemporary migration intake is entwined with the flow of international students to Australia, and this linkage is having a profound impact on migration patterns, student flows, and the Australian education system. This chapter will elaborate some of the main features of these education/migration linkages and postulate some lessons for other countries from Australia's decade of policy experimentation.

A decade ago Australia began to grant preferential treatment to applicants for permanent residence who held Australian higher education qualifications. The decision was based on longitudinal research on employment outcomes of earlier migrants, which showed that immigrants with Australian qualifications were more readily integrated into the labor market. A points system was introduced for skilled migration programs, and tertiary qualifications were assigned a specific number of points according to the level of study and perceived labor market demand for graduates in each discipline. Thus Australia launched into uncharted territory in international education policy development, and was closely watched by other countries, which recruit large numbers of international students and skilled migrants. This chapter provides an overview of the ways in which ensuing migration policy changes drove international student demand, and the ways in which educational institutions responded to this demand.

It quickly became apparent that a significant number of prospective international students were making course choices based upon the likelihood of attaining permanent residency with each type of educational qualification. In the ensuing decade, students seeking permanent residency, migration agents, educational institutions, and immigration officials have been engaged in an uneasy and unstable relationship with each other. Looking back over the past decade, a pattern is evident in which enrollments surge in those programs that provide the cheapest and shortest pathway to permanent residency. Educational institutions then expand those programs to meet booming demand. This leads within a few years to an oversupply of skilled migrants with particular qualifications, and immigration authorities respond by closing down those pathways. Student demand shifts quickly into the next best migration pathway and the cycle repeats.

The migration-education nexus, and in particular the perverse incentives it creates for educational institutions has in the past two years come to be seen as highly damaging to Australia's international reputation.

This chapter assesses the implications of Australia's experience for educational institutions and governments. It is clear that a high proportion of international students are attracted to the prospect of living and working after graduation in the country in which they study, either temporarily or permanently. It is in the interests of governments and students to make the criteria for granting such residency rights transparent and predictable—governments benefit by being able to process applications objectively and efficiently and students benefit by being able to make choices with a higher level of certainty about outcomes. The challenge for all countries that host significant numbers of international students is how to maximize the benefits that residency rights provide to students and the host country, while avoiding dramatic and unsustainable distortions in enrollment patterns.

Linking Student Recruitment with Skilled Migration

Since the 1990s Australia has laid great emphasis on skilled migration, increasing the number of tertiary qualified migrants at a much faster rate than other forms of migration such as family reunion and humanitarian programs. This growth in skilled migration intakes was uncontroversial in Australia until recently, with bipartisan political support, although the harsh treatment of refugees arriving by boat in Australian waters has been highly contentious, dividing public opinion. The preference for skilled migrants reflects labor market demand, since longitudinal research had shown that skilled workers had lower rates of unemployment, and the government's desire to use immigration to enhance the international competitiveness of the Australian economy by bringing in highly skilled workers from overseas. Between the mid-1990s and 2000, the proportion of skilled migrants in Australia's immigration intake increased from 29 percent to over half and continued to increase in the following years (Koleth 2010). The heightened selection of migrants based on skills and qualifications appeared to have significantly improved the employment outcomes for migrants who arrived around the turn of century compared with those who arrived in the early 1990s (Rizvi 2004; Hawthorne 2005).

Longitudinal studies of the employment outcomes of migrants who arrived during the 1990s showed that those with Australian tertiary qualifications fared significantly better than those who were educated abroad (Birrell and Hawthorne 1999). Former international students had several advantages over other migrants—qualifications that were readily recognized by employers, cultural familiarity, and established social networks, which were beneficial in finding employment.

Prior to 1998, former international students were able to apply for permanent residence, but were barred from applying for three years after graduation and were required to apply from outside Australia. Their applications were assessed on the same basis as graduates of other countries and there is no available data on the proportion of the migration intake that were former international students. There was, however, one large influx of international student migrants immediately after the 1989 Tiananmen Square protests, when 37,000 Chinese students were allowed to stay on compassionate grounds (Hawthorne 2005). Since the 1990s applicants for skilled migration have been rated using a points system that awards point for various qualities that the immigration authorities judge would lead to positive labor market outcomes, such as age, proficiency in English, occupational qualifications, and professional experience.

Starting in 1998, a range of measures was put in place to prioritize the recruitment of former international students as migrants. From 1998 five extra points were awarded for most Australian educational qualifications and from the following year ten points were awarded to applicants with an Australian doctorate. From 2001 international students were allowed to lodge permanent residency applications in Australia upon completion of their studies, whereas previously graduates had to leave the country before their student visa expired then apply for permanent residency from abroad, which is a major inconvenience. In 2003, bonus points for masters were increased to 10 points and 15 for doctorates, and an additional 5 points were awarded to students who resided in regional areas (Rizvi 2004).

These changes were highly effective in achieving their objectives; by 2002, international students comprised half of all applicants for skilled migration and there was early evidence that the migration pathway was stimulating demand for Australian education (Hawthorne 2005). Such an explicit and systematic linking of international education and migration outcomes was unprecedented, and was followed closely by the United Kingdom, Canada, and New Zealand, countries that are also destinations for large numbers of both international students and migrants. By 2004 more than a third of international students completing Australian university degrees were obtaining permanent residency. The rate of migration varied considerably by country of origin, as table 3.1 shows, with nearly three-quarters of graduates from South Asia obtaining permanent residency.

Table 3.1 International Students in Higher Education: Completions, Permanent Residency (PR) Visas Issued and Enrollment Growth

	Higher Education Completions 2004	PR Visas Issued 2004–2005 as % of 2004 Completions	Average Annual Rate of HE Enrolment Growth, 2000–2004
Sri Lanka	583	76.8	18.7
India	3,455	73.7	41.8
Bangladesh	681	69.8	51.7
South Korea	1,058	50.2	22.7
Indonesia	3,405	45.9	3.1
China (excluding HK)	7,061	39.7	69.6
Vietnam	714	35.2	14.5
Hong Kong	2,906	34.1	12.6
Japan	935	27.4	16.4
Malaysia	4,805	27.0	12.6
Taiwan	1,313	20.7	14.0
Singapore	3,226	15.7	1.5
Thailand	2,147	11.3	20.1
Canada	820	4.5	33.2
Other countries	9,186	24.2	12.9
Total	**42,295**	**34.1**	**20.0**

Source: Columns 2 and 3 from Birrell (2006), column 4 from Australian Education International, Commonwealth Department of Education, Employment and Workplace Relations, 2010.

Table 3.1 also shows the rates of enrollment growth across this period as the study-migration pathway was being established. For all nationalities, enrollments grew by 20 percent per year on average. The rate of growth for students from the top seven countries with the highest rates of permanent residence PR combined was 33.5 percent per annum, while the seven countries with the lowest rates of PR combined grew at only 11.6 percent per annum across this period. There are clearly many other factors driving enrollment levels for each country, and therefore much variation between countries with similar migration rates (e.g., China and Vietnam), but it is evident that enrollments grew significantly faster from those countries with higher migration rates.

During the first half of the decade many students seeking permanent residency in Australia undertook masters programs, usually in information technology and accounting. For graduates from overseas universities, these two-year programs offered extra points both because they are postgraduate qualifications and because these occupations were prioritized based on labor market demand for graduates. However, over time it became apparent that many international graduates of these programs were not subsequently employed in the fields for which they had studied. Immigration authorities worked with professional associations in information technology and accounting to fine-tune migration requirements, leading to a heightened emphasis on English proficiency and professional experience (Birrell and Rapson 2005).

New Entrants

In 2005, the Australian government increased the number of points international graduates needed to obtain permanent residency, meaning that many international students had to undertake further studies in an area of migration demand that would provide extra points. A number of trades (including hairdressing) had been included on the occupations in demand list for some time, and soon after raising the number of points required cooking was added to the list of occupations for which extra points would be awarded. Private colleges responded quickly by developing new cooking and hairdressing programs that would give students enough points to get through. Some private colleges are very high-quality institutions with a wide range of programs for local and international students, but there are low quality providers who cater almost exclusively to international students seeking fast and easy qualifications to support migration applications (for a description of these, see Jensen 2007).

The number of international students enrolled in vocational programs in private colleges grew extremely rapidly, from 37,061 in 2005 to 178,011 in 2009. For several years many in the Australian international education industry warned that the rapid growth of private college providers focused on migration pathway programs posed serious threats to vulnerable students, who were sometimes willing to pay hefty fees and tolerate poor facilities and teaching in return for a piece of paper that would assist them in gaining residency. There was also a concern that the actions of these colleges could bring the entire Australian education system into disrepute internationally. The industry group representing private educational institutions, the Australian Council for Private Education and Training, was the most outspoken voice calling for more active investigation and prosecution of substandard providers, recognizing that the organization's members had the most to lose from the actions of rogue providers (Morton and McKenzie 2007).

Enrollments in migration-oriented programs in private colleges continued to grow with no sign of slowing, however, the numbers of students in certain programs was beginning to far exceed Australia's workforce requirements in those occupations. The head of the Professional Hairdressers Association complained that private colleges were "bastardizing the industry," by taking in large numbers of international students intending to apply for permanent residency, very few of whom intended to work in the industry (Porter 2008). This situation has been compounded by rising unemployment in Australia, as elsewhere. A significant tightening of the student migration policy appears inevitable, but would be devastating for tens of thousands of young people who had invested heavily in study in Australia only to return home with qualifications of very limited value in their home country after wasting much time and money chasing permanent residency.

The Plight of Indian Students in Australia

It is clear that most Indian students who choose to study in Australia aspire to obtain permanent residency, but as Baas (2006) and Singh and Cabraal (2010) have shown, students' decisions are rarely purely concerned with migration; rather, these decisions reflect their personal career aspirations and extended family relationships both in Australia and India. Enrollments of Indian students in Australia have grown dramatically since the study-migration nexus was clearly established, as table 3.2 illustrates. Early growth up to 2005 was largely in public universities, however as

Table 3.2 Indian Students in Australian Tertiary Education

	2002	2005	2009
Higher Education—Public	8,742	21,930	26,345
Higher Education—Private	337	599	1,751
VET—Public	766	1,153	5,179
VET—Private	1,229	2,236	73,218
Total	**11,074**	**25,918**	**106,493**

Source: Australian Education International, Commonwealth Department of Education, Employment and Workplace Relations, 2011.

vocational programs came to represent a shorter and less costly route to permanent residency from 2005, most of the growth occurred in private vocational education and training colleges where enrollments of Indian students increased at a startling rate, from 2,236 in 2005 to 73,218 in 2009.

Australia's Indian student bubble has now well and truly burst, brought about by migration policy changes, which were widely expected, and by a sudden media storm arising from a series of assaults on Indian students. The number of Indian students starting tertiary studies in Australia fell by 28 percent in 2010 and is set to fall at a similar rate in 2011.

Looking at the factors that help explain the character of the media storm concerning Indian student welfare reveals much about the student migration boom, and highlights the enormous gulf between the reality on the ground and the Australian government's aspirations to recruit the best and the brightest into those areas of the labor market where labor shortages exist. In 2008, there were several cases of violent attacks on Indian taxi drivers, which led to highly publicized street protests. At around 3:00 a.m. on April 29, 2008, a 23-year-old Indian international student, Jalvinder Singh, working as a taxi driver in Melbourne was stabbed by a passenger. The following night Indian taxi drivers staged a 24-hour protest blocking one of the city's most prominent intersections, calling for improved security for drivers, including security screens to be installed in all taxis, and for improved security around suburban railway stations. The state government agreed to phase in security screens and to fully investigate all attacks. A 45-year-old man was charged with attempted murder. On May 18, 2008, in Adelaide, an Indian international student, Balraj Singh, driving a taxi was assaulted late at night by two 24-year-old men, who were subsequently charged with aggravated assault and robbery. Hundreds of taxi drivers staged protests in Adelaide, with similar demands to the Melbourne protests.

There has been a long history of violent attacks against taxi drivers in Australia, but what has changed is the ethnic composition of the workforce. A very large proportion of taxi drivers are now Indian, and the more experienced drivers, who are usually from more established migrant communities, tend to work day shifts while Indian students who study during the day and have less ability to pick and choose their shifts, are left to work night shifts, especially on weekends, which are notoriously dangerous. After the Adelaide attack the head of the Cab Drivers Association told local media, "We've got drivers out there that are not properly trained that the government refuses to recognize this—it's a critical issue in inflaming these assaults. We are exploiting our immigrants by getting them to become cheap labor in the taxi industry...I mean we should have the decency at least to train them properly, to skill them on what sort of situations they could face out there and we should have more interest in the work environment" (Bhandari 2008). These attacks led to discussions between the Indian consul general, South Australian government and police, as well as taxi industry, and drivers' representatives. However, while some branches of government were working hard to try to improve driver security, many international students driving taxis were in fear of immigration authorities that were carrying out inspections at taxi ranks to ensure that international students were not working more than the 20-hour limit imposed by student visas.

The government began to wind down the student migration program in December 2008 in response to the economic downturn that resulted from the global financial crisis (Evans 2008a, 2008b). The changes reduced the number of skilled migration places and made permanent residency more difficult for many international students already in migration oriented programs by prioritizing applicants sponsored by employers or governments and tightening the list of occupations eligible for bonus points. These changes negatively affected tens of thousands of students, some of whom were en route to commence their studies early in 2009, some were currently studying programs that they had expected would enable them to stay permanently, and others had already lodged applications based on previous studies.

In 2008, the attacks seemed confined to taxi drivers, but, in 2009, a series of serious assaults against Indian students in a one-month period in Melbourne and Sydney resulted in street protests in both cities and a media storm in India, with serious political repercussions in both countries. On May 9, 2009, Sourabh Sharma, 21, a hospitality management student was beaten up on a train by a group of teenagers. He was returning home in the evening after a shift at KFC (Johnston 2009). Four teenagers were charged over the assault. Security video footage of the attack, made public later in

May, was broadcast extensively in Australia and India, showing a group of teenage boys who appeared to be of diverse racial backgrounds repeatedly punching and kicking Sourabh, who sustained a broken jaw and extensive bruising from the attack. On May 25, 2009, Baljinder Singh, 25, an Indian cookery student, was stabbed in the stomach in an attempted robbery while leaving a suburban railway station. The following day four Indian students were attacked when a birthday party at their home was gate crashed by two teenage boys. One of the students, Sravan Kumar Theerthala, 25, who studied automotive technology in a private college, was stabbed in the head with a screwdriver by one of the intruders, putting him in a coma. A 17-year-old has been charged with attempted murder.

Photographs of Kumar and Singh, one unconscious in the hospital with head bandaged and tubes protruding from his nose and mouth, the other on a hospital bed displaying a large bandaged stab wound, were shown prominently on Indian television and in newspapers. Television current affairs programs and newspaper editorials speculated about the root causes of this apparent "wave of racist attacks." Was this caused by Australian resentment at India's growing status in the world and the newfound affluence of Indians abroad, some asked. As stories of previous assaults on Indians in Australia emerged others asked whether the Australian media had been covering up these racist attacks.

The political response in India was fast and furious. On May 29, Australia's high commissioner to India was summoned to a meeting with Indian Overseas Affairs minister Vayalar Ravi, who urged Australia to ensure the events were not repeated (Hodge and Clayfield 2011). India's high commissioner to Australia traveled to Melbourne to convey her government's concern to Victorian police, government, and educational representatives. The prime ministers and the foreign ministers of the two countries discussed the issue with their counterparts, all expressing their abhorrence at the attacks. On May 30, Indian film star Amitabh Bachchan announced he would turn down an honorary doctorate from the Queensland University of Technology that he had previously agreed to accept. On June 6, Bollywood's largest union, the Federation of Western India Cine Employees called on its members to stop filming in Australia. This comes after a string of big-budget Bollywood films that have been filmed and set in Australia in recent years.

In Australia, the response was quite different. Violent attacks by young men against other young men are not uncommon occurrences, and as around one in three people living in Melbourne and Sydney was born outside Australia it is very common for either the victim or perpetrator to be a foreigner. In Australia, debate hinged on whether the attacks were racially motivated, that is whether some young men (of various ethnic backgrounds) were targeting Indian students, or whether Indian students were finding themselves in the wrong places at the wrong times. For example, one senior editor with the Australian newspaper criticized the Victorian government for downplaying the racist character of the attacks, while other articles in that newspaper have pointed to the diverse ethnic and racial backgrounds of the perpetrators of the attacks. While there are some young Anglo-Australian men who are xenophobic and who have mounted ugly demonstrations against the "invasion" of their suburbs by immigrants (most famously in Cronulla in Sydney), there has been little indication that these particular assaults were motivated by such white racist backlash, though some surely are. The "survival tips" put forward by an Indian graduate from an Adelaide university paint a frightening picture of the threat posed by violent white teenagers. The student's advice, titled "Adopt their culture without compromising on yours," concludes, "Mostly all matured Australians are quite friendly with a great sense of humor. The whole Australian community should not be judged just because of the behavior and the manners of some of the most ill bred Aussie teenagers" (Defence Forum India 2011).

A major incident in early June in Sydney highlighted the complexity of the racial issues. On June 8 and 9, Indian students staged large protests in a low-income neighborhood where in recent years Indians have surpassed Lebanese as the largest ethnic group. The protests were sparked by an attack on an Indian student by a group of young men of Middle Eastern background. Indian students claimed that the police were not doing enough to protect them from Lebanese gangs. Indian protesters attacked three uninvolved Lebanese men and police brought in the reinforcements to control the crowd.

But why Indian students? Over 600,000 international students studied in Australia in 2009, but Indian students who make up around one sixth of the total seem to be the overrepresented as targets of violent assaults. The Indian students who are attracted to vocational programs in private colleges are from less affluent backgrounds, and have lower levels of English language proficiency, compared with those who enroll in university programs (Baas 2006; Singh and Cabraal 2010). These students are able to obtain loans with which they can pass the financial means test to obtain a student visa to Australia, but they are understandably reluctant to draw down on those loans and instead seek to earn enough in Australia to pay their tuition fees and living expenses. Compared with other international students in Australia, students from India appear to be more dependent upon income from shift work, such as driving taxis, stacking supermarket shelves, and working in convenience stores and as security guards. They are more likely to be living in outer suburbs with cheaper housing, and therefore traveling late on trains more often, and in areas where street violence is more common. Gender is an issue too, as assaults against strangers on and around public transport are generally perpetrated by young men on other young men, the vast majority of Indian students are male whereas East and Southeast Asian students are evenly split by gender. As a result one would expect a greater rate of assaults against Indian students.

Lessons Learned

Widening Access to International Education Can Create a Vulnerable Student Population

One of the unforeseen effects of the migration-education linkage was to broaden access to international higher education by allowing students from less affluent backgrounds to work while studying, and to have a good prospect of attaining residency after a relatively short academic program. Many of these students would not have been able to undertake a degree and then return home because of the difficulty of sourcing the funds to support years of study, and without the prospect of working in a high-income country upon graduation, could not be confident of a return on this investment if they were able to raise the funds through loans.

This episode demonstrated that these students who were attracted to private colleges providing migration-pathway programs were vulnerable to a lack of safety and quality of life that neither the Indian nor Australian communities could accept. Policing around public transport was improved for a short while, but the fact remained that youth violence had been a persistent problem in some Australian cities for a long time, and could not be fixed easily. As Markus (2012) has noted, violence and robbery had been a longstanding issue in many of the locations in which Indian students were assaulted, and the media attention that developed in India led to responses that local residents had long been calling for.

Quickly, Australian immigration authorities responded in a very different manner, tightening the financial means tests for students from less affluent countries, significantly increasing the amount of available funds for living expenses that prospective students were required to show in order to obtain a student visa. This served to again restrict access to education in Australia to more affluent students who are less likely to be exposed to the violent fringes of Australian society.

The Value of Permanent Residence to Students Can Easily be Exploited by Dishonest Providers and Migration Agents

The migration-driven nature of enrollments in many private colleges led to competition between providers on the basis of price and speed to gain one's desired qualification. Until this outpouring of frustration, neither students nor providers were primarily concerned with the quality of the education being provided. Anecdotal accounts of a cost relationship between less-than-honest students and less-than-honest colleges abounded, supported by evidence uncovered in raids by migration officials after the tide had begun to turn. Such perverse incentives could, and should, have been managed through a stringently enforced accreditation and quality assurance regime, however this was found to be severely lacking, which the industry had been calling for over many years (Morton and McKenzie 2007).

In particular, the vertical integration of student recruitment agencies, private colleges, migration agencies, accommodation providers, and employers led to many students being misinformed and directed on the basis of the commercial interests of interlinked business rather than the student's interests. Similar cases of insufficiently regulated private colleges targeting the international student market have been observed in the United Kingdom and New Zealand in the past decade. Educational and immigration authorities have been subjecting education providers to far higher levels of scrutiny since early 2009 in an effort to raise standards and to eliminate fraudulent practices.

Two-Step Migration Exposes Students to the Vagaries of Immigration Policies That are Prone to Frequent Review

Before the assaults on Indian students had hit the media, immigration authorities were removing lower-level vocational qualifications from the skilled migration points system (Evans 2008a). This posed significant risks to the pool of students that were at the time enrolled in these programs with the expectation of being able to apply for permanent residence, who numbered in the tens of thousands. Successive tightening of skilled migration intakes have left many tens of thousands of young people living in limbo in Australia on study visas and temporary bridging visas. Many are pursuing the remaining routes to permanent residency, including enrolling in higher education programs with a higher points weighting, and seeking employer or state government sponsorship. There are still routes to permanent residency but they are now more drawn out and less predictable for students.

References

Baas, Michiel. 2006. "Students of Migration: Indian Overseas Students and the Question of Permanent Residency." *People and Place* 14(1): 9–24.
Bhandari, Neena. 2008. "Taxi Drivers Protest Bashing of Indian Cabbie in Adelaide." *Indo-Asian News Service.* May 19, 2008.
Birrell, Bob. 2006. "Implications of Low English Standards Among Overseas Students at Australian Universities." *People and Place* 14(4): 53–64.
Birrell, Bob and Lesleyanne Hawthorne. 1999. "Skilled Migration Outcomes as of 1996," in *Review of the Independent and Skilled-Australian Linked Categories.* Canberra: Austrlian Government Department of Immigration, Multicultural and Aboriginal Affairs.
Birrell, Bob, and Virginia Rapson. 2005. *Migration and the Accounting Profession in Australia.* Melbourne: Monash University (for CPA Australia).
Defence Forum India. 2011. *Racist Attacks on Indians in Australia!.* Defence Forum India 2009. Available at: http://defenceforumindia.com/documentary/2050-racist-attacks-indians-australia-18.html (accessed July 30, 2011).
Evans, Chris. 2008a. *Changes to the 2008–09 Skilled Migration Program.* Canberra: Australian Government Department of Immigration and Citizenship.
———. 2008b. *Migration Program Gives Priority to Those with Skills Most Needed, Media Release.* Canberra: Commonwealth Department of Immigration and Citizenship.
Hawthorne, Lesleyanne. 2005. ""Picking Winners:" The Recent Transformation of Australia's Skill Migration Policy." *International Migration Review* 39(3): 663–696.
Hodge, Amanda and Matthew Clayfield. 2011. "Delhi Carpets Our Man Over Attacks." *The Australian.* May 30, 2011.
Jensen, Erik. 2007. "School's in for Stayers." *Sydney Morning Herald.* July 4, 2007.
Johnston, Chris. 2009. "Scarred, Scared and Wanting to Go Home." *The Age.* May 16, 2009.
Koleth, Elsa. 2010. Overseas Students: Immigration Policy Changes 1997–May 2010. Parliamentary Library Background Note. Canberra: Parliament of Australia.
Markus, Andrew. 2012. "Racism and International Students in Australia," in *A Home Away from Home? International Students in Australian and South African Higher Education*, ed. Ilana Snyder and John Nieuwenhuysen. Clayton: Monash University Press.
Morton, Adam and Nick McKenzie. 2007. "Canberra Failing to Regulate Colleges: Industry." *The Age.* March 15, 2007.

Porter, Jonathan. 2008. "Fast-Tracked Residents not Tied to Their Trades." *The Australian*. September 20, 2008.

Rizvi, Abul. 2004. "Immigration and International Education," in *Australian International Education Conference*. Sydney: IDP Education Australia.

Singh, Supriya and Anuja Cabraal. 2010. "Indian Student Migrants in Australia: Issues of Community Sustainability." *People and Place* 18(1): 19–30.

Chapter 4

"Shared Space" in Global Higher Education: A Southeast Asian Perspective

Morshidi Sirat

Introduction

The global higher education system can be conceptualized as a model comprising three components—the developed, the emerging, and the developing higher education systems—with overlapping area of exchanges and interactions, which can be termed as "shared space" for the purpose of collaboration and cooperation. This term or concept of shared space is different from the "common higher education area" in the European context or Southeast Asia's "common higher education space" as proposed by the Southeast Asian Ministers of Education Organization-Regional Centre for Higher Education and Development (SEAMEO-RIHED) in Bangkok. The common area or common space in the European Union (EU) and Southeast Asian contexts respectively is more geographical or rather geopolitical in nature. The shared space framework as proposed in this chapter (borrowed from sociologist Milton Santos 1975), builds upon functional relationships and networks, and thus would be nonphysical or nonspatial in character. Within this shared space we will notice that "circuits of exchange" (Sassen 2004) between the three components noted earlier are in terms of migration of ideas and persons. These circuits of exchanges within the shared space have important implications for the development of higher education institutions involved.

It is further envisaged that this shared space contains various activities connected to migration tendencies and mobility flows among academics/researchers, students, programs, and higher education institutions at various institutional scales or levels. Exchanges and interactions within this shared space and among different types of higher education institutions would exhibit the same set of variables but with different characteristics and intensity. This model would ultimately explain the nature of relationships, which is inherently dynamic, between systems within this functional shared space. Arguably, movement of persons would be more amenable to measurement and observation than the flow or migration of ideas. But, the migration of ideas between institutions could have more lasting impacts on participating institutions than just persons. Thus, it is important to have relationships and collaborations based on both the migration and mobility of persons and ideas from medium to longer term. Notably, flows of ideas were deemed to be borderless with the current explosion in communication technology (Wheeler et al. 2000). On the whole, these exchanges are postulated to have created areas of shared interests and mutual benefits, resulting in an abstract form of shared space between higher education institutions with its specific sociocultural implications. With sociocultural considerations being of prime importance in such an interaction and exchange, it is anticipated that the more socially and culturally conscious higher education institutions would normally initiate the development of this type of shared space.

This chapter, through an examination of the circuits of exchange and their impacts on higher education institutions, will attempt to illustrate the continued dominance of the developed higher education system within the shared space, particularly via the migration of ideas rather than persons. The chapter will proceed to argue that in the case of Malaysia, the migration of ideas rather than persons has had important implications for the development of higher education institutions and systems. Malaysia, through specific higher education institutions, is attempting to break away from such a "framework of influence" in its relation with countries within The Association of South East Asian nations (ASEAN) (Sirat 2009) and now beginning to infuse new approaches and thinking. In order to highlight Malaysia and its universities' effort at reconstructing the way we relate to other countries within the shared space framework, this chapter will assess migration and mobility patterns of academic programs, institutions, students, and academics/researchers at two levels: (1) Malaysia with countries well noted for their highly developed higher education system, and (2) Malaysia with the nations in Southeast Asia. Within this aggregate examination of the circuits of exchange, the specific experience of Universiti Sains Malaysia (USM) as Malaysia's first university selected to participate in the Accelerated Program for Excellence (APEX) will be highlighted. USM is very instrumental in mobilizing ideas relating to sustainability and development for the "bottom billions" not only within ASEAN but also expanding increasingly in other regions and groupings.

It is the contention of this chapter that even within the supposedly shared space of higher education between matured and emerging higher education systems, the circuits of exchanges have many characteristics of dominance, control, or even manipulation. In other words, while we may notice the dynamic relationships between the systems within the shared space that we could imagine and envisage, from the perspective of mobility and migration of persons, and more so with ideas, it is unequal and inequitable. There is indeed a need to reconceptualize and reconstruct generally accepted ideas and frameworks that govern relationships and collaborations within the shared space. In the Malaysian context, USM has initiated several discourses specifically to create awareness regarding such a possibility and challenge.

Shared Space, Circuits of Exchange in the Context of Higher Education: The Concept and Framework

Arguably, there are two related consumptions of higher education in developing countries, Malaysia included. There are many reasons for both domestic and external consumption of higher education (Sirat 2006). However, with cross-border higher education, improvement in Information and Computing Technology (ICT) and the increasing trade in education services, the distinction between domestic and external consumption has become blurred in terms of clients, provision, and providers (Sirat et al. 2009). Thus the explanation of what is domestic and what is external is far from perfect in many senses. It is noteworthy that higher education institutions were established to cater for domestic markets but they have transformed in order to serve external markets by providing higher education places to international students. Some have gone as far as franchising their programs and curriculum abroad while a few others have established branches overseas. These developments have created some sort of shared space of mutual benefits and concern between countries and institutions insofar as the developmental path of higher education is concerned. Their common or shared concern may revolve around the notion of social roles of higher education and how social objectives and priorities could be achieved through mobility and exchanges among academic staff, researchers, and students (Global University Network for Innovation 2008).

Notably, shared space may not necessarily involve neighboring countries, as there is no spatial connotation to this concept. As such, shared space could emerge between developed and developing higher education systems, between developing and emerging higher education systems, or as a result of a tripartite collaboration. Within these shared spaces, there exist circuits of exchange in the forms of migration of persons and ideas.

It is further postulated that circuits of exchange have peculiar characteristics, depending on whether they are vertical or lateral in direction. In other words, various activities in the exchanges operate within the context of certain provisions as determined by institutions involved. But generally we would assume that globally ranked higher education institutions would attract other institutions that are similarly ranked, if not one notch lower. They have a shared space and their circuits of exchange will be developed based on this premise and as such would be generally lateral or vertical in direction. There are however exceptions to this generalization, arising specifically out of a concern for equity and other social or human considerations. In this case, there will be a relationship with higher education institutions very much lower in global rankings and even with those not on the global radar at all.

USM is one higher education institution that is developing shared space with several higher education institutions in developing countries primarily because of the need to establish a conceptually different circuit of exchange with institutions outside of the mainstream of global ranking systems. Typically USM's circuit of exchange and that of the other four research universities in Malaysia are determined by the Ministry of Higher Education. But because USM is an APEX status university, it has, unlike other Malaysian public universities, the leeway to experiment with new concepts and approaches in developing shared space with other higher education institutions and implementing highly unconventional circuits of exchange with partnering institutions.

Malaysia Research Universities: Circuits of Exchange

In Malaysia, as a result of the government's preoccupation with global rankings and the desire for world-class stature for some of its universities, there is an expressed commitment to the creation of, in the first instance, research-focused universities. In this regard, the Malaysian Government has designated five universities—Universiti Malaya (UM), Universiti Sains Malaysia (USM), Universiti Putra Malaysia (UPM), Universiti Kebangsaan Malaysia (UKM), and Universiti Teknologi Malaysia (UTM)—as research universities. As research universities, each of these institutions has specific strengths in terms of exploiting opportunities created by expanding shared space in the Asia-Pacific region.

Research collaborations in these research universities take many forms, including research links, networks, and partnerships. Research collaborations frequently consist of networks, which are characterized by horizontal exchanges of information and activities and many would subsequently be adopted as arrangements that are long term in nature. The majority of research collaborations involve smart partnerships between researchers in planning, conducting, managing, and facilitating research activities that enable the production or the application of scientific knowledge. Ultimately, research collaborations are expected to contribute to the research and innovation processes in terms of academic mobility, joint postgraduate supervision, coauthorship of publications, joint product development in relation to commercialization of research products, and technology transfer.

Research Collaboration: Objectives, Modes, and Forms

The internationalization of research and academic researchers has been on the agenda of research universities in Malaysia (Sarjit et al. 2007), and was further emphasized in the recently released *National Higher Education Strategic Plan Approaching 2020* and the accompanying document on *National Higher Education Action Plan 2007–2010*. It is argued that the transnational engagement of researchers is expected to strategically position Malaysian university researchers within the global knowledge societies. The growing importance of worldwide or international rankings of universities, generally according to research criteria, has also changed the scope and nature of research (and publications) in Malaysian universities. In addition, Malaysia's higher education policy, which has been realigned to be in line with the objective of creating "world class" research universities (Kementerian Pengajian Tinggi Malaysia 2007), has presented Malaysian universities with the opportunities to position them accordingly. This objective is to be achieved through a systemic and sustained effort at making research more responsive to the requirements and challenges of internationalization. Toward this end, it is immediately acknowledged that efforts must be directed toward international research cooperation and cross-border networking. (Unfortunately, migration and mobility of persons in the current Malaysia's strategy is based on conventional or western construct and as a result Malaysia will continue to play a catching-up game.)

Research universities' engagement in collaborative research, be it bilateral or multilateral, is increasingly important to Malaysia's position in the global knowledge economy. The quality and impact of internationalization of research should be mapped in terms of international networking and linkages, leadership, and representation in international professional bodies, competitive international research grants, and quantity of international postgraduate students (Kementerian Pengajian Tinggi Malaysia 2007).

The common platform for cooperation is the desire to develop academic exchange programs and cooperation in teaching and research in the furtherance of the advancement and dissemination of learning. This may include various modes that are designed to suit the nature of width and spread of collaborative activities agreed by the partners. These measures include activities commonly practiced by many other universities in Malaysia as follows: exchange of staff and students in teaching and research programs, exchange of scientific materials, publications and information, joint curriculum development, and research collaboration.

In practical terms there are two forms of collaboration as follows:

1. A Memorandum of Understanding (MoU)—the general format is based on an intention to create a relationship with no specific obligations from parties involved, thus is not legally binding.
2. A Memorandum of Agreement (MoA)—this entails a detailed format of cooperation with specific obligations by the parties involved thus is considered legally binding.

The procedures for MoUs/MoAs are, by and large, fairly well established in all universities in Malaysia, including research universities. The process would normally involve a critical phase of institutional matching, whereby intentions are created and parties get together to discuss and identify areas of common interest. This is then followed by official approval by top university management and the University senate if necessary. There have been occasions when formal representations by Malaysian government officials and diplomatic corps were deemed necessary in order to highlight ventures of significance not only to respective Malaysian universities but also to Malaysia. Suffice to say that in all Malaysian universities, there are available guidelines that detail the necessary work process in facilitating collaborative efforts.

A number of mobility schemes have emerged in recent years in the Asia-Pacific region, some related to students and their study abroad, others related to professional mobility (Lenn 2004). The common exchange programs in most Malaysian universities usually involve mainly staff exchange for both academic and administrative staff.

Each research university has specific strengths where strategic links to research (at the international level) are very evident. UM is looking to the West (Europe), but UKM and USM are emphasizing on the Asia Pacific. Postgraduate and staff mobility are still low, although Malaysia is increasingly viewed as an important player in the higher education market with a new group of learners from the Middle East and Southeast Asia. Malaysia has recognized the significance of being a learner in knowledge production, economic wealth creation, and labor movement within a rapidly expanding higher education markets in the Asia Pacific (see Sirat et al. 2010 for details of circuits of exchanges at the aggregate level).

Admittedly, the framework for establishing shared spaces with higher education institutions in other countries is based on conventional and mainstream ideas and constructs. USM has attempted to reconstruct this framework by infusing new ideas and thinking based on sustainability issues and concern for the "bottom billions." Migration and mobility of ideas and persons within shared space with like-minded higher education institutions in other higher education systems should take cognizance of these issues and concerns.

Universiti Sains Malaysia[1]

Universiti Sains Malaysia, established in 1969, is the second oldest university in Malaysia after Universiti Malaya in Kuala Lumpur. By definition, USM as a public university is state controlled and incorporated as a statutory body. As such, the university implements duties and responsibilities in line with the government's objectives and aspirations (Sirat 2009). Following a myriad of education reforms in 1996, the Malaysian government introduced corporate governance for state-controlled universities in 1997 by amending the 1971 University and University Colleges Act (UUCA) 1971. With the passing of a law on the corporatization of state-controlled universities, USM was subsequently corporatized in 1998. The new governance structure implied that the university was expected to operate as an efficient, transparent, and financially able entity. It is important to note that even though USM is corporatized, it is not an independent administrative entity. The government still retains explicit control on the institution.

In 2005, USM was accorded a research university status and subsequently in September 2008 was the only university in Malaysia to be selected as an APEX university. Notably, USM has a history of intentional, systematic, and strategic responses to issues involving higher education and its role and contribution to development and progress of society in the developing world. In this context, USM is at the forefront in acknowledging (and at the same time confronting) the influence of western constructs and ideas in the higher education landscape in Asia, in particular, Southeast Asia. USM focuses on the impacts of the globalization era and the internationalization of higher education with a view of identifying partners and formulating issues of common concern as a basis for the construction of shared space. USM endeavors to achieve the shared space by adopting the Blue Ocean Strategy (BOS) of Kim and Mauborgne (2005). Using BOS as a tool and in connection with the task of transforming its higher education agenda, USM has set out to achieve the following goals: eliminate/reduce bureaucracy, the resource gap, and talent mismatch; raise its global agenda, autonomy, accountability, quality of services, and future relevance; create "people-led" local solutions; and promote sustainability in its functions.

In developing a shared space with partner institutions based on the objectives noted above, circuits of exchange are collectively developed, implemented, monitored, and evaluated. This can be very complex and may involve a range of stakeholders. But, the USM leadership has charted and implemented a systematic program to carry them out effectively by incorporating all activities in the strategic planning process. For instance in 2006, USM's vice-chancellor, focusing on the "university-for-tomorrow," initiated and mobilized selected academics to conduct a series of workshops and brainstorming sessions that were designed to disseminate different scenarios of the "university-of-tomorrow" in preparation for the increasingly globalized higher education environment. These workshops involved 400 academics, administrators, students, support staff, and USM alumni (Universiti Sains Malaysia 2007a). Five alternative scenarios and their respective future triangles were presented by the working committee and they included: The A'la Carte University (market-student-led), The Invisible University (market-tech-led), The Corporate University (commerce-led), The State University (state-led), and The University in the Garden (scholar-led) (Universiti Sains Malaysia 2007b, 37). These scenarios were presented first to the USM community and subsequently at a UNESCO forum on higher education in Paris and the Association of Southeast Asian Institutions of Higher Learning (ASAIHIL) conference in Penang. Since then USM has been sharing its ideas with like-minded institutions in both developed and developing countries—its shared space.

As the only Regional Centre of Expertise (RCE) on Education for Sustainable Development in the ASEAN region, a designation received in 2005, USM has brought forward the issue of sustainable development in many forums. In its proposal for the APEX, the University set forth its strategic mission to become a sustainability-led institution. The objective is to integrate sustainable development into the higher education system so that future generations can be nurtured and imbued with the need to embrace ecological protection, conservation of resources, and human development (Razak and Ramli 2008).

Universiti Sains Malaysia: Shared Space and Circuits of Exchange

As observed by P. Altbach (2004), for many higher education institutions the new era of globalization is characterized by international agreements and arrangements that help to manage global interactions. Admittedly, these arrangements range from bilateral agreements relating to student and faculty exchanges to mutual recognition of degrees. Assumed under these agreements are the flows of ideas between partnering institutions. Many groups of institutions representing various forms of shared space (and interests) have been formed to conduct educational activities and research. The member institutions may differ in size and focus, but through these networks, they agree to common functions and objectives, for example, to promote collaborative studies and research programs in priority areas identified for the region, and/or to enhance development of academic and professional human resources in the region. USM has had active links with the following groups, networks, and countries since 2000 (Farhan 2008; Sirat et al. 2010).

- University Mobility in Asia and the Pacific (UMAP)
- International Association of Universities (IAU)
- Global University Network for Innovation Asia and the Asia Pacific (GUNI-AP)
- Association of Southeast Asia Institutions of Higher Learning (ASAIHL)
- ASEAN University Network (AUN)
- The Association of Commonwealth Universities (ACU)
- Association of Universities of Asia Pacific (ACAP)
- University Cooperation for Internationalization (UNICOFIN)
- Asia Pacific Professional Leaders in Education (APPLE)

- United Nations Universities, Regional Centre for Education for Sustainable Development (RCE)
- Association of International Education
- SEAMEO-RIHED, Bangkok
- Asean University Network
- UNESCO, Bangkok
- Cuba
- Cambodia, Lao PDR, Vietnam (CLV countries)

Involvement in international groups or networks allows USM to share its experience in various fields and activities with others. From early 2000, its participation in international organizations has increased tremendously especially with USM leadership roles such as the appointment of the vice-chancellor as president of ASAIHL, a board member of UMAP, a vice president of IAU, and a member of the Advisory Committee for Asia-Europe Foundation (ASEF). In the Commonwealth Universities Study Abroad Consortium, the University was elected as Asian representative for three consecutive terms beginning in 2000 and chaired the Executive Committee for two terms. While the flows of ideas are real in many instances where USM is involved, admittedly, the notion of tracking the migration of ideas is very daunting indeed. However, in many forums where USM was the representative, issues of the domination of western constructs (for instance internationalization) in many higher education policies of the developing south are frequently raised. For USM this is "business unusual" and is within the BOS operating environment.

Conclusion

Milton Santo's "shared space" and Saskia Sassen's "circuits of exchange" were adopted in this chapter in order to develop a framework to examine Malaysia's and finally USM's engagements with other higher education institutions and systems. With these as basis, we were able to explore and argue about the nature and justifications for shared spaces in global higher education insofar as Malaysia and USM are concerned. We have identified elements and items that are linked by a given circuit, what is exchanged within it, and how much is exchanged. While not very detailed yet at this stage, it gives some indication of how these circuits of exchange have operated and how they have impacted collaborative institutions. The questions regarding who benefits or loses from the changes generated by such exchanges and who controls or regulates the exchanges require further analysis.

Note

1. The discussion in this section was drawn extensively from several drafts chapters as follows: Sarjit Kaur, Morshidi Sirat, and Norpisah Mat Isa. (2010). "Strategic Responses to Globalization: The Case of Universiti Sains Malaysia," which was subsequently published as Sarjit Kaur, Morshidi Sirat and Norpisah Mat Isa (2011) "Strategic Responses to Globalization: The Case of Universiti Sains Malaysia" in Simon Marginson, Sarjit Kaur, Erlenawati Sawir (eds.) *Higher Education in the Asia-Pacific. Strategic Responses to Globalization.* New York: Springer, 179–198; Morshidi Sirat and Abdul Razak Ahmad (2009) "University Governance Structure in Challenging Times: The Case of Malaysia's First Apex University (Universiti Sains Malaysia)," which was subsequently published as Morshidi Sirat and Abdul Razak Ahmad (2010) "University Governance Structure in Challenging Times. The Case of Malaysia's First APEX University (Universiti Sains Malaysia)," in Ka-Ho Mok (ed). *The Search for New Governance of Higher Education in Asia.* Hampshire: Palgrave Macmillan, 125–138.

References

Altbach, Philip G. 2004. "Globalization and the University: Myths and Realities in an Unequal World." *Tertiary Education and Management,* 10 (1), pp. 3–25.
Farhan, Ahmad M. S. 2008. "Case Study of Universiti Sains Malaysia: Networking @ USM." Paper Presented at the Regional Education Markets in the Asia Pacific Region and Links to Research Activities and Collaboration in Malaysia. Round Table discussion, Bangi, Selangor.
Global University Network for Innovation. 2008. *Higher Education: New Challenges and Emerging Roles for Human and Social Development.* Higher Education in the World 3, GUNI Series on the Social Commitment of Universities 3. New York: Palgrave Macmillan.
Kementerian Pengajian Tinggi Malaysia. 2007. *Pelan Strategik Pengajian Tinggi Negara Melangkaui Tahun 2000* (National Higher Education Strategic Plan). Putrajaya: Kementerian Pengajian Tinggi Malaysia.
Kim, Chan W., and R. Mauborgne. 2005. *Blue Ocean Strategy.* Boston: Harvard Business School Press.
Lenn, M. P. 2004. "*Quality Assurance and Accreditation in Higher Education in East Asia and the Pacific.*" World Bank Paper Series, Paper No. 2004–6, August.
Razak, Dzulkifli Abdul and M. Ramli. 2008. *The APEX University. Universiti Sains Malaysia—Transforming Higher Education for a Sustainable Tomorrow.* Penang: Universiti Sains Malaysia.
Santos, Milton. 1975. *The Shared Space.* London and New York: Methuen.
Sarjit, Kaur, S. Morshidi, and A. Norzaini. 2007. *Globalization and Internationalization of Higher Education in Malaysia.* Penang: Universiti Sains Malaysia Publisher and Institut Penyelidikan Pendidikan Tinggi Negara.

Sassen, Saskia. 2004. "Economic Globalization and World Migration as Factors in the Mapping of Today's Advanced Urban Economy." Paper Commissioned for the Globalization Research Network, www.global.grn.org. Available at: http://globalgrn.files.wordpress.com/2009/08/sassen.pdf (accessed June 12, 2010).

Sirat, Morshidi. 2006. "Malaysia," in *Higher Education in South-East Asia*. Asia Pacific Program of Educational Innovation for Development (APEID). Bangkok: UNESCO.

———. 2009. "Trends in International Higher Education and Regionalism: Issues and Challenges for Malaysia." GIARI Working Paper, WASEDA University Global COE Program, Global Institute for Asian Regional Integration.

Sirat, Morshidi, A. Abdul Razak, and Y. L. Koo. 2009. "Trade in Services and its Policy Implications: The Case of Cross-Border/Transnational Higher Education in Malaysia." *Journal of Studies in International Education* OnlineFirst, published on May 21, 2009, as doi:10.1177/1028315309334878.

Sirat, Morshidi, Ahman Farban Sadullah, Ibrahim Komoo, Koo Yew Lie, N. S. Nik Meriam, A. Norzaini, Y. Farina, and W. Wong. 2010. "Research and Collaboration in an Expanding Higher Education Market in the Asia-Pacific: The Experience of Malaysian Universities," in *Globalization and Tertiary Education in the Asia-Pacific. The Changing Nature of a Dynamic Market*, ed. Christopher Findlay and W. G. Tierney. Singapore: World Scientific Publishing Company.

Universiti Sains Malaysia. 1996. *Laporan Cadangan Pengkorporatan Universiti*. Penang: Universiti Sains Malaysia.

———. 2007a. *Annual Report 2006*. Penang: Sinaran Bros. Sdn Bhd.

———. 2007b. *Constructing Future Higher Education Scenarios: Insights from Universiti Sains Malaysia, Celebrating 50 years of Nationhood*. Penang: Universiti Sains Malaysia Press.

Wheeler, James O., Y. Aoyama, and B. Warf. 2000. *Cities in the Telecommunication Age. The Fracturing of Geographies*. New York and London: Routledge.

Chapter 5

International Mobility of Faculty and Its Impacts on Korean Higher Education

Jung-Cheol Shin

Introduction

With the rapid internationalization of higher education, student and faculty mobility is an attractive policy issue as well as a subject of academic research. Studying abroad to earn a degree then returning is a long standing pattern of South Korean academics. According to the Korean Center for Education Statistics, 39 percent of academics received their PhD from a foreign university in 2009. The share of foreign degree holders has been consistent since the 1960s in Korean universities. Although there were controversies on the large share of foreign degree holders in Korean universities, they have contributed in the upgrading of teaching and research in various ways (Lee 1989). They have contributed in developing new curriculum, bringing new instructional methods, and introducing scientific research methods. Especially, current scientific development is mainly accomplished by these study-abroad scholars.

Concerning the internationalization of higher education, the Korean government has recently implemented an aggressive initiative. It has been setting aside government budget monies to hire international scholars in national universities since 2008. According to the plan, the Korean government allocated funds to hire 200 additional international scholars in

2008 alone; the plan will be renewed annually through 2012 (Korean Ministry of Education, Science and Technology 2008). Before this government initiative, Korean universities did not hire many foreign scholars for reasons such as language barriers, salary gaps, the need to provide education for their children, and so on. Recently, however, Korean universities have begun to aggressively hire international scholars. According to the Korean Center for Education Statistics, currently, 6.7 percent of academics in four-year universities are international scholars.

These foreign degree holders and foreign professors may bring changes to Korean higher education institutions. For example, foreign university degree holders may engage in different patterns of activities in their teaching and research compared to their peers with domestic degrees. Also, international scholars may pursue different teaching and research activities compared with their Korean peers. Further, they may change the academic culture of their academic unit. Therefore, this chapter focuses on the impacts that foreign university degree holders and international scholars have brought to Korean higher education. The chapter is not an evaluative study, but shows how and whether foreign degree holders (including international scholars) differ in their activity, performance, and affects on academic climate.

International Mobility and Faculty Career Path

According to the Organization for Economic Co-operation and Development (OECD) data, the most popular place to study abroad for Korean students is at US universities followed by Japan, Australia, the United Kingdom, Germany, and France. These countries are economically developed and also advanced in their academic research as well as providing better living environments. For Korean academics, having studied abroad creates a signal that the individual is a qualified researcher. Most Korean academics study at advanced knowledge levels in their major fields at highly reputed research universities. Further, study abroad opens opportunities to establish networks with international scholars. Language is a critical factor in deciding on studying abroad. Many universities require publishing in international journals; even further, some universities require teaching courses in English. In the global market, college graduates are required to speak and write in English to be employed by globalized Korean companies as well as international companies.

A brief discussion on the Korean contexts of academic career paths helps to illustrate the degree of tertiary mobility in Korea. Currently, 39 percent of professors in four-year institutions earned their PhDs from a foreign university (Korean Center for Education Statistics 2009). The proportion of Korean academics who have obtained their PhDs from a foreign country is quite high compared with other advanced countries. The percentage of academics who obtain PhDs from a domestic university is 97 percent in the United States and Japan, 94 percent in Germany and China, 91 percent in Italy, and 86 percent in the United Kingdom, Brazil, and Norway (International Center for Higher Education Research Kassel 2009). The high proportion of foreign degree holders is directly related to the growth of the higher education market in Korea. Most PhD holders from foreign countries have been hired at professorial ranks during recent expansion periods (in the 1980s and 1990s) although some exceptions exist.

We can discern three distinctive academic career paths in Korea. In both (Pattern 1 and Pattern 2) the postdoctoral researcher (postdoc), or researcher position is a normal career path for academics in hard disciplines. Even in some "soft disciplines," for example, education, sociology, public administration, social studies, and so on, the postdoc or researcher position is becoming the norm. In addition, some research universities require prior job experience at a research university in other countries (Pattern 3). Currently, obtaining faculty employment at Korean universities requires longer preparation and is also much harder to obtain.

- Pattern 1: bachelor's in Korea—master's in Korea—*PhD in Korea*—(postdoc or researcher)—professor in a Korean university
- Pattern 2: bachelor's in Korea—master's in Korea—*PhD in a foreign university* (postdoc or researcher)—professor in a Korean university
- Pattern 3: bachelor's in Korea—master's in Korea—PhD in a foreign university (postdoc or researcher in a foreign country)—*professor in a foreign university*—professor in a Korean university

In brief, study abroad brings benefits to Korean higher education though there is a controversy on the training of Korean academics in foreign universities (Lee 1989), especially, the foreign degree holders that have contributed much to upgrading the research productivity of Korean academics. For example, in terms of rapidity of growth of Science Citation Indexed (SCI) journal article publication among the OECD countries Korea ranks as the highest country. In addition, foreign degree holders have contributed to upgrading instructional methods and curriculum at both undergraduate and graduate levels. Further, international degree holders have contributed to networking with international scholars.

Method

The data for this study are based on two sources: surveys and interviews. The survey data was collected for the international comparative study of the Changing Academic Profession (CAP) of 2008. The CAP 2008 survey is the follow up study of the Carnegie Foundation survey conducted in 1992. The survey items cover faculty education, their career paths, and their teaching and research activities. The data provide answers as to whether foreign degree holders display differences in their activities compared with their peers with domestic degrees. In addition, the data show whether they bring different instructional methods to their classroom, and how foreign PhD holders perceive the academic culture of their institutions compared to their Korean university PhD holding counterparts.

The population of this study is the 52,763 full-time faculty in bachelor degree granting institutions in Korea. The sample is randomly drawn to yield a sample size of 9,139 from the database of the Korean Research Foundation (KRF). The data was collected through an online survey. Overall 6,827 faculty accessed the survey and 900 completed it for a return rate of 13.2 percent. Among the 900 completed surveys, we excluded 95 cases and have 819 cases that satisfy the purpose of this study (which focuses on the origin of PhD degrees from the six countries as shown in table 5.1). According to the descriptive data, 57 percent of Korean academics earned a PhD in a Korean university while 43 percent of academics earned their PhDs from a foreign university. To make a parsimonious comparison, we grouped the countries into: PhD earned from a Korean university (*Korean PhD*), a US university (*US PhD*), and grouped together Japanese, the United Kingdom, German, and French universities (*European PhD*). Although the groping is rough, our main research interest is how academics who graduated from a Korean university differ from those with a US and other university degrees.

Table 5.1 Distribution of Sample by County of PhD Earned

Country	Soft Discipline		Hard Discipline		Total	
	Number	Percent	Number	Percent	Number	Percent
Korea	237	50	233	50	470	57
United States	117	49	122	51	239	29
UK, Germany, France, Japan	63	66	33	34	96	12
Others	11	79	3	21	14	2
Total	428	52	391	48	819	100

In addition to the survey data, a small-scale interview was conducted to explore in-depth information on how international scholars differ in their academic activity and their perception on academic climates of their universities. For the interview, an academic unit that has three international scholars was chosen. The three international scholars have quite various academic backgrounds. Their major areas are humanities, social science, and natural science. To collect better inside views, a department chair, a program head, or close observer were also contacted. The interview questions are semistructured and focused on the international scholars' teaching and research activity, academic performance, how they adjust themselves in a new environment, and how they communicate with their Korean colleagues.

Findings and Discussions

The findings are based on survey and interview data. For this study, statistical significance is not our main interest. Instead, this chapter focuses on how the faculty activity and their perceptions differ between domestic and foreign PhD degrees. For that, the findings and discussions are based on descriptive data of the CAP survey. In addition, the interview data was presented where it is relevant. The main findings are organized by academic activities (teaching and research, internationalization), academic productivity (research productivity), and their perception of their institutional academic climate.

Academic Activities

Professors who earned a PhD from a domestic university may differ from a foreign degree holder in both teaching and/or research activities. Most degree holders have been trained at a research-oriented university, and thus may have a stronger preference toward research than their colleagues who are domestic degree holders. Foreign degree holders may use various instructional methods because foreign university, especially US universities emphasize interactive instructional methods in their classroom teaching, while domestic degree holders are relatively conservative in their teaching. With respect to research, foreign degree holders, especially US PhDs, may lean toward more applied and practice-based research than pure and theory-based research because US universities emphasize practical values. As a natural trend, finally, foreign degree holders may have better international perspectives than their colleagues with domestic PhDs in teaching and research.

Perception on Teaching and Research

Academics who have been trained in a strong research-oriented university may have stronger preferences toward research than their colleagues in less research-oriented universities. Most Korean academics that hold PhDs from a US university or a Japanese university have been trained from a strong research tradition. However, PhDs from universities other than these may or may not be research oriented. Even French universities, though they train many international scholars, do not emphasize research itself because research is the responsibility of research institutes in France. Readers may be reminded that historically France has long made the distinction and division of labor between the university sector and research institutes.

This preference may be clearly demonstrated when we compare domestic and foreign PhD holders. For simplicity, this chapter has categorized Korean academics' PhD background as a Korean university degree holder, US PhD holder, or European PhD holders. As shown in table 5.2, academics that earned PhDs from a US or European university have stronger research preferences than their peers with a Korean PhD. The finding implies that Korean foreign PhD holders prioritize research compared with domestic PhD holders. However, a strong research preference may or may not be a positive contribution to higher education.

As many empirical studies have shown, research may or may not have impacts on their faculty members' teaching activity (Shin 2011a). Research may even conflict with teaching when academics spend most of their time on research and shortchange their undergraduate teaching (Feldman 1987; Hattie and Marsh 1996). These empirical studies are not consistent with academic perceptions of their own activities. Controversy exists between empirical quantitative and qualitative studies of teaching and research. Interestingly, much academic research based on qualitative data has reported that their research has positive impacts on classroom teaching (Shin 2011a). The same findings are reported in this survey. As shown in table 5.2, academics "perceive" that research reinforces teaching regardless the origin of PhDs.

There has been serious discussion on academic scholarships, especially since Ernest L. Boyer proposed four dimensions of academic scholarship in his famous report, *Academic Scholarship Reconsidered* (1990). Boyer proposed four such dimensions: the scholarship of teaching, discovery, application, and synthesis. Its effect has been to prompt academics and higher education institutions to pay attention to the other three types of scholarship (teaching, application, and synthesis) as well as the scholarship of discovery (research). The CAP data includes academics' perception on

Table 5.2 Faculty Perception, Performance, and Culture

Perception, Performance, and Culture		Korea	United States	Europe	Total
Research Preference	Research preference	63.6	73.6	77.1	68.2
	Research reinforces teaching	84.3	87.4	81.3	84.8
Academic Scholarship	Discovery	77.0	78.7	78.1	77.6
	Application	82.6	84.9	75.0	82.4
	Synthesis	90.2	93.3	82.3	90.2
Instructional Methods	Lecturing	98.1	97.5	96.9	97.8
	Individualized Instruction	54.7	63.6	55.2	57.4
	Project-based	47.9	46.0	44.8	47.0
	Practice-based	50.9	48.5	47.9	49.8
Research Focuses	Basic/theoretical	57.4	63.2	63.5	59.9
	Applied/practically-oriented	73.2	70.3	74.0	72.4
	Commercially oriented	19.1	17.2	17.7	18.4
	Single discipline-based	43.6	47.7	43.8	44.8
	Multi discipline-based	50.4	53.6	47.9	51.1
Internationalization	Teaching international perspective	73.6	76.6	76.0	74.8
	Teaching in other language experience	26.6	40.6	33.3	31.6
	Research in international orientation	31.5	31.4	29.2	31.2
	International collaboration	26.4	34.3	34.4	29.7
Academic Productivity	Book publication	1.64	1.51	1.69	1.61
	Domestic journal article	6.48	6.09	6.15	6.33
	SCI journal article	3.62	5.01	2.83	3.95
Academic Culture	Academic freedom	48.2	54.8	43.8	49.6
	Collegiality	20.2	15.5	14.6	18.1

Note: The number is the percentage of academics who agreed or strongly agreed with the survey question.

academic scholarship. According to table 5.2, most academics perceive synthesis as a scholarship followed by application and discovery. Interestingly, however, European PhDs place less weight on application and synthesis than their peers with a domestic or US PhD. It is quite interesting to know that European degree holders put less weight on synthesis as a scholarship pathway. Traditionally, European scholars prefer to conduct theory grounded research than their US counterparts.

Teaching Method

Since Boyer proposed the four dimensions of academic scholarships in 1990, many US universities have begun to emphasize teaching competency in their hiring and promotion decisions. This emphasis on teaching is even broadly applied in many US research focused universities. In addition, many universities moved to establish teaching support units to support faculty teaching. Within this context, teaching became a critical component of quality assurance in many countries. Korean universities also emphasize the quality of teaching by their faculty personnel, though still place more relative weight on research productivity. This has been supported by government's initiative in providing funds for teaching quality enhancement since 2008.

Nevertheless, academics cannot be said to have transformed their teaching practices. Although many universities established support centers for teaching and learning, there is no clear evidence that academics are transforming their instructional methods. As shown in table 5.2, derived from the CAP data most academics (97.8 percent) use lecturing as a main method of instruction regardless of their PhD origin, and fewer use individualized instruction, project-based, and practice-based instructions. Presumably, academics use lecturing as the main instructional method and use these other methods as a teaching supplement. Again we observe no critical difference by country of origin for the PhD. This may be related to Korean academics' preference toward research, as they predispose toward research and pay less attention to classroom teaching, in part because faculty hiring and promotion are based mainly on research. Although considered as a factor in Korean university personnel decisions, teaching is not regarded as critical.

Table 5.2 indicates that US PhD holders use more individualized instruction (e.g., class discussion) methods than their other peers, reflecting this aspect of doctoral training in individualized teaching environments. However, those trained in a Korean university or a European university were so different in their use of individualized instruction methods. This fact may reflect the academic atmosphere of Korean and European university training compared with the United States. A relatively rigid hierarchy exists between students and professors in Korean and European universities whereas the relationship between professor and student is softer and friendlier in US academic culture, attributes that presumably influence the selection of instructional methods.

This has been supported by the interviews. The three interviewees mentioned that international scholars are very active in their personal contacts with students and they tend to use interactive instructional methods. The course satisfaction of these international scholars looks quite high and students have good relationships with their professors. However, this does not mean that the quality of course content is qualitatively high. According to one interview, although students expressed their satisfaction on the class instruction in general, some students complained about the quality of content covered by an international professor. The complaint may relate to the failure of adjusting the level of content covered in the course or may relate to the academic preparation of the international professor. Sometimes, academics are assigned to teach a course for which he/she is not fully qualified.

In general, the findings and their interpretations imply that a university may not transform instructional methods and may not update them by establishing systematic reforms such as establishing centers for teaching and learning. This may be activated by changing personnel policy and academic culture. In the long run the cultural change may require being embedded in Korean society where rigid hierarchy has been institutionalized for quite a long time. Changes in instructional methods may contribute to the change in academic culture or vise versa.

Research Focus

Controversy exists over the relative merits of pure and applied research. The CAP data include academics' perspectives on pure and applied research and as indicated in table 5.2, in general, Korean academics give more weight to practical and applied research (72.4 percent) than to pure and theory-based research (59.9 percent). Table 5.2 provides the interesting fact that Korean university PhDs put less weight on basic or theoretical research (57.4 percent) than their peers with foreign university PhDs; and they spend more time on applied or practically oriented research (73.2 percent) than foreign degree holders. The finding implies that Korean universities are increasingly leaning toward practical and applied research in their PhD training. This finding is also consistent with government policy, which has been prioritizing research relevant to economic development.

Nevertheless, Korean academics are less commercially oriented (18.4 percent) in general. These findings are a bit complicated to interpret because while Korean academics work more on applied and practice-oriented research than pure research, they are nevertheless less commercially oriented. This may require more in-depth research on the research patterns of Korean academics. One interpretation is that they may not pay much attention to the commercial utility of their research even though the research may have social relevance. Korean universities are not quite as ready for commercialization of their research outputs and Korean government policy may not yet effectively support its commercialization. However, this may require a more in-depth study to explore why academics pay limited attention to research commercialization.

Alternatively, we may find a persuasive reason from the academic structure of Korean universities in which professors are affiliated with a discrete academic unit that functions like a basic unit by providing courses, hiring faculty, admitting students for undergraduate and graduate levels, and as a research unit. In most cases, the academic unit is based in a discrete academic field and most of its activities are conducted within it, and tend not to crossover to other units. Within this context, a strong internal academic culture has long been institutionalized and interdisciplinary research is uncommon. Consequently, academic research, most of which is applied and practically oriented, may lack practical relevance because it is based on a single discipline. That is why government policy emphasizes multidisciplinary research in its research funding policy.

It is quite disappointing that many applied and practice oriented researchers do not produce commercial applications. In our research approximately half of Korean academics (51.1 percent) reported having conducted multidisciplinary research, a figure that currently may or may not be higher. However, the proportion that conducts multidisciplinary research is relatively low when we consider the fact that 72.4 percent conduct applied and practice oriented research. Simplistically, 21.3 percent (the difference between 72.4 and 51.1 percent) of the applied and practice oriented research was not based on multidisciplinary research. As indicated above, research based on a single discipline may have more limitations than the multidisciplinary work in its application to social contexts. This may deserve further in-depth study in the future.

International Perspective in Teaching and Research

An international perspective in teaching and research is increasingly emphasized in the global economy. To comply with internationalization

Korean academics choose global topics and course materials, and provide their courses in other languages, primarily English. Regardless of where they earned their PhDs Korean academics tend to emphasize global perspectives in their course design and in choosing course materials. In this regard they are sensitive to advanced theories and practices developed in advanced countries, especially the United States, largely a result of having importing theory and course materials (books and journals) from western societies and Japan. In this context Korean academics emphasize global perspectives regardless of their PhD origins, a conclusion supported by the CAP data in table 5.2.

Foreign degree holders may be more active in choosing research topics with international perspectives and collaborating with their international colleagues. Presumably, foreign degree holders may have networks among their former classmates and former professors. Foreign degree holders, especially academics who are early in their careers, may not be significantly independent from their PhD training when developing research topics. Although foreign degree holders develop academic research topics after returning to Korea, adjusting to Korean research contexts requires time. Most early career academics tend to apply what they have learned from their PhD training into Korean contexts. However, interestingly, foreign degree holders are not different from their domestic counterparts in their international research orientations as shown in table 5.2.

Here, our query is why domestic PhDs holders and their foreign counterparts possess similar international orientations. One explanation may relate to the texts and theories that are covered in graduate education. Most professors, regardless of degree origination use foreign textbooks in their graduate courses. In addition, Korean academics tend to stay current with theoretical developments in Western academic contexts. In this regard, Korean academics tend to embrace international perspectives in their research, borrowing theoretical frameworks from Western scholars even when the subject at hand is purely Korean.

Foreign degree holders may be more collaborative with their international colleagues than domestic PhDs. Foreign degree holders may have connections with international colleagues and maintain connections with former professors. Recently, working collaboratively with international colleagues has been emphasized by government policy, which reinforces publication in SCI journals. In this respect foreign degree holders are also benefited in faculty job searches. Foreign degree holders also benefit from international collaborations that emerge from study-abroad opportunities that result from close friendship with international students. This trend has been supported by the CAP data as shown in table 5.2.

International scholars in general tend to have stronger collaborations with colleagues abroad that lead to attending academic conferences with former colleagues and friends. These linkages allow them to maintain currency with recent research trends and explore opportunities for collaboration. Ironically, these pathways toward international collaboration may have negative effects on collaboration with Korean colleagues, as international obligations require them to spend more time adjusting to the culture of a Korean university, even as their international linkages may lead to negative perceptions by their Korean colleagues who have to work with their international colleagues in their local contexts.

Academic Productivity

The Korean government did not pay much attention to PhD training until the early 1990s when the government began to support graduate education as a requirement for competing in a knowledge-based economy and gaining better trained human resources for industry. Since then, the Korean government has aggressively adopted evaluation-based funding systems in which research performance makes up the key indicators. In addition, the government created the Brain Korea (BK) 21 project directed toward building world-class universities in 1999 and has adopted follow-up projects to support faculty research. These include Humanity Korea (HK) and Social Science Korea (SSK) as well as a second step of the BK 21 project (Shin 2011b). These aggressive initiatives have enabled Korean academics to intensify their research efforts.

Under these government initiatives academic productivity has been rapidly increasing since the mid-1990s, especially as represented by publication in international journals, changes highlighted by many foreign media and by academics. For example, the US National Science Board (2010) reported that Korea achieved the highest growth rate among OECD countries in publishing in science, technology, engineering, and medical sciences during the ten years from 1995 to 2005. Also CAP data show that Korean academics are the most productive among the participating countries. Korean academics on average published 1.6 books during the period 2005 to 2007, and 10.94 articles in international and/or domestic journals.

Concerning these differences, foreign PhDs, most of whom earned their PhDs from a research-focused foreign university, tend to produce more papers than their domestic counterparts, no doubt reflecting their more intensive research-oriented graduate training. In contrast, domestic PhD holders received relatively less rigorous training for research. On balance domestic PhD holders may seek to publish papers in domestic journals, but tend not to do so in internationally competitive journals. This has been supported by CAP data as shown in table 5.2. US trained academics publish more papers in international journals compared to their domestic or European-trained colleagues. They tend to have learned cutting-edge knowledge in the leading research universities, are well grounded in research methodology, and also maintain established networks with former classmates in the United States.

Interestingly European PhDs are relatively less productive, performing even lower than Korean PhD's in international journal publication. This may reflect disciplinary choices of European PhDs, many of whom are in the humanities and social sciences where relatively fewer articles are published than in natural sciences, engineering, and medical science. Professors in the soft disciplines (arts and humanities, and social sciences) prefer to disseminate their research in the form of books rather than journal articles. This interpretation is supported by CAP data that indicates that European PhDs produce more books than domestic or US PhDs, while the Europeans publish fewer journal papers overall. In general, domestic PhD holders publish more in domestic journals than the other two colleague groups.

When interviewees were asked about the potential productivity of newly hired international scholars, they did not exhibit confidence, which may reflect on the perceived academic competency of the new hires or the lack of support systems of Korean universities for their research, or both. Alternatively, this may reflect different viewpoints on what constitutes academic research. Korean universities tend to emphasize article publication in their evaluation processes, whereas more internationally oriented researchers think in terms of both book and journal publications and look as well to service-oriented research to satisfy local demands. However, book publication and service research are not weighed in faculty evaluation processes, and thus from this perspective international scholars with these perspectives would be viewed as not active in "academic" research.

Also of interest are the high expectations that Korean academics have for international scholars. As discussed, many Korean academics trained in a US university have strong admiration for their "home" university, which leads them to have high academic expectations toward foreign academics, especially those from the United States. This may lead Korean academics to collaborate with international scholars and have them lead their Korean colleagues in research. Conversely, these international scholars may wish Korean academics to lead research endeavors given their own lack of familiarity with the local university contexts, and expect their Korean colleagues to perform a mentoring role in establishing research settings. These perceptional differences may lead Korean academics to perceive that their international peers may lack promise as high academic performers.

Perceptions of Academic Culture

Korean higher education institutions and their related academic culture are quite complicated to understand because while their formal system is close to the United States, their internal culture is closer to the academic culture of a German university. The Korean government tends not to be involved in academic issues such as choosing research topics and course content as is the case in classic continental European universities. However, the notion of academic freedom is slightly different in the US higher education. A continental European university has a stronger notion of academic freedom than a US university. On the other hand, a rigid hierarchy exists between senior and junior professors within a German university. The *academic chair* in a German university (chair systems) has strong power while the multiple professors who are at a full-professor position of a US department are equal in rank (Clark 1983).

These cultural differences between European and US universities may produce different perceptions of academic cultures in our two classes of PhD holders. Europeans may perceive that Korean academic culture has less academic freedom than that enjoyed by their European colleagues, while a US PhD holder may see the range of freedom enjoyed by his Korean colleagues as superior to American colleagues. On the other hand, European PhD's may perceive that in status terms they are more equal than their European colleagues while a US PhD may perceive Korean academics as less collegial than US colleagues.

The CAP data show interesting findings. As expected, domestic PhD holders are between US PhD holders and European PhD holders in terms of their perception of the extent of academic freedom in a Korean university. On the other hand, both US and European PhDs perceive that they are less collegial than their Korean PhD holding colleagues. Given that academic freedom is related to government policy, it is not surprising that academics perceive that they are free from government in their academic affairs. Concerning faculty collegiality, on the other hand, Korean academics perceive that their institutional leaders are not collegial in their academic decision making. Only 18.1 percent of Korean academics perceive that campus-wide decision making is collegial (table 5.2). This is quite interesting because faculty members are strongly represented in academic affairs in many universities, especially national universities. This may be related to broader issues of institutional governance and leadership of institutional leaders (for details, see Shin 2011c).

Domestic degree holders are more likely to find collegiality in campus-wide decision making than their foreign degree colleagues. This finding may require a more in-depth elaboration. One explanation is that domestic

PhDs are more familiar with campus-wide decision-making styles. For example, many critical decisions tend to be coordinated through informal meetings and discussions. Domestic degree holders are likely to be more familiar with these internal processes and frequently attend them, whereas foreign degree holders may be less invited into such processes. These informal discussions are quite influential when combined with high levels of academic inbreeding. The result is an informal but highly functioning in-group / out-group structure operating within many institutions. These network structures operate to channel information exchange and collect opinions for higher ranking administrators. Foreign degree holders may be isolated from this pattern of campus-wide decision making.

Faculty collegiality is a serious matter for international scholars. Western academic culture tends to organize decision making through formal meetings. Even though Korean academics do make critical decisions through such meetings, international scholars may not be fully understanding of the contexts, language, and culture within which they take place. Accordingly, international scholars view themselves as isolated in campus-wide decision making. The three interviewees mentioned that international scholars tend to double check what the Korean faculty members decided at the meeting by reviewing official email with their colleagues. On the other hand, organizational culture has been changing in the departments where international scholars are working. Korean academics, especially department chairs and program coordinators increasingly adopt the role of a cultural channel between international scholars and their Korean colleagues.

Through a mutual adjustment process, academic culture in an academic unit has been transforming from informal to formal, and from closed to open. Although many academic units with international scholars are confronted with these changes, national universities may experience more challenges by hiring international professors than private universities. International academics may also pay attention to cultural differences between their home country and local context and work to adjust themselves to local circumstances. Regardless of whether the government initiated such cultural changes by hiring international scholars, these changes become a basis for enhancing the competitiveness of Korean universities in the long run.

Concluding Remarks

This chapter focused on how academics differ in their perception, activity, and academic performance by their country of PhDs origin. This chapter paid special attention to Korean academics who earned PhDs from a

Korean university and those with a foreign university degree. Additional efforts were made to understand how international scholars teaching in a Korean university differ from their Korean counterparts in their perceptions, academic activity, and performance. This chapter used the CAP data and conducted a semistructured interview to address a range of issues. Using descriptive analysis, this study found:

- Foreign PhDs are more research focused than domestic PhDs.
- Korean academics use lecturing as the main instructional method regardless of whether they are domestic or foreign degree holders.
- Korean academics give more weight to applied than pure research, but their research is not very commercially oriented.
- Foreign PhD holders are more actively involved in international collaboration than their domestic PhDs colleagues.
- Domestic PhD holders contribute more articles to domestic journals than the foreign PhDs, but less to international journals.
- Foreign PhD holders perceive that campus-wide decision making is less collegial than domestic PhD holders.

Although these findings are based on descriptive data, they add to our understanding of how Korean academics differ by PhD origin. However, such differences are complicated by the aggressive hiring of international scholars since 2008. According to semistructured interviews, international scholars may or may not be research productive; but they are engaged in interactive classroom teaching. Another interesting issue was the collegiality culture in Korean universities. Decision making in Korean universities has been changing from informal to formal communications since international scholars have joined Korean university. These findings and discussions should be further studied and theorized to investigate how international degrees and the hiring of international scholars may affect Korean higher education in the future.

Acknowledgments: Partial fulfillment of this work was supported by the National Research Foundation of Korea Grant funded by the Korean Government (NRF-2010–330-B00232).

References

Boyer, Ernest L. 1990. *Scholarship Reconsidered: Priorities of the Professoriate.* Princeton, NJ: Carnegie Foundation for the Advancement of Teaching.

Clark, Burton R. 1983. *The Higher Education System: Academic Organization in Cross-National Perspective.* CA: University of California Press.

Feldman, Kenneth A. 1987. "Research Productivity and Scholarly Accomplishment of College Teachers as Related to Their Instructional Effectiveness: A Review and Exploration." *Research in Higher Education* 26(3): 227–298.

Hattie, John and Herbert W. Marsh. 1996. "The Relationship between Research and Teaching: A Meta-analysis." *Review of Educational Research* 66(4): 507–542.

International Center for Higher Education Research Kassel. 2009. "Changing Academic Profession (CAP)." International Center for Higher Education Research, Germany.

Korean Center for Education Statistics. 2009. *Yearly Education Statistics*. Seoul: Korean Center for Education Statistics.

Korean Ministry of Education, Science and Technology. 2008. "Annual Strategic Plan Report to President in Education, Science and Technology." Seoul: Korean Ministry of Education, Science and Technology.

Lee, Sungho. 1989. "The Emergence of the Modern University in Korea." *Higher Education* 18(1): 87–116.

Shin, Jung C. 2011a. "Teaching and Research Nexuses in a Research University in South Korea. *Studies in Higher Education* 36(5): 485–503.

———. 2011b. *Higher Education Development in Korea: Western University Ideas, Confucian Tradition, and Economic Development.* Unpublished Working Paper.

———. 2011c. "South Korea: Decentralized Centralization—Fading Shared Governance and Rising Managerialism," in *Governance and Management in Higher Education: The Perspective of the Academy,* ed. William Locke, William Cummings, and Donald Fisher. The Netherlands: Springer.

US National Science Board. 2010. *Science and Engineering Indicators: 2010.* Available at: http://www.nsf.gov/statistics/seind10/ (accessed March 1, 2011).

Chapter 6

The Changing Structure of Japanese Higher Education: Globalization, Mobility, and Massification

Reiko Yamada

Introduction

Over the past ten years, Japanese universities and colleges have experienced sweeping and sudden changes. Two phenomena have contributed much to these developments. First, globalization has encouraged Japanese universities to compete in and adapt to a newly internationalized knowledge-based society. In a knowledge-based society, the transfer of knowledge and human personnel is associated with mobility or internationalization. As a result, Japanese universities have felt obliged to tailor research as well as teaching and learning to a more global world. Second, Japan's birth rate has declined rapidly over the past 18 years. In other words, Japanese universities have entered a period of universalization, in which almost 50 percent of college-aged students have access to higher education (Trow 1974). In Japan, such universalization is often referred to as "taishuka," which roughly translates into "massification." With 49.9 percent of recent high school graduates enrolling in higher education in 2003, Japan entered the massification phase (The Ministry of Education, Culture, Sports, Science, and Technology [MEXT] 2004). At present, this means that almost every student who wishes to attend university is given admission. As an implicit result, students less prepared for university study, lacking basic knowledge, the appropriate study skills, and the necessary motivation, are entering higher education. In response, Japanese universities have been encouraged to develop more learning-centered programs to equip such ill-prepared students for the rigors of university life.

Taken together, these two phenomena have led to the growth of accountability in Japanese higher education. Put slightly differently, Japanese universities now feel obliged to ensure greater quality in undergraduate education. One sign of increased responsibility is university evaluation and faculty development. In 2008, for instance, the Central Council for Education in Japan presented a report entitled "For Restructuring Undergraduate Education." The report, which included several proposals for improving undergraduate education, has triggered a shift toward teaching- and learning-oriented policy in Japanese higher education. Such "quality assurance" has rushed higher education into curricular, program, and pedagogical reforms that have forced universities to adapt to the demands of massification as well as the emergence of something like global educational standards.

What then are the effects of globalization, mobility, and massification on Japanese higher education? The goal of this chapter is to account for changes in government policy toward higher education, the current environment of Japanese higher education, and the changing structure of Japanese higher education, all of which have attempted to address globalization, mobility, and massification. How then has Japanese higher education changed in recent years? After examining student data, I show the ways in which Japanese higher education has dealt with massification. It is obvious that globalization and mobility affect both research and learning. However, in this chapter, I would like to focus on learning in particular. In the next section, I present policy changes implemented in Japanese higher education.

Japanese Higher Education Policy in a Knowledge-Based Society

Reflecting the environmental change in Japanese higher education, a new reform movement has emerged, embodied in new MEXT policies. The reform is economic centered, market conscious, and influenced by a government policy shift toward deregulation, reflecting governmental concerns about global competition in the twenty-first century and Japan's ability to cope with both a rapidly aging population and a declining birth rate. In an aging society with a declining birth rate, financial loss and retrenchment become serious issues. After the 1980s, a shift to policies based on neoliberalism can be observed worldwide. The question is what sort of effect neoliberal policies have on higher education. According to neoliberalist theory, education and research are regarded as indispensable to national development. Although less public money is available overall for education, much more of the budget tends to be funneled into technology, science, and market-related fields.

At the same time, serious competition resulting from globalization forces university research to shift toward science and technology, becoming more sensitive to industrial policy and intellectual-property strategies (Slaughter 1998). In other words, educational institutions are obliged to pursue two functions simultaneously: the cultivation of elites and the education of greater and greater numbers of students. The Central Council of Education (CCE), for example, issued a report entitled the "Future of Japanese Higher Education." In it, the council claims that the twenty-first century is the age of the knowledge-based society and that, as a result, in such a society higher education has become more important, not only for individuals (so-called Personality Development), but also for the government (the National Strategy). Accordingly, the Japanese government has invested heavily in certain aspects of education, encouraging both research and educational programs that cultivate highly skilled students. Such programs focus explicitly on the challenges of globalization and mobility in the twenty-first century. Consider, for instance, the Global 30. Started in 2009, the Global 30 program is one aspect of MEXT's "300,000 International Students Plan," which seeks to increase the number of foreign students studying in Japan. The program aims to elevate the international competitiveness of Japanese universities while taking advantage of the mobility of students in international markets and promoting cosmopolitan campuses with a greater number of English courses and more international content. The program includes courses taught exclusively in English, the movement of students and researchers into overseas campuses, and joint-degree opportunities. Thirteen Japanese universities were given grants to promote the Global 30 programs in 2009. The selected universities are expected to develop themselves as Japan's leading internationalization hubs: they will provide high-quality education and an environment that makes it easy for both Japanese and international students to compete internationally (Japan Society for Promotion of Science 2011).

At the same time, however, the need for greater accountability has emerged as a result of the neoliberal framework within which such policy shifts have been enacted. Increasingly, attention is being directed to broad social uses and economic rationalizations for university functions (Van

Vaught and Westerjeojden 1994). Today, for instance, universities are required to demonstrate that they have met their objectives. Frans A. Van Vaught and Don F. Westerjeojden (1994) have found that the concerns of governments and other interest groups tend to be concerns about accountability (1994). Robert O. Berdahl and Thomas R. McConnell (1994) have defined accountability as being answerable to various constituencies for the responsible performance of duties. This requires the evaluation and measurement of performance; in education, this means monitoring the functions of a university (Albornoz 1996). Put another way, the general public has become more concerned with higher education and has, as a result, sought ways to assess the outcomes of both educational and research objectives. Moreover, the public at large tends to criticize educational institutions that it feels are performing below standard. In other words, educational outcomes are the means by which universities ensure the quality of their research and educational agendas and the primary means by which they prove their institutional accountability.

However, it has often been claimed that the heavily research-oriented academic culture of Japanese universities has long prevented substantive improvements to teaching practices. Between 1992 and 1993, the Carnegie Foundation for the Advancement of Teaching conducted an international survey of the academic profession in 14 countries. Importantly, the survey revealed Japanese professors for the most part viewed themselves as researchers rather than teachers (Arimoto and Ehara 1996). Using the findings of this survey, Takekazu Ehara (1998) identified three types of faculty. Using the 13 countries and 1 region selected for this survey, he produced three views of higher education: the Latin-American, the Anglo-American, and the German. In the Latin-American model, which included faculty from Chile, Mexico, Brazil, and Russia, professors ranked teaching highest among their responsibilities. In the German model, which included faculty from Japan, Israel, Sweden, the Netherlands, and, of course, Germany, professors ranked research activities above their other responsibilities. In the Anglo-American model, which included faculty from the United States and United Kingdom, fell somewhere in between the Latin-American and German models, ranking both research and teaching activities high among their responsibilities. At Japanese universities, a mere 27.5 percent of participating faculty members—second-to-last among the 13 countries—assigned a high rank to teaching activities.

Such a research-oriented academic culture has long prevented substantive efforts to improve university pedagogy in Japan. In hopes of encouraging Japanese universities to focus more on teaching and not just research, MEXT developed competitive grants that offered universities opportunities to transform themselves into more learning-centered environments. This increased attention on effective teaching has forced even research-centered universities to focus more on teaching and learning. As a result, though a small percentage of research-centered universities that are highly competitive worldwide still exist, since 2000 the overwhelming majority of four-year institutions in Japan have become more learning and teaching oriented.

Such environmental changes in Japanese higher education are forcing institutions to attend more to teaching, learning, and their ultimate effects on student learning outcomes. In particular, universities are held to account through institutional evaluations and faculty development. For instance, a report issued by The Central Council for Education (2008) contained a proposal to develop some form of quality assurance, specifically in reference to educational outcomes, for graduating students. Since then, the issue of learning outcomes has become critical in Japanese higher education. In the same report, a common standard of "learning outcome" was recommended, using "graduate attributes" as a point of reference. Such graduate attributes included the following: (1) inter- and multicultural understanding of human culture, society, and nature; (2) generic competence, including communication skills, quantitative skills, information-literacy skills, logical-thinking skills, and problem-solving skills; (3) the adoption of attitudes that demonstrate self-control, ethical behavior, and citizenship; the ability to work in teams, collaborate, and lead; and a commitment to lifelong learning; and (4) evidence of cohesive learning experiences and creative thinking (The Central Council for Education 2008).

Although such "graduate attributes" are particular to the recommendations of Japan's Central Council for Education, universities across several countries share much in common with the council's directives. For example, a report conducted by the Task Force on General Education at the Faculty of Arts and Sciences at Harvard University (2007) also noted several key features of a general undergraduate education at Harvard. The University of Melbourne likewise proposed a set of "Attributes of the Melbourne Graduate" in 2007. In both Harvard's and Melbourne's reports—and much like the Council's report—learning outcomes include logical-thinking skills, problem-solving skills, the ability to work in teams and collaborate, ethical development, inter- and multicultural literacy, and communication skills. In all three reports, such skills and attributes are regarded as "universal skills" required in the knowledge-based world of the twenty-first century. A quick search of educational agendas at other universities in other countries produces a similar impression. As a result, it is obvious that many universities today, the world over, are directing their strategies and policies toward producing students ready for the demands of the twenty-first century. In the past, institutions of higher education used to make *local* educational policies, designing systems, course content, and educational services around the local needs of their students. Today, however, in a global society, universities are forced to address and conform to *universal* or *international* standards. It is believed that having similar graduate attributes across all nations will improve and expedite the international mobility of students, through common or similar curricula. As a result, we can see the ways in which this most recent shift in Japanese policy toward learning-centered approaches in higher education may indirectly promote the mobility and migration of Japanese graduates while attracting international students to Japan.

At the same time, though universities today must meet the demands of an "international" education, they must also solve the "local issue." In Japan, the local issue—massification itself, which has rapidly accelerated in recent years, is particular and acute, one that all Japanese institutions of higher education must address. Unsurprisingly, the Council report also recommended the development of First Year Experience (FYE) programs, to accommodate the growing number of students accepted to universities, despite not having taken any type of scholastic entrance examination, especially at smaller private institutions. The report thus required universities to issue a clear "admission policy" that emphasized the importance of the FYE program as a prerequisite to and preparation for university study, after they had enrolled at the institution. The report explains that the FYE program can effectively support the transition of students from secondary to postsecondary education and urges universities to introduce the FYE program as a normal, credited component of the undergraduate curriculum, in order to improve learning outcomes (The Central Council for Education 2008).

In the next section, I take up in closer detail the local issue in Japanese higher education, offering a comparison of student data from both the United States and Japan.

Learning Outcomes and Assessment in Japanese Higher Education

There are several ways to assess learning outcomes. For instance, learning outcomes can be examined as the knowledge acquired through a university education. They can also be measured by outcome-assessment tools. In any case, the definition of learning outcome is broad and complicated. It covers the field of general education, academic disciplines, and the method of assessment. In the United States, various tests have been developed in order to assess the learning outcomes in general education, academic disciplines, and high school learning. In Japan, however, techniques for assessing students are not well developed. Few, if any, metrics beyond a student's score in English examinations, like the Test of English as a Foreign Language (TOEFL) or the Test of English for International Communication (TOEIC), exist at Japanese universities.

Conversely, in the United States, many metrics have been devised, researched, and implemented. The Spellings' Commission on the Future of Higher Education (2006),[1] for instance, issued a report that considered the introduction of national tests for assessment. However, as Trudy W. Banta (2007) has noted, in the 1990s, when national-level or at least state-level testing of college students was proposed, the context for considering a national test for college students was actually much fuller than in 2006, and the approach for designing and administering the test was more careful and deliberate. Over the years, much research had been done on and many arguments have been made about the efficacy and accuracy of student assessments. In other words, many researchers have dedicated their work to measuring, testing, and assessing student learning outcomes in the Unites States and have developed various tools for gauging the cognitive, educational, and affective progress of students.

Conversely, in Japan little research on student assessment has been undertaken. As a result, it is extremely difficult to define assessment within and apply the principles of assessment to Japanese higher education. Nonetheless, there remain two kinds of outcome assessment in Japan. We can divide these into direct and indirect assessment. Direct assessment gauges the direct learning outcome of students through tests, essays, portfolios, graduation examinations, graduation research papers, and standardized tests in both general and discipline-based education. Indirect assessment gauges the learning process, using student surveys about learning behaviors, student experiences, self-perception, and satisfaction. These surveys are offered to students upon entering college, at the end of the first year, at the end of the senior year, and after graduation. When used in tandem, indirect and direct assessments complement one another.

In this chapter, I focus on indirect assessment, using it to measure the process of student learning. However, we should proceed with caution. In Japan, few assessment tools have been developed on the basis of research and a sound theory of development. Further, Japanese student surveys are frequently used with little theoretical background. Since 2003, I have been developing student surveys as an assessment tool for gauging the developmental model of students' affective and behavioral engagement in education. My theoretical approach picks up on Alexander W. Astin's early work. Since 1966, Astin has been developing an input-environment-output (I-E-O) model, which theorizes student outcomes through a consideration of multiple factors, within college-impact theory, which examines the origins and processes of change. Examples of assessment tools developed through such studies include the Cooperative Institutional Research Program (CIRP) and the College Student Survey (CSS). These surveys emphasize affective aspects of students' outcomes and are used by many universities as an assessment tool. The I-E-O model is based on college-impact theory, which is closely associated with student development. The model suggests that college outcomes should be regarded as the integrated product of inputs (e.g., demographic characteristics of the student, and his or her gender, family background, and academic and social experiences at high school), environments (e.g., programs, disciplines, policies, cultures, group dynamics of peers, relationships with faculty, and experiences through college life), and outcomes (i.e., outputs, for example, goals, career, gained knowledge and skills, attitudes, values, beliefs, behaviors, and satisfaction toward college life). Inputs can directly lead to outcomes, but outcomes are also often indirectly affected by environmental factors.

Based on diverse studies using the I-E-O model, Astin (1985) has developed a "theory of involvement": students learn by becoming involved in various kinds of college activities, such as studying, peer relationships, faculty relationships, cocurricular activities, and curricular activities. Astin (1985) proposes five basic postulates for the theory of involvement: (1) involvement requires the investment of psychological as well as physical energy in such things as tasks, people, and activities; (2) involvement is a continuous concept; (3) involvement has both quantitative and qualitative features; (4) the amount of learning or development is directly proportional to the quality and quantity of involvement; and (5) the educational effectiveness of any policy or practice is associated with its capacity to induce student involvement.

Learning outcomes can be measured in two ways. First, they can be measured on the basis of "external effects" (i.e., in reference to the efficacy of factors outside of the formal educational system). Second, they can be measured by "internal effects," also known as "college impact" (i.e., by demonstrating the degree and extent of quality pedagogy and student involvement). College-impact theory concentrates not on any individual process of student growth; rather, it focuses on the contexts in which a student acts and thinks: the institutional structures, policies, programs, and services; and the attitudes, values, and behaviors of others in institutional environments (Pascarella and Terenzini 2005). Astin's theory of involvement and his I-E-O model offer a basic conceptual and analytic foundation for college-impact research, influencing the educational policies of colleges and universities that aim to achieve more productive learning and teaching environments.

Many theorists have followed Astin, building upon and proposing several models of college impact, which focus variously on student characteristics, institutional environments, and learning outcomes. In the United States in particular, many researchers have spent much energy developing and studying college-impact theory (Astin 1993; Pascarella and Terenzini 2005). Thanks to Astin's pioneering research, college-impact theorists have developed a family of theories and models. Ernest T. Pascarella (1985), for instance, has suggested a reformed model of I-E-O. In his model, Pascarella seeks to clarify the causal relationship between students' backgrounds and their precollege characteristics and the structural and organizational features of an institution. According to him, the institutional structure has both an indirect and a direct influence on a student's development in tandem with the college environment, the effort the student puts in, and the student's interactions with other students and faculty.

Issues Facing Japanese Higher Education and Results of Student-Survey

Results of CSS and JCSS

With the approval of the Higher Education Research Institute (HERI) at University of California, Los Angeles (UCLA), my research fellows and I developed in 2005 a Japanese version of the College Student Survey (JCSS); then, in 2008, we developed the Japanese Freshman Survey (JFS). In the following, I review the results of these two surveys. First, however, I offer a brief account of both surveys. Both the JCSS and the JFS are derived from two preexisting surveys—the CSS and CIRP Freshman Survey (TFS) both of which were designed by the HERI at UCLA. Following a pilot study in 2004, we administered the JCSS, in 2005, 2007, and 2009. We administered the JFS in 2008 and 2009. The surveys track learning behaviors, experiences, values, motivation, and student self-assessment.

Both of these surveys focus on environmental aspects of college. Three major research questions are presented for analysis:

1. What are the differences and similarities of students' experiences and self-evaluation between the United States and Japan?

2. What is the effect of environmental factors on student development?
3. What is the relationship between environmental factors and learning outcomes?

I assume that student learning is related closely to the student's involvement in his or her studies, its quantity, and quality. Further, I assume that the institution's educational policies and practices and its faculty's involvement with a student affect a student's ultimate learning outcome. As a result, I analyze the findings of the JCSS 2005 and 2007 using the college-impact model (Yamada 2009).

Table 6.1 compares the experiences of American and Japanese students. The graph indicates overall that Japanese students have fewer learning experiences than their American counterparts. Nonetheless, Japanese students demonstrated a couple interesting educational advantages: a substantial percentage of students, for instance, discussed course content with their peers. Further, continuous data shows that the learning experiences of Japanese students tend to improve over time.

Table 6.2 compares American and Japanese students' self-evaluation of their learning outcomes. From the table we can see, according to students,

Table 6.1 Learning Experiences of Japanese and American Students

	CSS 2005 (US)	JCSS 2005 (Japan)	JCSS 2007 (Japan)
Took interdisciplinary courses	66.0	30.4	53.4
Worked on independent study projects	58.0	24.0	30.9
Discussed course content with students outside of class	64.6	73.9	71.8
Have been a guest in a faculty's home	45.0	31.1	37.1
Failed to complete homework on time	60.0	42.1	50.2
Have been bored in class	27.0	45.7	47.9
Used the internet for research or homework	84.4	70.1	74.9
Missed class due to employment	25.0	34.4	28.6
Tutored another college student	45.3	9.1	10.0
Total of frequently and occasionally(%)			

Source: JCSS Survey 2005, 2007.

Table 6.2 Student Self-Evaluation of Learning Outcomes: USA and Japan

	USA 2005	Japan 2005	Japan 2007
General knowledge	46.1	9.5	7.8
Analytical and problem solving skills	35.1	7.3	8.1
Knowledge of discipline and major	59.5	23.6	24.1
Ability to think critically	38.7	10	9.8
Knowledge of people from different races/ cultures	21	6.2	7.5
Leadership abilities	27.5	4.7	6.2
Interpersonal skills	32.4	11.8	11.7
Ability to get along with different races/cultures	20.7	3.1	3.8
Understanding of the problems facing your community	19.5	3.6	3.7
Understanding of the problems facing your nation	25.9	5.4	4.8
Writing skills	30.2	6	6.8
Oral presentation skills	28.1	7	8.7
Mathematical skills	14.1	3.3	4.2
Computer skills	27	19.5	16.1
Understanding of global issues	26.1	5.9	4.7
Foreign language ability	13	4.8	4.7

Source: JCSS Survey 2005, 2007.

a massive chasm between the learning outcomes of Japanese and American students: according to them, Japanese students demonstrate at best modest learning outcomes. Despite the seemingly clear-cut difference between American and Japanese students, however, we ought to take into consideration the typical modesty of Japanese students and carefully examine the comparative standard between both sets of students. We should note immediately, for instance, disparities between the approaches and attitudes of both sets of students to higher education, such as their learning behaviors, abilities, skills, and values. Put more generally, we could say that there are cultural and structural differences in higher education that might explain the significance of certain perceived differences in the gains students make in college. As a result, it is best to present such data as an *international* comparison: rather than set a single national benchmark for certain outcomes, it makes more sense to accommodate and consider a range of institutional structures and cultural differences. Looking at student outcomes and experiences in the context of different institutional and cultural arrangements in turn provides new insight into learning outcomes useful to educators the world over.

Results of the JFS 2008

In this section, I analyze the data collected in the JFS 2008. We gave this survey to first-year students between June and July of 2008, three or four months after enrollment. 163 four-year colleges and universities participated in the survey, offering us a sample size of approximately 20,000. The proportion sampled for the JFS fits the proportion of overall Japanese national, public, and private four-year universities. Though not a random sampling of all Japanese higher education institutions (HEIs), the sample population comes pretty close.

I divided the students into types based on their skills. In particular, I classified them based on their learning behavior in high school, using a latent classification method. Accordingly, students were divided into six types (figure 6.1). To clarify, I divided "Inquiry-oriented" students into in an (A) and (B) type for one reason: although both groups of students experienced active learning in order to expedite problem discovering and solving in their high-school days, type (A) students could not understand the significance of active learning and type (B) students were able to relate their high-school experiences of active learning to their college-level experiences. Further, "entrance-exam-oriented" students were divided into (A) and (B) for a similar reason: while entrance-exam-oriented (A) students studied in order simply to pass their entrance examinations, (B) type students studied with a clear goal of what their college major might be.

Unlike the JCSS, the JFS has been consciously focused on Japanese high school, college, and entrance-exam systems. It thus suits the Japanese higher-education system better than the JCSS does.

As the figure 6.1 shows, the largest number of students takes remedial English. We can divide them based on the student skills that I outlined above. Obedient, guidance-oriented students tend to be successful in high school and willfully submissive to their teachers' guidance. Many of these students take remedial classes. What does this mean? We hypothesize that obedient, guidance-oriented students fail to develop the kinds of self-motivated learning skills in high school that prove integral to university-level study.

The data these surveys present document several issues that Japanese universities face. First, unlike their American counterparts, Japanese students experience a far less rich educational experience—on top of which,

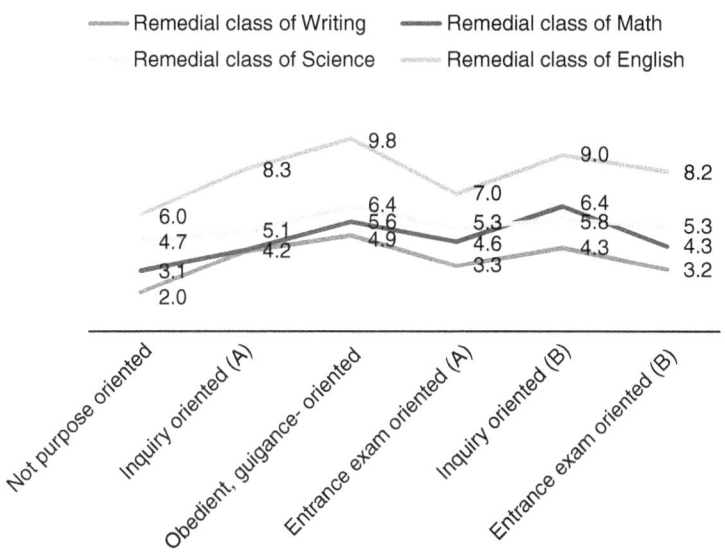

Figure 6.1 The Proportion of Students Who Take Remedial Classes.
Source: JFS 2008.

many Japanese students expect to take remedial classes. Also, as noted earlier, Japanese students' self-evaluation of their learning outcomes were lower than American students'. Nonetheless, we can, through a longitudinal study, examine how the educational reform movement in Japanese higher education that aims at improving teaching and learning has proven effective.

In the next section, I present the first-year experience program Japanese universities have developed over the past ten years as an embodiment of the educational reform movement.

The First-Year Experiences (FYE) Programs and Challenges

FYE programs introduced in recent years seem to be closely connected to these issues. First-year seminars, which originally developed in the United States in the early twentieth century and were popularized in the 1980s, have been evaluated for their capacity to motivate teaching reforms and to improve retention rates (Yamada 2004). John N. Gardner et al. (2001) observe eight factors that affect the evaluation of first-year experiences by college students. These factors include: (1) tax payers' reluctance to tolerate continuing higher education expenditures; (2) fund providers' demand to raise the productivity of students; (3) pressure to raise admission standards; (4) pressure to redistribute more students to the less costly two-year sector; (5) pressure to teach more students through distance education to reduce costs; (6) pressure to shorten time-to-degree; (7) pressure to provide remedial education; and (8) the emergence of serious competition with the private-for-profit sector. All of these factors are products of and influenced by the pressures of accountability and they have forced institutions of higher education to direct energy away from research toward teaching.

A survey conducted by the National Resource Center (2002) for the First-Year Experience & Students in Transition at University of South Carolina found that FYE programs facilitated the transition to college life. Fidler and Hunter (1989) suggest that freshman success can be defined in six ways: a student must develop academic and intellectual competence; establish and maintain interpersonal relationships; develop a personal identity; decide on a career and lifestyle; maintain personal health and wellness; and develop an integrated philosophy of life. Quite obviously, then, the success of first-year students can be accounted for in ways beyond a good grade-point average. Moreover, several researchers have found that there is a higher retention rate between the first and second year of college among first-year students who have taken first-year seminars (Fidler and Hunter 1989). In the United States, first-year seminars have steadily developed to the point of indispensability: today they rank high among policymakers, fund providers, and rank-and-file faculty and administration (Upcraft et al. 2005). Further, they point out that credible assessment studies have emerged demonstrating the ways in which such FYE programs have assisted the success of first-year students.

In 1998, Reiko Yamada conducted the first survey of first-year programs in Japan.[2] Her study revealed that learning ability, learning motivation, and note-taking skills of students in four-year universities and colleges had declined over the preceding five years. For this reason, many universities and colleges reported a newfound need to address their students' lack of readiness for higher education. Private universities in particular reported the greatest concern about the deterioration of scholastic achievement, self-motivation, and social skills. The survey results also demonstrated that there was little agreement among institutions of higher education in Japan about what a FYE program was: some faculty members and departments defined a first-year program as remedial education; others thought of the program as a regular feature of the first-year curriculum. This confusion was also apparent in the diverse array of courses and pedagogical methods that comprised first-year programs in Japanese universities. Because the conditions of education are changing rapidly in Japan, it was my hypothesis that the status of a first-year program has also changed since the 1998 survey. To test that hypothesis, I conducted a survey of 1,170 deans and academic provosts at private universities in 2001. Comparing the results of the 1998 and 2001 surveys allowed me to determine the then current and changing status of first-year seminar programs in Japan. Again, in 2007, other researchers conducted almost the same survey on all national and private four-year universities in order to compare the progress of FYE programs over the course of the decade.

A Decade of FYE Programs in Japan

As seen in table 6.3, 80.9 percent of Japanese universities integrated a first-year seminar into their curricula in 2001. By 2007, the integration rate had increased to 97 percent. Today, FYE programs are a prevalent feature of Japanese higher education. Moreover, it can be credibly claimed that spread of FYE programs in Japan has occurred against the backdrop of reform in higher education and has been accompanied by a recent emphasis on teaching and learning at universities and colleges in Japan. FYE programs are now a stable component of higher education in Japan, an answer to the challenges posed by the newfound demands of students in an era of massification.

Table 6.3 demonstrates the growth and omnipresence of FYE programs in Japanese universities, regardless of discipline. As a result, we can assume that a wide range of researchers from various disciplines have come to participate in the FYE movement in Japan over the course of the past decade.

Table 6.3 Proportion of Integration of First-Year Seminars in the Curriculum in Japanese Higher Education

	Humanities (%)	Social sciences (%)	Sciences & Technology (%)	Others (%)	Total (%)
2001	76.1	84.9	86.7	73.2	80.9
2007	96.7	96.3	98.0	96.2	97.0
*<.05					

Source: JFS 2008.

Although confusion existed about the precise definition of a FYE program in 1998 and 2001, the surveys revealed by 2007 that there were seven explicitly defined types of FYE programs in Japan. They included: (1) remedial education covering high-school-level educational content; (2) study skills, such as report writing, reading comprehension, and IT skill; (3) social skills, manners, and general knowledge required for university success; and (4) the transition to majors, including general and special knowledge in the major. Beyond which, FYE programs sought to cultivate: (5) career education; (6) student skills; and (7) a sense of attachment to the campus. Over the course of this decade, then, course content in FYE programs grew markedly.

Though in the past some educators had tried to make a general education in liberal arts a standard feature of first-year education in university, systematized or organized FYE classes were not a regular component of university education in Japan until the late 1990s. As it became apparent to universities and colleges that students were having difficulty adapting to college-level learning, such institutions gradually turned their attention to the first year of study. But concerns early on were largely *academic*: in Japan, FYE programs started as a feature of regular course work. The FYE movement has also been promoted externally by the "good practice" grants that have been administered and managed by the Ministry of Education, Culture, Sports, Science, and Technology: such grants have encouraged competition among institutions to secure funding and their survival in the future. At the same time, however, internal pressure has also promoted the growth and refinement of FYE programs: universities and colleges themselves, even before the introduction of the grants, were troubled by the prevalence of underachieving and ill-motivated students.

Nonetheless, Japanese FYE programs still face a host of difficulties. For instance, Japanese students, unlike their American counterparts, rank the study and generic skills they acquired in college below those they developed in high school. Though many Japanese students have gained specialized knowledge of their major, few on the other hand seem to feel that that knowledge in tangible. Moreover, it appears that a great chasm, in terms of both the objectives of education as well as the style of pedagogy, has opened up between what students learn in high school and what they learn at colleges and universities (Yamada 2010).

Of the first column in figure 6.2 illustrates the lack of articulation between primary and secondary schools and secondary and postsecondary education. In both instances, there remains a disparity between early and later educational goals and pedagogical practices. Japanese secondary schools, for instance, tend to put more emphasis on the "banking style" of teaching—teachers impart information to students; students

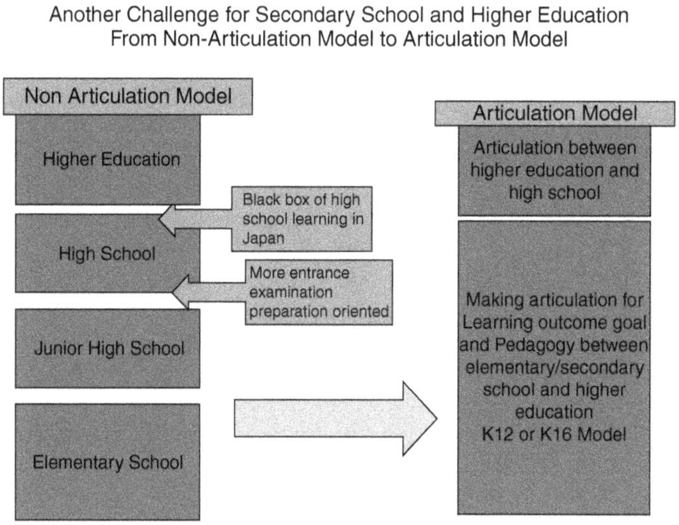

Another Challenge for Secondary School and Higher Education
From Non-Articulation Model to Articulation Model

Non Articulation Model
- Higher Education
  - ← Black box of high school learning in Japan
- High School
  - ← More entrance examination preparation oriented
- Junior High School
- Elementary School

Articulation Model
- Articulation between higher education and high school
- Making articulation for Learning outcome goal and Pedagogy between elementary/secondary school and higher education K12 or K16 Model

Figure 6.2 Non-Articulation Model and Articulation Model between Secondary School and Higher Education in Japan.
Source: JFS 2008.

memorize what the teacher imparts—while students tend to memorize knowledge solely to pass examinations. Conversely, in the United States, for example, there is an "advance placement" system, the goal of which is to prepare high-school students for college-level learning and teaching. Unlike their American counterparts, then, Japanese students are not being fully prepared for postsecondary education, despite the proposals of the Central Council for Education in 2008. Instead, educators should be pursuing an articulation model—that is, educators on the whole need to share a set of goals and expectations for students. Collaboration and the development of effective pedagogical methods need to span from the primary all the way to the postsecondary level, as seen in figure 6.2.

Moreover, Japanese FYE programs face the new challenge of massification: more and more students—some motivated and some not, some high performers and some low—are being funneled into higher education. To address the emergent needs of this newly diversified student body, FYE programs must accommodate a wider range of student abilities and needs. For example, Japanese FYE programs need to develop honors programs for high-achieving students, such as courses taught in English to meet the demands of globalization as well as study-skills programs for low-achieving students.

Conclusion

In this chapter, I have offered an account of the issues and challenges that globalization, mobility, and massification have presented for Japanese higher education. Above all, these issues have raised the question of quality assurance and accountability when it comes to undergraduate education, learning outcomes, and internationalization, as the "universal standard" has become indispensable to functioning in today's knowledge-based, global society. In particular, we can view the Global 30 program as a symbol of the desire among Japanese universities to promote and accommodate internationalization and global mobility, by providing education to promising, qualified students from all around the world while generating opportunities for students to share and collaborate on research projects on a global scale. Globally, both governments through policy and universities through teaching have sought to offer such international opportunities while ensuring accountability. At the same time, Japanese universities still face a local issue: massification requires universities to educate greater and greater numbers of students, who may or may not be fully prepared for the demands of postsecondary education. In even the most recent past, the Japanese viewed colleges and universities as "gatekeepers," institutions that conferred social status, secure elite occupations, and guarantee both social and financial benefits through the screening process of college entry. Consequently, the effect of social "charters"—that is, an *external* effect—has been more pronounced than internal effects in Japanese higher education. Nonetheless, as I have argued in this chapter, the internal effects of Japanese higher education— namely college impact—already function to yield educational outcomes. Moreover, the "good practice" grants system as well as policy enacted by the Ministry of Education, Culture, Sports, Science, and Technology have contributed to the transformation of Japanese universities into institutions of teaching and learning, and not research alone. As a result of this policy shift, Japanese universities have developed assessment systems to measure learning outcomes. Such policy shifts along with the introduction of FYE programs are responses to the challenge that massification has issued. As a result, I have argued in this chapter that Japanese higher education policy and higher-education institutions are obliged to pursue both universal and local issues in a more global context.

Notes

1. The Spellings' Commission on the Future of Higher Education issued the report in 2006. However, the author's name and the report was publicly U.S.

Department of Education 2006. *A Test of Leadership: Charting the Future of American Higher Education.*
2. The survey was conducted 1998 at 209 four-year universities and colleges in Japan in order to gather information about freshman seminar or remedial education course offerings. The final respondent rate was 54 percent. Medical, engineering, economics, intercultural studies, and communication and language departments participated.

REFERENCES

Albornoz, O. 1996. "Autonomy and Accountability in Higher Education," in *Higher Education in an International Perspective*, ed. Z. Morsy and P. G. Altbach. New York: Garland Publishing, 36–45.

Arimoto, A. and T. Ehara, eds. 1996. *Daigaku Kyouiku no Kokusai Hikaku* [International Comparison of the Academic Profession]. Tokyo: Tamagawa University Press.

Astin, Alexander W. 1985. *Achieving Educational Excellence: A Critical Assessment of Priorities and Practices in Higher Education.* San Francisco: Jossey-Bass.

———. 1993. *Assessment for Excellence: The Philosophy and Practice of Assessment and Evaluation in Higher Education.* Phoenix: ORYX Press.

Astin, H. S. and A. L. Antonio. 2004. "The Impact of College on Character Development."*New Directions for Institutional Research* 122: 55–64.

Banta, T. W. ed. 2007. *Assessing Student Achievement in General Education.* San Francisco, CA: Jossey-Bass. A Willey Company.

Berdahl, R. O. and T. R. McConnell. 1994. "Autonomy and Accountability: Some Fundamental Issues," in *Higher Education in American Society*, ed. P. G. Altbach, R. O. Berdahl, and P. J. Gumport. Amherst, NY: Prometheus, 55–72.

Ehara, T. 1998. "Research and Teaching: the Dilemma from an International Comparative Perspective." *Daigaku Ronshu* 28: 133–154.

Fidler, P. P. and M. S. Hunter. 1989. "How Seminars Enhance Student Success," in *The Freshman Year Experience*, ed. M. L. Upcraft et al. San Francisco, CA: Jossey-Bass, 216–237.

Gardner, J. N., Barefoot, B. O., and Swing, R. L. 2001. *Guidelines for Evaluating the First-year Experience at Four-year Colleges* (2nd Edition), Columbia: National Resource Center for the First-Year Experience & Students in Transition, University of South Carolina.

Harvard University. 2007. "Task Force on General Education at the Faculty of Arts and Sciences at Harvard University." Available at: http://isites.harvard.edu/fs/docs/icb.topic624259.files/report.pdf (accessed August 12, 2011).

Japan Society for Promotion of Science. 2011. Available at: http://www.jsps.go.jp/english/e-kokusaika/index.html (accessed August 2, 2011).

National Resource Center. 2002. The First-Year Experience & Students in Transition. 2002. *University 101: Success Starts Here: Tools for Tomorrow.*: Columbia, NRC.

Pascarella, E. T. 1985. "College Environmental Influences on Learning and Cognitive Development; A Critical Review and Synthesis, " in *Higher Education: Handbook of Theory and Research*, ed. J. Smart, Vol 1. New York: Agathon Press, 1–64. Pascarella, E. T. and P. T. Terenzini. 2005. *How College Affects Students*. San Francisco: Jossey-Bass.

Slaughter, S. 1998. "National Higher Education Policies in a Global Economy," in *Universities and Globalization: Critical Perspectives,* ed. J. Currie. and J. Newson. London: Sage Publications, 45–70.

The Central Council for Education. 2008. *A Report: Structuring Undergraduate Education*. Tokyo: MEXT.

The Ministry of Education, Culture, Sports, Science and Technology (MEXT). 2004. *Higher Education Agency Material*. Tokyo: MEXT.

Trow, M. 1974. "Problems in the Transition from Elite to Mass Higher Education." *Policy for Higher Education*. Paris: Organisation for Economic Co-operation and Development, 51–101.

U.S. Department of Education. 2006. *A Test of Leadership: Charting the Future of American Higher Education*, Report of the Commission Appointed by Secretary of Education Margaret Spellings. Washington DC: US Department of Education.

University of Melbourne. 2007. "Attributes of the Melbourne Graduate." Available at: http://www.unimelb.edu.au/about/attributes.html, (accessed August 2, 2011).

Upcraft, M. L., Gardner, J. J., and Barefoot, B. O. 2005. "Introduction: The Fist Year of College Revisited," in *Challenging & Supporting The First-Year Students: A Handbook for Improving The First Year of College,* ed. Upcraft et al. San Francisco: Jossey-Bass, 1–12.

Van Vaught, F. A. and D. F. Westerheijden. 1994. "Towards a General Model of Quality Assessment in Higher Education." *Higher Education* 28(3): 355–371.

Yamada, R. ed. 1998. *The Current Status of Freshman Seminar Course in Japanese Universities*. Osaka: Poole Gakuin University.

———. 2004. "The Development of First-Year Education and the Practice in Doshisha Univeristy," in Mizogami, S. ed., *University Teaching to Support Students' Learning*. Tokyo: Toshindo, 246–272.

———. 2009. "Comparative Student Analysis between Universities through JCSS," in *Science of Undergraduate Education: Comparative Analysis of Student Assessment*. ed. Reiko Yamada. Tokyo: Toshindo, 41–62.

———. 2010. "Current Status and the Future of First-Year Experience," in *University Education 30 Years of Study and Reform*, ed. Editors of the Liberal and General Education Society of Japan, Tokyo: Toshindo, 29–48.

Part 2

Institutional Responses to Mobility and Migration in Asian Pacific Higher Education

Chapter 7

The Rhetoric and Reality of Mobility and Migration in Higher Education: The Case of the University of California, Los Angeles

John N. Hawkins

Mobility, Migration, and Higher Education Transformation: The View from the Asia-Pacific Region

It is not difficult to find in the very large literature on mobility and migration (M&M) in higher education (HE) soaring language about how the world has forever or is in the process of being changed by globalization and internationalization and how these social phenomena have particularly impacted the world's universities and colleges. It is noted that the movement of students, scholars, skilled talent, ideas, institutional structures, the structure of knowledge, and almost everything else associated with what I will refer to going forward as M&M, are a key part of these phenomena, ushering in a new age of HE particularly in the Asia-Pacific region (for bibliographic citations of the breadth of this literature and discussion of these trends see Childress 2010; Kell and Vogl 2010; Wildavsky 2010 among others). Much of the literature is focused, as one might expect, on the movement of students and scholars through the region (here meant to include the United States as a Pacific nation); less attention has been placed on institutional change as a result of these and other movements. And the bulk of the literature on M&M places it squarely in the context of the broader mega trends of globalization and its predecessor, internationalization.

It is useful to keep in mind the distinctions among these terms, all of which describe social phenomenon that have been with us for some time, some would say a very long time. Students and scholars have roamed the world seeking new knowledge and experiences since the advent of higher learning, and despite the relative newness of the term "globalization" it too has a long history, and higher education institutions (HEIs) have been experiencing internationalization since the first foreign student or scholar walked through their doors. Yet we recognize that the contemporary use of these concepts is what is being discussed here, that is, globalization as defined by Neubauer (2007), Held (2004), among others, and characterized by scope, pace, networking, and technology. Then, one can consider internationalization as something that HEI policymakers seek to either pursue or restrict, but that has measurable outcomes, and M&M as one of the more significant of those outcomes.

In general, there appears to be some consensus that internationalization of HE and the M&M characteristics that help define it, is moving forward at a rapid pace, a juggernaut in the context of globalization. The Association of Pacific Rim Universities (APRU) and the Pacific Economic Cooperation Council (PECC) state clearly in their various reports that globalization is increasing internationalization that is leading a second wave of M&M (the first being the simple movement of students and faculty, increases in foreign language study, courses with international content, and perspectives between HEIs, etc.). It is noted that since 1999 there has been a 57 percent increase in the number of students worldwide who are pursuing HE outside of their own country. The second wave will include not only the movement of students, faculty, scholars but whole institutions into overseas markets, complete with joint degrees, distance learning, cross-border supply of educational services, commercialization of educational services, and so on (Findlay and Tierney 2008). The reports also conclude that the Asia-Pacific region will account for the bulk of this expanded movement and mobility. Recognizing that there remain restrictions to this expansive M&M movement, a multitude of barriers to its realization, the reports recommend the removal of such barriers through regional cooperation in the following four areas:

1. Government cooperation to provide more openness in modes of supply beyond what GATS (General Agreement on Trade in Services) suggests.
2. Increase regulation of the quality of these ventures.

3. Link the ventures with cooperative research.
4. Reform migration policies so that countries are poised for the forthcoming "war for skills" that will characterize the future (Findlay and Tierney 2008).

Others (Glassman 2010; Wildavsky 2010) have written about "The Great Brain Race" and "Minds on the Move" and how nations are competing for international students, the best students, and how this free trade in minds has numerous beneficial advantages to the receiving and sending nations.

The picture that is painted in these and other reports is that M&M is destined to develop broader and deeper, extending beyond simple exchange, student and faculty mobility, and into such areas as institutional mobility, the movement of ideas, and structural reform including the liberalization of migration policies to accommodate this insatiable hunger for a global, internationalized HE framework; truly, a major global transformation of HE.

There are a number of intriguing minitrends of M&M in the region that have yet to coalesce into anything resembling a recognizable megatrend. For example, there has been a shift away from human resource mobility per se and the social and cultural impact it might have toward the economic impact of M&M as well as skill distribution. While in the United States, M&M is reported to have contributed $17.6 billion to the US economy; it has not yet been seen to be the income generator that it has for the United Kingdom and Australia. The establishment of differential fees for international students, for example, is beginning to be seen in Europe, the United Kingdom, and Australia (and of course in the United States, this has always been the case in the public universities that have residential and nonresidential fees). There is also increased competition for the best students among the top receiving countries such as the United States, United Kingdom, Germany, France, and Australia and now beginning to be seen in China, Malaysia, Taiwan, and other emerging Asian economies. This is related to a shift from massive to selective recruitment for international students so that they feed the needs of the knowledge economy for receiving nations. And finally, a regionalization is taking place as students and faculty seem to be increasingly expressing their mobility by moving within their own region.

One outcome of this shift toward highly skilled students and faculty is that the notion of "brain drain" is back on the agenda, as newly emerging economies like Vietnam are particularly hard hit by the siphoning off of their best students not only to the usual destinations (Europe, United States, United Kingdom, Australia) but to Asian destinations as well. One irony to all of this is that as the young, bright brains move to other sites, those nations most effected by this are recruiting, more senior, foreign brains to fill faculty slots that would otherwise be filled by their own graduates (de Witt 2010). In any case, what is perhaps most striking is that the numbers being talked about in the current Asia-Pacific M&M movement of people, are considered to be quite small, so small that (with the exception of Australia), most receiving nations are recommending at a minimum a doubling of the numbers in the near future (this is true for the United States—Douglass and Edelstein 2010; Japan, Malaysia, Singapore, and Taiwan—de Witt 2010). Furthermore, it is not often noted that though mobility has increased in terms of absolute numbers of students and scholars, when compared with the increase in enrollments and faculty hiring as a result of massification, as O'Hara notes: "it is nothing explosive like we would expect" (O'Hara 2010).

Whatever the scale, how much impact has all of this movement had on the HEIs involved? We really do not have good case study data to know the particulars of this "flow" in specific HEIs. One could argue that given the flow of students, scholars, research projects, ideas, and notions about HE structure and governance that some of this would have rubbed off on the institutions most involved. We might expect to see changes of at least three types:

1. An upward trend in the percentages of students and scholars going abroad and coming from abroad, in the context of the parallel increase in enrollments and faculty hiring that has accompanied HE massification.
2. Institutional adaptation to better handle the scale of M&M activities, that is, structural, curricular, human resource changes that would involve the establishment of new offices, structures, protocols, policies, and so on.
3. Institutional transformation. That is, the HEI itself would begin to adopt HE practices and policies of the nations with which it is most involved; in other words, institutional evolution not just adaptation would begin to occur.

We really don't know how much of this has occurred. The president of the Woodrow Wilson National Fellowship Foundation notes that it is inevitable that HEIs in most nations will become more internationalized as a result of increased M&M, but simply having an array of study-abroad programs and other international activities do not make an institution "internationalized" or represent any substantive change in their organizational structure. He suggests that there will be a need for much more cross-institutional integration before we "…wake up to an entirely different university" (Fischer 2010c, 1). This observation is echoed by the chancellor of the largest public university system in the Unites States (Nancy L. Zimpher-SUNY) who notes that there is a large gap between the rhetoric and the reality (at least in the Unites States) of internationalized HE. She argues that a great deal of strategic planning, establishment of measurable outcomes, and accountability will be necessary before the "thousand points of light uncoordinated" can be harnessed to have any real impact or transformative change on the university (Fischer 2010b).

The universe of M&M activity in the Asia-Pacific region is dynamic and diverse, changing quickly and representing a wide range of activity. Some settings like Australia are clearly at the dynamic end of the spectrum as a receiving country with a total of 26 percent of all enrollees in public universities coming from abroad. As Marginson notes: "Education is the third largest export sector in Australia—below coal and iron ore but ahead of tourism, beef, wheat, and manufacturing" (Marginson 2009, 6). Other nations are retreating from their previous role as a sending nation while still seeking to become a receiving nation. Japan, historically a leader in sending students and scholars abroad, now shows a consistent decline in enrollments abroad at both the undergraduate and graduate levels. Japanese students are now reported to be "grass eaters," that is, more content to stay at home and graze where it is comfortable, at the same time as the government is seeking to double the number of foreign students and scholars coming to Japan. There are many reasons for this decline in mobility on the part of Japanese students, including the difficult economy Japan has been facing in recent years. But the reasons are more profound than that, including a propensity toward insularity, and an increasing lack of competitiveness when compared to Indian, Chinese, Korean, and Taiwan students (Fukushima 2010). Japan may be demonstrating that M&M activity is cyclical and related to levels of economic development as well as sociocultural shifts (*Washington Post* April 11, 2011). Yet, the question still remains, despite this surge or lack thereof of M&M activity in Asia Pacific, what impact if any is it having on HEIs in the countries most involved, especially in the three areas referred to above? This chapter addresses this question by moving the focus to the United States and more specifically to one major research institution to dig below the surface of the rhetoric of M&M and internationalization.

The US Context of Internationalization

One of the primary impacts of globalization, internationalization, and M&M has been the impact this has had on some of the demographics of American HEIs. Those of us who call these places our homes over the years have seen the results of this in our daily lives as teachers, researchers, administrators, and so on. And, we have experienced this as well by being part of the worldwide movement of ideas in our joint research with our colleagues abroad and through our interaction with visiting scholars in our home institutions. Even in the smallest liberal arts colleges, study-abroad programs have sprung up and of course in the largest research universities these and other programs have become part of the academic landscape in some cases, going so far as to have branch campuses located overseas.

We can thank the American Council on Education (ACE) for providing us with survey data on the extent to which this M&M phenomenon has actually impacted the American academy. The results have been intriguing, both the 2001 survey and the more recent 2006 survey. The survey results bring into relief a picture of M&M, internationalization, and globalization and elicited surprise and to some degree astonishment among academics and scholars in the United States and elsewhere. Here we will only summarize the 2006 study in order to provide a context for the later discussion of one particular institution (for details of the entire study see Green, Luu, and Burris 2008).

The ACE survey, entitled, "Mapping Internationalization in U.S. Campuses" gathered data from almost 3,000 US HEIs according to the following indicators:

- Institutional support and structure
- Academic requirements (curriculum among others)
- Faculty policies and opportunities, the academic culture
- International students.

The report begins with a statement that is worth quoting in full:

> Given the geopolitical realties of the world after September 11, the growing pace of globalization, and the repeated national calls for 'globally competent college graduates,' one might expect that U.S. colleges and universities today would be working avidly, perhaps urgently, to retool their curricula, policies, and practices to position themselves to fully prepare students for work and life in this changed world...we might have anticipated that that the survey would illustrate that U.S. higher education institutions were redoubling their efforts to produce college graduates with strong intercultural skills by working diligently to intensify language study, infuse their curricula with international study, and institute policies and practices that promote campus internationalization. *The findings of this study do not suggest that this is happening.* (Green et al. 2008, 81)

More specifically, the study found that most US HEIs have not made a public commitment to internationalization and support of M&M through such mechanisms as mission statements, strategic plans, task force studies, and other strategies to recognize that such a phenomenon is taking place and that it occupies an important place in their institution. It appears that for the most part, over 50 percent of all US HEIs seem unaware that M&M is occurring. And, among those who have taken some steps to address this movement, what they do about it does not constitute a coherent strategy according to the ACE study. Most efforts reported are unsystematic, scattered, and lack traction illustrating once again, how difficult it is to enact change in the face of the dominant paradigm of US HE.

Among those institutions that appear to have developed some sort of strategy for M&M, there exists a large gap between institutional rhetoric and reality; the former utilized largely to project a marketing/branding image of being "with it" with respect to internationalization. This conclusion coincides with that of NASULGC's *National Agenda* (2007) study, which reached a similar conclusion regarding the degree to which US HEIs are preparing students and faculty for the increasingly globalized world. Institutionally, most American universities and colleges have not taken structural steps or felt the need to take steps to foster and support internationalization in the face of M&M.

While much is said and written about international student mobility and migration throughout the Asia-Pacific region and the United States, the ACE study found that students in the United States generally receive little or no exposure to global learning, the complexities of the world, or encounter the realities of the M&M that is taking place around them. The curriculum is the least changed of all elements of HE in the United States when it comes to M&M. Study-abroad programs have increased in number and impact in recent years but still only account for a very small percentage of all students enrolled (in 2006, US undergraduate and graduate enrollments nationwide were about 17,000,000; US students participating in study abroad were 220,200 or slightly over 1 percent [Green et al. 2008, 82]; Chow and Chambers and the Statistical Abstract for 2010 show some higher figures, totaling 4 percent and 3 percent respectively). Furthermore, even for those who stay home, there is little indication that they will ever take a course that remotely deals with the issues of globalization, internationalization, or M&M. Only 37 percent of all institutions surveyed had any courses that could be called international in their general education (GE) requirements and roughly 60 percent of undergraduates graduate without ever having a course or other curricular experience that falls in this area of globalization/internationalization (Green et al. 2008, 82).

Given the increasing mobility of businesses, labor, and professionals in the globalized economy one would think that at least in the area of foreign language preparation there would be an uptick in enrollments but even here there has been a decline falling back to 1965 levels. Only 18 percent of doctorate granting institutions require a foreign language either for admission or graduation (Green et al. 2008, 83). Finally, as referenced above, most institutions have not invested in structural changes that will promote or support internationalization through the establishment of specific offices, administration positions, staff support, and so on. Those who have done this have relied on part-time employees and one or two committed faculty members who generally donate their time. The faculty reward structure has not evolved to encourage faculty to engage in international linkage activities and the study noted that in fact, in many cases, the opposite is true (Green et al. 2008, 88). This dire assessment of the internationality of HE the United States is not encouraging and certainly does not support a view of a rapidly expanding scope of mobility and migration of US students abroad.

Looked at the other way, that is, the number of international students attending US HEIs, the news is more supportive of the M&M rhetoric, as these numbers have been increasing over the years. Yet they still only amount to about only 4 percent of the total student body, both graduate and undergraduate in the United States in 2009 (Fischer 2009). Other changes have been even less encouraging. The Council of Graduate Schools in the United States shows that the number of foreign students in US graduate programs has remained flat for the last five years with decreases in the critical STEM areas and in business, where they were expected to grow modestly (Douglass and Edelstein 2010). While the world and especially the Asia-Pacific region may experience an expansion of international students and increased M&M, how this is distributed seems to be a key factor. New competitors have emerged and the market has shifted toward countries such as Australia, New Zealand, Japan, and Canada; the Unites States has lost 20 to 25 percent of its market share in the period 2000 to 2006 (Douglass and Edelstein 2010). In short, the Unites States does not seem to be a model of M&M in any sense, and statistically in terms of student circuits of exchange, appears to be a very domestic, parochial nation. To probe a little deeper into this seeming disconnect to the M&M, globalization, internationalization literature, it is time to turn to our case study of one major research institution in the United States, the University of California, Los Angeles to see how one institution, ranked among the top ten of "internationalized" US universities, looks with respect to the ACE criteria we have just reviewed (Kivowitz 2007).

UCLA's Internationalization in the Context of Globalization, Mobility, and Migration

UCLA was established in 1919 as the Southern Branch of the University of California, and functioned as a community college and teacher training school. It was renamed the University of California, Los Angeles (UCLA) in 1927 with 5,000 students enrolled at its current location in Westwood. It currently has a teaching faculty of over 4,000, undergraduate enrollments of 26,687 (2009 to 2010), and graduate enrollments of 11,863 for a total enrolment of 38,550 (the total reported is slightly higher as nondegree students, interns and others are counted). It is the largest in enrollments of all of the University of California campuses and consists of a College of Letters and Sciences and eleven professional schools including a medical school. There are 118 undergraduate degree programs and 200 graduate degree programs. In short, it is a major Tier One research university ranked highly in a number of fields of study and overall ranked twenty-fourth nationally and fourth among public universities (Best Colleges 2010).

Located on the west coast of the United States, UCLA has naturally come to represent a university defined and characterized by great diversity, both ethnically (drawing upon Latino, Asian, and African-American populations in the Los Angeles area) and internationally due to its proximity to the Asia-Pacific region and Latin America. It is little wonder, then, that UCLA has a reputation as being one of the most diverse and internationalized of US universities (ranked in the top ten by *Open Doors* with respect to foreign students and students studying abroad) (Kivowitz 2007). Indeed, two major administrative units have been in existence for over a quarter of a century to oversee this internationality: The Dashew Center for International Students and Scholars, and the UCLA International Institute.

Structural Impact of M&M

The Dashew Center for International Students and Scholars was established 30 years ago and more recently through a priority fund-raising effort, Bradley Hall was constructed, an attractive, signature building to showcase UCLA's commitment to M&M. In their mission statement, the Dashew Center notes: "The Dashew Center for International Students and Scholars enhances the UCLA experience for international students and scholars and promotes global connection through services to the university community." The Center provides a wealth of services for foreign students and scholars including offering advice and counsel to students and scholars from abroad, interpreting immigration regulations, understanding employment options, and helping with educational, personal, and cultural adjustments to university life. The Center also provides educational activities for foreign students and scholars including English language conversation classes, seminars, and workshops on global development issues, social activities, and programs to engage UCLA students and faculty and the community at large. The Center is generally recognized as unique and broad in scope among American universities and colleges.

The UCLA International Institute is the focal point for international research and teaching at UCLA. It has a long history, having gone through various iterations but was conceived and implemented as UCLA's administrative unit to oversee interdisciplinary area studies centers, other international centers and programs, international academic and exchange agreements, and a variety of other outreach and educational activities.[1] The chief administrative officer is currently a vice provost and therefore well represented among UCLA's top administrators. As an example of its scope and breadth, the Institute currently oversees the operations of 18 multidisciplinary centers and programs (e.g., NDEA Title VI centers such as the Latin American Institute, and the Asia Institute), and engages in a broad range of community and lifelong learning accredited training programs for global affairs. The University of California's well-known Education Abroad Program is also under this administrative umbrella.

UCLA's steady interaction with the world at large, and the impact of this M&M flow over the years, has resulted in an evolving administrative adaptation as represented by these two units. In this sense, M&M has indeed made an impact on the campus and its organizational structure. The Dashew Center addresses a discrete population with special needs and many if not most American universities have such a structure. The International Institute has a broader mission, and is more academic and educational in scope. When put into the context of the entire university, however, the question remains as to how deep M&M really is at UCLA when expressed in terms of the numbers of students, scholars, and faculty actually engaged in this globalized flow. It is to this question that we now turn.

The Flow of International Students and Scholars

As was noted before, UCLA has been recognized as among the top ten universities in the United States with respect to M&M, that is, sending and receiving students to and from abroad (Kivowitz 2007). The flagship program for UCLA is the system-wide Education Abroad Program (EAP), which is a smoothly running, first-rate program, admired by many US universities. This program and many others not associated with EAP are coordinated by the International Education Office (IEO), part of the International Institute referred to above. The IEO was only formed in 2007 but it has brought more order to bear on UCLA's M&M efforts, through more effective outreach and marketing. As noted in their brochure, "we are working harder than ever to get the message across that study abroad is for everyone, and not only for financially privileged and academically outstanding students" (*UCLA Newsroom* 2009). The flow of students in and out of UCLA for study abroad has a reach of over 60 countries. EAP, which is highly selective, offers more than 140 programs in 30 countries. Clearly there has been a major commitment within the University of California system (UC) and at UCLA to offer high quality and well-organized programs for study abroad and for receiving international students. The institutional impact in the form of offices, staff, and budget of global M&M is easily recognized on this campus.

Yet it is important to take a closer look at the actual scope and trends of this activity to see how it compares with M&M flows in other countries and how the rhetoric compares with the realities of students moving in and out of the institution. The most recent news release for study abroad (November 2009) notes that UCLA ranked eighth in the United States in foreign students and fifth in number of students studying abroad (more than any other UC campus) (*UCLA Newsroom* November 9, 2010). What were these numbers? Specifically, the number of foreign students during 2009 to 2010 academic year was 5,685, the largest share of this coming from South Korea, China, India, Hong Kong, Taiwan, and Japan (despite that nation's recent retrenchment). These included graduate and undergraduate students, as well as students in UCLA's nondegree Extension Program and those on internship visas, and English as Second Language (ESL) students. Of the total, 2,282 were enrolled in degree granting graduate programs, and 1,737 in undergraduate programs (thus occupying about 10 percent of the total UCLA degree enrollment) (UCLA Open Doors Report 2010).

Looked at another way, as a percentage of freshman applicants, in 2010, international students comprised 7 percent of the total number of applicants. This percentage held constant as they ended up being 7 percent of those admitted. Over a ten year period these percentages have hovered around 4 to 5 percent of both applications and those admitted and have increased 1 percent a year for the past three years, the highest ever. Thus, it is possible to state, as has been done, that since 2006 (when the percentage of admits was 3.6 percent) international students at UCLA have doubled in number. Yet, the fact remains that these are fairly constant, and low percentages, by no means a rapid trend in M&M upward ("*Undergraduate Admissions and Relations with Schools, Profile of Admitted Freshman*" 2010). In comparison, the number of UCLA students studying abroad (a topic to which we will return) for this same period, in all programs (not just EAP) totaled 2,330 or 5.8 percent of the total undergraduate enrollment. These students primarily went to the United Kingdom, France, Italy, Spain, and China. So with the exception of the new fascination with China, EAP and other UCLA students are still quite Eurocentric choosing as sites for study those nations that have traditionally been the focus of US study abroad and those programs where English is used as the medium of instruction.

Returning to the profile of international students coming to UCLA, however, we find some asymmetry in several important respects. These numbers and percentages, while not large, are respectable enough to be able to say that international students occupy a modest share of UCLA's total undergraduate and graduate enrollments. The graduate numbers are, however, skewed somewhat toward graduate enrollments in specific disciplines such as engineering, management, and the sciences. The other asymmetry is that incoming international students are about three times the number of outgoing UCLA students. The third trend that is revealed is that UCLA's study-abroad students are bimodal, that is, by far the bulk of them are participating in study-abroad programs that are not part of the prestigious EAP program (622 in EAP for 2008–2009 out of a total of 2,230). Non-EAP students may go abroad for a summer program, or for one quarter, or even for a month or so. EAP students are required to spend at least one quarter and more often the entire junior year abroad with a highly structured program, including a faculty adviser, which may include foreign language study. If one looks only at the officially sanctioned EAP program, for the past five years (2004 to 2009) the numbers have averaged about 557 students (low of 465, high of 622) or about 2 percent of the total of undergraduates (UCEAP Annual Statistics 2010). The fourth asymmetry is that international students are disproportionately from Asia and the US students studying abroad go disproportionately to Europe, despite the rhetoric about the dawning of the Asia-Pacific century and California's place on the Pacific Rim. While increases in the number of UCLA students going to Asia can be documented especially for South Korea, China, India, Thailand, and Taiwan, the majorities of these participants are "heritage" students and represent a small and particularized subset of the UCLA student body. A final observation would be that while efforts have been made to capitalize on the internationality that does take place at UCLA through the organizations discussed above (The Dashew Center and the International Institute) both study-abroad students and international students remain generally marginalized and unintegrated with the main student body. It is difficult to claim that they have a particular impact on the social, intellectual, or cultural life of UCLA as a whole. A conclusion seems to be that for both groups, the numbers are rather small and not growing much in the context of the size of UCLA, and hardly constitute a surge over time in M&M and globalization of the UCLA student body.

The M&M of visiting scholars and faculty is another important measure in judging the rate and pace, of internationalization, mobility, and migration in HE. At UCLA as has been noted, the Dashew Center and its predecessor the International Student and Scholar Office have been allocated space, personnel, and funds to market UCLA abroad and to efficiently receive and host visiting scholars for over 40 years. At the forefront of most US universities UCLA has a reputation of making visiting scholars feel welcome.

This is reflected in the rather steady number of visiting scholars who each year arrives at UCLA and who are dispersed across the many departments and divisions. Data for the past six years shows the number of international scholars who were registered at UCLA as follows:

2008 586
2007 574
2006 669
2005 609
2003 538
2002 556
(UCLA Graduate Division 2010a)

What is most noticeable is that the total number each year represents on average about 14 percent of UCLA's regular ladder faculty count, which is now (2010) 4,000+. Yet what is also noticeable is that the numbers have not changed much over this period. There does not appear to be any M&M acceleration due to increased globalization and internationalization.

When probed a bit deeper (looking at the year 2007 as a representative year), we find that well over half of the international scholars come from China, India, Japan, and South Korea with the next largest grouping coming from Germany, France, and the United Kingdom. We also find that they are overwhelmingly clustered in the sciences, engineering, and medicine (UCLA Graduate Division 2010b). Thus, the mobility of scholars from abroad seems to be relatively limited to two (albeit, large) regions (Asia and Europe) and distributed throughout a particular segment of campus and has been in a steady state over the past several years. The numbers are rather small and clearly do not support an argument that the

M&M of scholars at least to UCLA has increased much over the years nor show a trend for such increase. However, the argument that the Asia-Pacific region is becoming a dominant force in what mobility there is, does seem to be substantiated. It is likely that this movement of scholars into the sciences and technical areas has had some impact on those fields; this is difficult to judge. However, there seems to be little that can be said about how this movement has impacted the institution as a whole. The Graduate Division makes efforts to bring the scholars together in various social events and to assist along with the International and Students and Scholars Office to meet faculty in their discipline but beyond those few efforts the scholars appear to be on their own, devoted to their individual research projects.[2]

Institutional Priorities and Curricular Impact

The ACE study referenced above utilized as one measure of internationalization that a clear statement be made by top-level institutional administrators that internationalization was a high priority (even if it is only one among other priorities). Statements such as this usually appeared in either or both of the institutional-mission statements and institutional-level strategic plans. The current UCLA mission statement is one page long and contains the following two sentences: "UCLA's primary purpose as a public research university is the creation, dissemination, preservation, and application of knowledge for the betterment of our global society. Located on the Pacific Rim in one of the world's most diverse and vibrant cities, UCLA reaches beyond campus boundaries to establish partnerships locally and globally" (UCLA Mission Statement 2010). However, in the current (2010) university-wide strategic plan, global and/or international priorities are not listed as one of the core priorities of UCLA. This represents a departure from strategic plans issued by the previous two chancellors. The priorities listed now focus on the United States, California, and ethnic diversity. There appears to be a refocusing of priorities on local California and Los Angeles social and economic issues, which may arguably be a function of the difficult state-funding environment in which the University of California has found itself and the political pressure exerted on the University of California by the legislature, the Board of Regents and the governor.

With respect to the undergraduate and graduate curriculum UCLA's course offerings are rich in international and global content, over 1,600 in all that fall in this category. In addition, although students are not required to take a foreign language, over 40 are offered should they wish to do so

(International Institute Brochure 2010). More importantly, as the ACE study suggests, one critical measure of internationalization is the degree to which undergraduates are exposed to global and international topics in the general education requirements. Thus, while there is little mention of internationality in the chancellor's current strategic plan, UCLA offers a unique and innovative GE cluster approach that includes several global and international courses as well as those focused specifically on Asia and the Pacific Rim (for example, "The Global Environment: a Multidisciplinary Perspective," and "Politics, Society, and Urban Culture in East Asia," to name two). On the whole, however, the GE offerings in the social sciences have a strong focus on the United States.

Finally, as the ACE study points out, one institutional feature of M&M is the degree to which institutions are proactive and supportive in the establishment of joint degrees, branch campuses and other international collaborative curricular and institutional programs. It should be noted at the outset that the University of California system has long had a policy of not supporting branch campuses. That said, one would think that the opportunities that now present themselves for joint degrees and other collaborative programs, especially from the Asia-Pacific region, would be welcomed and facilitated by the various UC campuses. That does not appear to be the case. It appears that at UCLA there are perhaps fewer than ten such programs (data have not been collected at this time—email from Vice Provost Nicholas Entrekin, International Institute, UCLA, April 19, 2010).

Discussion

It is hard to escape the conclusion that UCLA, a highly ranked "international" university, is in fact, predominantly domestic, and perhaps even local with respect to the M&M criteria utilized by the ACE study. There are indeed circuits of exchange that have a global reach but most of the international flows do not represent large percentages of the key cohorts of incoming and outgoing faculty, students, visiting scholars, or seem to have effected in any significant way the key components of the university such as the strategic plan, curriculum, structure of knowledge, support personnel, or institutional forms. Furthermore, and perhaps more significant, the flows, such as they are, appear to be fairly flat over the past five to ten years.

Clearly there are some forces that resist M&M and the volume of flow and exchange, more of a "short" circuit of exchange at least with respect to UCLA. As a public university (although given the state financial withdrawal over the past several years, that appellation could be disputed) UCLA is required to admit at the undergraduate level predetermined percentages of California residents. This introduces a barrier to the number of international undergraduates that might be admitted. A new policy however, driven by economic contingencies, is proposing an increase in full-fee paying nonresident students, largely from Asia. Yet, one finds that international student applications have not changed dramatically over the past ten years. One might suspect that if there were an international trend pushing M&M applications would be up. It may be that international students learn there are limits to the admissions process for international students and concentrate their applications on private institutions where no such limitations exist.

Graduate student international enrollments are better but are skewed toward a few "pragmatic" disciplines and come from a narrow band of countries. UCLA students, for their part, have remained fairly traditional with their education abroad choices, going mostly to European destinations (with the exception of China), and in low numbers that remain largely constant. Foreign scholars do not come to UCLA in large numbers nor has the volume increased over the last decade.

UCLA can be credited with vision in that institutional structures have been put in place to encourage and accommodate what M&M exists, and course offerings are plentiful with respect to globalized content (although I suspect the data would show enrollments in such courses have not dramatically risen over the past few years), yet international GE offerings are few and foreign language requirements are absent despite the large array of languages that are offered.

Taken as whole, the volume and scope of M&M, internationalization, and globalization at UCLA is minimal, and what one finds is skewed toward a few countries and a few disciplines. Hardly the impact one would predict given the rhetoric of M&M literature and the assumptions regarding globalization and internationalization of HE.

The parochialism of an institution such as UCLA brings into question some of the more expansive notions of M&M, especially ideas such as "brain circulation" and "the brain race." From the perspective of UCLA this circulation and race still seems to be asymmetric, that is, international talent coming to UCLA (although in relatively small numbers, and then either staying or increasingly, returning home), while UCLA students foray out in even smaller numbers and then to the most familiar destinations; the same can be said for visiting scholars. While statements such as those by Wildavsky may hold true in the abstract, and be rhetorically espoused by political and educational leaders ("a well-educated person today must be exposed to ideas and people without regard to national boundaries") in practice, one must look carefully at the national and institutional level to see exactly how much of this exposure is actually occurring and in what manner (Solimano 2008; Wildavsky 2010, 23). It is clearly occurring in some settings, especially where the fervor of building "world-class universities" is the hottest. China and India are often used as examples and there is certainly much to be observed in their quest for knowledge and new forms of HE through borrowing and adaptation. How significant this will be in the long run and how much globalization can be credited with the pace and scope of M&M remains to be seen. As was noted above, the high percentages of student and scholar mobility must be measured against the worldwide growth of enrollments and faculty hiring. Looked at that way, these numbers are not so impressive. Furthermore, as the new IIE study notes, it is likely that while the raw numbers may continue to increase modestly, the rate of growth has slowed and will continue to slow with the worldwide recession, meaning that the hyperbole that we have entered a new era of dramatic M&M and "how global universities are reshaping the world" (Wildavsky 2010) must taken with some degree of skepticism. A first step in assessing these trends would be more case studies of HEIs at the forefront of this movement to measure M&M as well as its impact on the structure and culture of the institutions in question. As it stands now, there exist many asymmetries, including the fact that only eight countries worldwide host 72 percent of the world's students (the United States, United Kingdom, Germany, France, Australia, China, Canada, and Japan—*Higher Education on the Move* 2010). Perhaps as Bigalke (2009) has provocatively suggested with respect to the public-private debate, the United States might be an outlier with respect to M&M as well, and the nature of the circuits of exchange may still be primarily unidirectional; in essence, a short circuit of exchange. This certainly seems to be the case at UCLA.

Notes

1. The author served for 13 years as the Dean of this unit when it was known as International Studies and Overseas Programs (ISOP).
2. It was not possible to get any accurate estimation on the outflow of UCLA faculty as visiting scholars to other HEIs. From my experience as Dean of international studies it is clear that UCLA faculty travel abroad regularly for academic purposes, participate in the Fulbright program as well as other such programs. Yet, as the recent IIE study has shown, US faculty members are among the least

mobile worldwide, ranked last among the top 14 of developed nations (*Higher Education on the Move* 2010).

References

2010 Statistical Abstract. 2010. *U.S. Census Bureau*. Available online at: *http://www.census.gov/compendia/statab/cats/education/higher_education_institutions _and_enrollment.html* (accessed July 30, 2011).
Best Colleges 2010. *US News and World Report* (May 1, 2010).
Bigalke, T. W. 2009. "Increasing Privatization of U.S. Higher Education: Forerunner or Deviant Case," in *Higher Education in Asia Pacific: Quality and the Public Good*, ed. Bigalke T. W. and Neubauer D. New York: Palgrave MacMillan Press.
Block, G. 2010. *UC Regents Meeting, UCLA Strategic Plan Presentation*. Available online at: http://chancellor.ucla.edu/updates/remarks-delivered-to-regents.pdf (accessed July 30, 2011).
Chow, P. and J. Chambers. 2010. "International Enrollments in the United States." *IHE*, No. 59.
Childress, L. K. 2010. *The Twenty-First Century University: Developing Faculty Engagement in International Education*. New York: Peter Lang Publishers.
De Witt, H. 2010. "Trends and Issues in International Student Mobility." *IHE*, No. 59.
Douglass, J. A. and R. Edelstein. 2010. "The Global Market for International Students: American Perspectives." *IHE*, No. 59.
Findlay, C. and W. Tierney. 2008. *The Globalization of Education: The Next Wave*. Association of Pacific Rim Universities. Unpublished manuscript.
Fischer, K. 2009. "The Number of Foreign Students in the U.S. Hit a New High Last Year." *CHE* (November 16, 2009).
———. 2010a. "More Colleges Coach Professors to Lead Study-Abroad Trips." *CHE* (February 7, 2010).
———. 2010b. "College Chiefs should Walk the Walk on Internationalizing Campuses, Says SUNY Chancellor." *CHE* (February 16, 2010).
———. 2010c. "Internationalized Academe is Inevitable But Its Form is Not, Says Arthur Levine." *CHE* (February 17, 2010).
Fukushima, G. 2010. "Reverse Japan's Insularity." *Japan Times* (April 26, 2010).
Glassman, J. K. 2010. "Minds on the Move: a New Kind of Free Trade as Universities Around the World Compete for Students and Schools." *Wall Street Journal* (www.wallstreetjournal.com) (May 20, 2010).
Green, M. F. and K. Koch. 2010. "Competition for International Students." *IHE*, No. 59.
Green, M. F., D. Luu, and B. Burris. 2008. *Mapping Internationalization on U.S. Campuses*. Washington. DC: American Council on Education.
Head, S. K. 2010. "U.S.: Fees Worth $18 Billion to Economy." *UWN* Issue 108 (January 24, 2010).

Held, D. 2004. "Inescapabely Side by Side." *Global Policy Forum.* Available online at: http://www.globalpolicy.org/globalization/defining-globalization/27670.html (accessed July 30, 2011).
Higher Education on the Move: New Developments in Global Mobility 2010. Washington DC: Institute of International Education.
International Education Office. 2010. Available online at: http://www.ieo.ucla.edu/ (accessed July 30, 2011).
Kell, P. and G. Vogl. 2010. *Global Student Mobility in the Asia Pacific: Mobility, Migration, Security and Well Being of International Students.* New Castle: Cambridge Scholars Publishing.
Kivowitz, E. 2007. November 15, "UCLA Rated in Top 10 in U.S. for Foreign Students, Students Studying Abroad." *UCLA Newsroom.* Available online at: www.newsroom.ucla.edu (accessed July, 30 2011).
Marginson, S. 2009. "Is Australia Overdependent on International Students?" *IHE,* No. 54: 10–12.
A National Action Agenda for Internationalizing Higher Education. 2007. NASULGC, Washington DC.
Neubauer, D. 2007. "Globalization and Education: Characteristics, Dynamics, Implications," in *Changing Education: Leadership, Innovation, and Development in a Globalizing Asia Pacific,* ed. Hershock, P. D., M. Mason, and J. N. Hawkins. Hong Kong: Springer Press.
O'Hara, S. 2010. *Higher Education on the Move: New Developments in Global Mobility.* Washington DC: Institute of International Education.
Solimano, A. ed. 2008. *The International Mobility of Talent: Types, Causes, and Development Impact.* Oxford: Oxford University Press.
UCLA Graduate Division. 2010a. *About Post-Doctoral Scholars.* Available online at: http://www.gdnet.ucla.edu/gss/postdoc/aboutpostdocs.htm
———. 2010b. *Post Doc 411.* Available online at: http://www.gdnet.ucla.edu/gss/postdoc/aboutpostdocs.htm.
———. 2010c. *Program Profile Report.* Available online at: http://www.gdnet.ucla.edu/asis/progprofile/result.asp?selectmajor=0TTT&search DeptButton=Display+Report (accessed July 30, 2011).
UCEAP Annual Statistics. 2010. *UOEAP Research.* Available online at: http://eap.ucop.edu/staff/research/annual_stats/general_stats.shtm (accessed July 30, 2011).
Undergraduate Admissions and Relations with Schools, Profile of Admitted Freshman. 2010. Available online at: http://www.admissions.ucla.edu/Prospect/Adm_fr/Frosh_Prof.htm (accessed: July 30, 2011).
Wildavsky, B. 2010. *The Great Brain Race: How Global Universities are Reshaping the World."* Princeton: Princeton University Press.

Chapter 8

Internationalization Strategies and Academic Mobility in Europe: Sciences Po and the London School of Economics

Marie Scot

Sciences Po (Rain 1963; Osborne 1983; Descoings 2007) and the London School of Economics and Political Science (LSE) (Dahrendorf 1995; Scot 2011a) are remarkably internationalized European higher education establishments: in 2010, the proportion of international students making up their respective student bodies totaled 40 and 70 percent, with nonnationals accounting for 12.5 percent and 45 percent of their respective faculty. They describe themselves as *world-class universities*, veritable top training grounds for global elites. They are therefore genuine laboratories of academic internationalization strategies in Europe, as well as outstanding observatories of academic mobility and the institutional and intellectual transformations that result from the internationalization of European higher education (Huisman and Van der Wende 2004, 2005; Corbett 2005; Musselin and Mignot 2005; Ravinet 2007; Mangset 2009).

This chapter outlines the successive phases of internationalization undergone by both institutions and examines their underlying reasons and purposes. This historical approach shows that academic internationalization is neither a recent phenomenon, nor is it a linear process, but rather alternates between phases of openness and withdrawal.

This chapter also compares the expansion strategies of the two establishments in order to examine whether a "European model" of higher education internationalization exists. Sciences Po and the LSE are often portrayed as sister universities in terms of their goals, status, and size, though in fact they underwent very different processes of internationalization in light of their distinct institutional identities, specific national contexts in tertiary education not to mention differences in their very internationalization strategies. This comparison calls existing models into question: there is not *one* "European model" of higher education internationalization, but rather *many* distinct paths to internationalization, calling for a microlevel study of institutions.

Academic mobility and migration (Charle et al. 2004; Byram and Dervin 2008) are two among many indicators of the internationalization of higher education. The presence of "foreigners" in the student and teaching body of a university is considered to be a measure of teaching quality and research excellence. In addition, specific policies to encourage mobility and the *brain drain* were implemented by academic institutions and the state (Commonwealth Fellowships in the United Kingdom, Lavoisier scholarships in France, Erasmus and Erasmus Mundus programs, Pierre and Marie Curie scholarships in Europe). Examining internationalization in terms of flows compares the reality of academic openness with institutional claims and self-congratulatory discourse. While the definitions and underlying causes of the internationalization of the student body and faculty differ, studies on the qualitative impact of the university presence of foreign nationals also underline the complexity of mobility itself, questioning theories of "creative marginality" and the inherent boon of intellectual migration (Ben-David and Collins 1966; Ash and Sollner 1996; Clifford 1997; Assayag and Benei 2003; Jeanpierre 2004; Scot 2011b).

Early Internationalizations, Tradition, and Heritage

University internationalization is often reduced to the sole criteria of mobility and student and teacher migration. To this extent, statistical reconstructions of the migratory flows affecting Sciences Po and the LSE from their respective foundations in 1871 and 1895[1] to today attest to the precocity and persistence of their internationalization.

Pre–World War II Internationalization

Foreign students made up 21 percent of the Sciences Po student body between 1890 and 1914, and 26 percent between 1919 and 1939. During the interwar period, foreign nationals accounted for between 20 and 30 percent of the London School of Economics' student body. These figures are exceptional for the time and point to a first phase of international openness at the very same time that *national* higher education systems were organized and flourishing throughout Europe.

This mobility is not simply the result of the advanced development of a European and international higher education environment (Karady 2002), but also of strategies and policies of international advocacy put in place by both institutions. From 1907, Sciences Po established a certificate of studies and special conferences aimed at visiting or occasional foreign students. LSE also developed offerings for overseas students: special certificates, English as a foreign language, as well as British civilization courses. In a show of even greater goodwill, the LSE encouraged and organized student and faculty mobility from the 1920s onwards, by relying on British diplomacy in China and Egypt or by signing exchange agreements in Europe, for example, with Sciences Po. In the 1930s, William Beveridge, the school's director, rallied to ensure that foreign scholars were hired, including the economist Friedrich Von Hayek, and that hospitality was given to refugee scholars, such as sociologist Karl Mannheim, demographer and statistician Robert Kuzcynski, or legal scholars Ernst Lauterpacht and Otto Kahn-Freud.

Diverging Internationalization Strategies

Yet from the outset, the reasons for both schools' international openness differed in light of their institutional specificities and their respective positions within national higher education.

Founded by liberal intellectual reformers after France's humiliating defeat against Germany and the 1870 declaration of the Third Republic, Sciences Po (Favre 1981; Damamme 1987) is an institution dedicated to training a new French élite: the political, administrative, economic, and intellectual executives of the young republican system. This typically French set of goals made Sciences Po a central and dominant establishment in the country's tertiary education landscape. In addition, the reasons for the international advocacy of the Paris school are "national" above all: competing with the proven success of the German university system and adding to the spread of French culture and pedagogy. The particular countries of origin of the foreign students that came to Paris between 1900 and 1939 point to the very "diplomatic" nature of the school's international advancement: France's strategic allies—Romanians, Greeks, Bulgarians, Poles, and Russians—were high in number whereas Sciences Po struggled to attract Americans, Scandinavians, or the Swiss, invariably drawn to German research universities (Laurent 1991).

The LSE, on the other hand, was founded by Fabian intellectuals and, from the very outset, it was a marginal establishment within an English tertiary education landscape dominated by the Ancient Universities of Oxford and Cambridge that had a monopoly on the education of British elites. Given its pioneering[2] intellectual agenda, the LSE struggled to draw English applicants and so catered its enrollment policy to European and colonial students from the very beginning. International enrollment was a condition of the school's financial viability,[3] yet also of its intellectual survival insofar as foreign students undertook the bulk of research duties that the English students shunned. In addition, overseas students were mainly graduates (making up 30 to 50 percent of student researchers at the LSE in the 1930s) arriving from the USA, the Dominions, and Europe (notably Germany, Scandinavia, the Balkans, and Central and Eastern Europe), but also Asia, in particular India.

The Paradox of Imperial Openness after World War II

From 1945 onwards, both Sciences Po and the LSE experienced a "National Moment." Punished for its conservative elitism and its stance during the German occupation, Sciences Po was partly nationalized and incorporated into the *Université de Paris* in 1945 (Rain and Chapsal 1963; Charle 1991; Jeanneney 1997); the LSE finally attained national university status, heralded by a significant public grant, a surge in English applicants as well as involvement in British political life.

Paradoxically, this "National Moment" failed to undermine further internationalization. Sciences Po welcomed over 20 percent of mainly Francophone foreign students in the 1960s, while the figure swung between 30 and 40 percent for the LSE during the 1960s and 1970s. Mapping this period's enrollments reveals significant changes in foreign students' countries of origin to the benefit of Imperial, Asian, and African elites. While Europe and North America remain Sciences Po and the LSE's privileged partners, Asia and Africa are exceptionally well represented. Asian students account for 25 to 30 percent of the LSE's foreign enrollments, compared with 10 to 13 percent for African students. At Sciences Po, the opposite is true: Francophone elites from Africa (5 to 17 percent), North Africa (13 to 20 percent), and the Middle East make up more than 25 percent of the foreign student body, compared with just 5 to 8 percent for Asian elites.

Compared with previous and subsequent periods in the history of both institutions, the 1950s, 1960s, and 1970s display striking geographic and cultural diversity in foreign student enrollments, reflecting unmatched openness to the South.

From the end of the nineteenth century, European higher education is characterized by significant scholarly mobility; nationalization of university life and international advocacy are not contradictory but parallel and often intimately linked phenomena (through cultural diplomacy or imperial policy) (Charle 1994). Furthermore, Sciences Po and the LSE provide a remarkable yet differentiated international openness in light of their respective national standing: Sciences Po is France's flagship training ground for the nation's administrative and political elites, while the LSE's marginal place in the British national landscape conversely explains its international profile's extremely early development.

Internationalization and Globalization (1970–2010), Strategic and Motivational Analysis

The gradual development of a global higher education market throughout the last 40 years has affected Sciences Po and the LSE in various ways, both schools having pioneering internationalization strategies and having established themselves in the profitable niche of training global elites. Nevertheless, once again their underlying reasons and strategies were radically different.

The LSE's International Recruitment Strategy: Foreign Student Enrollment as a Survival Tactic[4]

The LSE's last push for internationalization was brought on out of necessity in the 1970s: the breakdown of public financing combined with inflation as well as the Malthusian and nationalist education policies of both Labor and Conservative parties (that penalized foreign enrollment) all forced the school's directors to produce a policy alternative to total national retreat. To sustain development in a time of financial crisis while also maintaining its institutional identity as a research university, the LSE turned to foreign student enrollment *en masse* and overseas student fees. Commitment to international development at the expense of a fragile national fate, such was *the* solution chosen by the LSE to shore up both its independence and financial viability. The internationalization strategy was therefore drafted in response to financial imperatives as well as to a national context of higher education crisis.

Financial concerns are the defining motif of the LSE's international strategy, structured along three lines: foreign enrollments rallying and relying upon the entire academic community, fund-raising, in particular from foreign alumni,[5] and, from the 1990s onwards, the accumulation and multiplication of lucrative initiatives aimed at foreign students (specialized courses, summer schools, accreditations, and franchising) (Clark 1998; Larsen and Vincent-Lancrin 2002). The results of this strategy were spectacular. The London School, Britain's least English university, experienced a singular and extreme internationalization, not so much exemplary as it was atypical. The number of overseas students jumped from 1,850 to 2,558 between 1978 and 1990 (41 percent increase), then to 4,477 in 2000 (74 percent increase) before reaching 6,885 in 2010 (54 percent increase). In 1975, international students made up 37 percent of the student body. In 1990, that figure was over 50 percent and, two decades on, reached 67 percent. In 2010, international students outnumbered British nationals two to one. Overall, 51 percent of all undergraduates were British nationals whereas 80 percent of graduate students were international. Over a quarter of these students were American and Canadian, with 33 percent coming from Europe and a further 40 percent from Asia. At the same time, the proportion of non-British faculty grew from 20 percent in the early 1990s to 45 percent in 2010.

To meet the challenge of continued growth while maintaining its elitist image and urban London campus, the LSE developed a novel means of international influence at the end of the 1980s: virtual deterritorialization through franchising and accreditation and the transfer of higher education authority[6] (McBurnie and Ziguras 2007; Becker 2009). Updating and reinstating the University of London's revered system of External Degrees established in 1856 and revived in the name of Empire after the World War II (so-called special relationships administrated by the Inter University Council for Higher Education in the Colonies), the London School oversees a network of foreign institutions that have purchased the right to prepare and assess their students for LSE diplomas. In 2010, the LSE thus had more virtual students around the world than it did regular students in London. This undertaking relies on distance education and virtual teaching insofar as neither teachers nor classrooms are required. It thus offers maximum profitability and a huge scope for further expansion. This network of affiliate institutions, primarily based in emerging countries, enables the LSE to export its curricula and educational content.

Sciences Po and Internationalization as a Means to Attract French Elites, the Policy of Exit Flows[7]

The reasons for Sciences Po's internationalization are far different. The school's latest international push is much more recent, dating back to the middle of the 1990s. It is a direct follow-on from the Institute's traditional mission statement: retaining a monopoly on training French elites who, faced with the decline of French influence around the world, invest in international capital to shore up their strategies of distinction. Unlike the LSE, which deliberately privileged foreign enrollment at the expense of domestic enrollment, Sciences Po welcomed international students to allow its own French students to study abroad and thereby maintain its appeal and dominant position within the landscape of French tertiary education. Unlike the LSE that acted under financial duress, money was not an initial motivating factor for Sciences Po's recent internationalization, and for good reason—the school does not benefit from the dominant position that Anglo-American institutions have nor does it have a strong enough scientific reputation to curry favor in the international landscape of higher education.

Sciences Po's international policy is structured along two lines: sending French students abroad through an active policy of foreign exchanges on the one hand, and seeking master's-level foreign student enrollment in small numbers but of high quality on the other.

Having become aware of the necessity of increased international openness to retain the most ambitious French students, Sciences Po instituted the "compulsory third-year-abroad" in 1999 as an integral part of its prestigious and typically French curriculum. This reform was a runaway success, with French students positively enthused at the idea of a highly international tertiary education within a network of prestigious foreign partner institutions. The third-year-abroad reform produced an *unintended* yet no less *radical* consequence: in order to send a thousand students to foreign universities each year, Sciences Po had to open its doors more than ever to foreign students to ensure mutual and balanced university exchanges.

Sciences Po's priority during an initial phase (1996–2000) was to provide foreign placements for its French undergraduate students. A large number of partnerships were signed, first of all with American and European universities within the Erasmus program framework, and then, to counterbalance English and American partners, with English-speaking Asian higher education establishments. Given the primary objective of exporting French students, Sciences Po first paid little attention to the quality of foreign students coming to Paris for a short period (either a semester or an academic year) within the context of specialized and nondegree programs.

In subsequent years, student exchanges have been leveraged to recruit high-quality and proven foreign students, particularly within the institute's graduate student body. Sciences Po, an established and very French institution, sought to remedy its lack of international reputation (cf. international rankings[8]) and the decline of French cultural influence globally. The school thus decided to commit itself to firming up its standing (*positionnement*) within the international higher education landscape. Two strategies were devised to establish the school's reputation around the world: the "American detour" and the creation of dual-degree programs. Between 1995 and 2005, Sciences Po resolved to develop partnerships with prestigious American universities, a necessary precondition for international recognition. From 2005 onwards, Sciences Po developed joint degrees offerings, devised and dispensed collectively with certain prestigious partners (Columbia and the LSE, for example) so as to attract the best and brightest students.

In response to the enthusiasm of French applicants and a surge in foreign exchange students, Sciences Po also had to rise to the challenge of rapid growth in its student body. Like the LSE, Sciences Po refused to give up its urban Paris campus and elitism, however it chose not to "outsource" its teaching to accredited institutions abroad. To increase its capacity, Sciences Po opted for an expected solution: opening various undergraduate campuses in certain cities of the oft-maligned French *Province* (Nancy, Dijon, Reims, Le Havre, Poitiers, and Menton). To attract French and foreign students to campuses away from the capital, Sciences Po put forward an attractive sales pitch involving specialized training in campus-specific international settings. Foreign students account for over 50 percent of the student body in each of the provincial campuses, teaching is provided in English and each site is devoted to an area-specific specialization: the Nancy campus is dedicated to Franco-German affairs, the Dijon campus specializes in Central and Eastern Europe, Menton in the Mediterranean and Middle East, Poitiers focuses on Latin America, and Le Havre in Asian studies.[9] Sciences Po's provincial "satellite" campuses were designed to respond to the challenge of ongoing expansion and better establishing Sciences Po's hold in France itself, but their success and continued development has been the result of their international scope. They have enabled a small-scale version of educational import-export between France and key international geographic zones.

The LSE's international development model thus combined international enrollment and the foreign export of its training through a system of institutional accreditation. The international development model devised by Sciences Po, on the other hand, relies on exporting French students to the world and importing a miniaturized version of the world to France via the school's provincial campuses.

The Myths and Realities of Internationalization

The analysis of entry and exit flows, or mobility and migration, is a pertinent means to describe the rhythm and scope of internationalization. Yet its limits become swiftly apparent when assessing the movement's depth and penetration, and especially the quality of the resulting academic exchanges.

Shifting Definitions of Foreignness and Internationality

Measuring the scope of internationalization in terms of mobility presents a first difficulty in terms of defining "overseas" students and faculty. In the shadow of rankings and marketing speak, it is easy to mistake "real" (permanent and established) for "fake" (occasional and transiting) foreign students and faculty (Marginson and Sawir 2005; Rivza and Teichler 2007).

For example, while the LSE has favored a policy of integrating foreign students into its degree programs since the 1940s, Sciences Po directed foreign students towards special and nondegree programs up until the beginning of the 2000s (political studies certificates, exchange semesters). This policy can be largely explained in terms of the language barrier: given that the degree program was undertaken in French, academic "segregation" was the result of a linguistic imperative. Only very recently, the Paris school has understood the need to offer foreign (and French) students degree programs entirely in English. The differentiated treatment of foreign students at Sciences Po and the LSE explains why the internationalization of the regular student body is far reaching at the LSE, but more superficial at Sciences Po. For, though the proportion of foreign students jumped from 20 percent in 1998 to 40 percent in 2010, in actual fact only 30 percent of these are "regular students."

The internationalization of faculty (Altbach 1996; Welch 1997, 2005) at both institutions is far less comprehensive, and its assessment criteria are just as problematic: is "foreignness" determined by a scholar's nationality, the country in which they attended university, undertook their PhD, postdoc, or later teaching positions? The choice of criteria can dramatically affect the measure of internationalization. In 2010, 12.5 percent of Sciences Po's faculty was made up of foreign nationals and scholars with a PhD from a non-French university. Those with a foreign degree and having taught overseas made up 22 percent and 24 percent. This figure reaches 50 percent when taking into account the number of visiting professors. Nevertheless, strong national recruitment continues to define Sciences Po, despite an increase in foreign recruitment since 2005.[10]

Inconstant Internationalization

Furthermore, internationalization is far from homogeneous and varies considerably according to academic discipline. Foreign nationals made up less than half of the total LSE faculty in 2010, yet while foreign nationals accounted for a quarter of the Sociology and Social Policy departments, that figure reached 67 percent for the school's four economics departments (124 of the 184 members). 10 of the 25 members of the traditional English Accounting department were foreign born, while 40 of the 71 Management Institute faculty and 46 of the 66 Economics faculty were non-British, but the record went to the Finance department with over 90 percent being born overseas. The same observation can be made at Sciences Po, where the highest proportions of foreign nationals are to be found at the recently created Law School and Economics department.

Internationalization, Westernization, Europeanization, and Anglo-Americanization

On closer examination, the geographic origins of overseas attendees provides a more nuanced understanding of the self-congratulatory discourse framing the "globalization" of higher education, often misinterpreted as the galloping westernization or Anglo-Americanization of the student and teaching body.

Thus, the resurgence of the Europe-US-Asia axis characterizes the enrollment pools of the most recent phase of internationalization at Sciences Po and the LSE: in 2010, the European basin covered 30 percent of LSE enrollments and over 56 percent of those at Sciences Po; North American accounted for 20 to 25 percent of foreign students, and the significant number of Asian students enrolled at the LSE (40 percent) was the only major counterweight to both schools' decidedly "Western" composition. Sciences Po no longer turns to Francophone countries, having abandoned the French-speaking pools that it had won over (in 2010: North Africa accounted for just 6 percent of enrollments, and the Middle East 3 percent). This policy can be explained by the priority given to departing student flows, with English-speaking geographies holding more appeal to French students leaving abroad. Sciences Po thus forewent potential Francophone talent and pegged its approach to regional policies devised by Anglophone universities, though without the same historic clout. Despite the high number of Asian enrollments at the LSE, the foreign student body of both schools is thus resoundingly Anglo-European.

The same observation can be made regarding faculty (Scot 2011a). While 45 percent of scholars at the LSE are foreign nationals, is it fair to qualify nonnationals trained at the LSE or in the United States as "international?" In 1991, the thoroughly Western aspect of the so-called cosmopolitan faculty was striking, with over three-quarters of foreign professors being American, Canadian, or European. In 2010, the LSE's academic staff appeared to be a far more internationalized body. The four economics departments, for instance, numbered 26 different nationalities. American dominance seemed a forgotten memory with only 18 Americans and 2 Canadians for 63 Europeans,[11] 19 Asians, and 7 Latin Americans. Nonetheless, the vast majority of foreign scholars at the LSE (99 out of 124) completed their studies (PhD) in American universities (76) or at the LSE (26). The truly varied nationalities of the LSE faculty mask their homogeneous academic training. Furthermore, given that many British scholars at the LSE have been trained in the Unites States, in particular Harvard economists and Yale law scholars, it is fair to say that though the LSE faculty is no longer Anglo-American by birth, they remain Anglo-Americanized by academic training. The Sciences Po faculty is unreservedly less "internationalized" and yet, paradoxically, it displays greater diversity in terms of nationality and intellectual heritage, though remaining highly European and Anglo-centric.[12]

One of the Institutional Consequences of Internationalization: Curriculum Driven by Demand

In spite of the above, the presence of foreign students and scholars at Sciences Po and the LSE undeniably led to significant changes in both institutions' curricula.

To attract increasing numbers of high-fee-paying students, the LSE had to subscribe to the international higher education market's logic. Until recently, course offerings were the purview of the academic community: the development of a competitive market where consumer-clients—the students—were interested parties led to the transformation and expansion of the training on offer. In a first notable change, the LSE devised new educational products that lacked any real scientific merit yet were profitable and user-friendly, responding to both competition and demand (summer schools; refresher courses [cramming]; language classes; nondegree programs). Yet the transformation not only affected the range of educational products on offer (whether straight additions or adjuncts to degree programs), it also affected degree programs themselves that in turn had to be adapted to student demands and the needs of the job market. The undergraduate program was traditionally multidisciplinary yet has since become specialized and professionalized. Within the Graduate School, professionalized masters are more in demand than research degrees (MPhil and PhD): master's students accounted for 56 percent of the Graduate School in 1983, 66 percent in 1993, and 75 percent in 2010. Eighty percent of those enrolled are not British nationals. Nevertheless, the academic community managed to retain certain specificities allowing it to distinguish its teaching offerings from competitors: thus, it refused to offer a classic MBA for a long time, preferring an original system with a more theoretical and generalist master's of management.

To reconcile an academic logic grounded in excellence and the market logic of client-consumer satisfaction, the LSE's scientific community has also had to modify its institutional culture and reach certain compromises. During the early 1980s, the priority given to increasing the number of high-fees foreign students inevitably ran contrary to the push for excellence. With less attention given to the quality of applicants[13] and the number of faculty available to train them, teaching staff observed a generally lower level and worrying rate of failure at final exams. Faced with these challenges, the school's reaction was swift: a compromise was developed in the 1990s that allowed profitable streams and degrees (diplomas, educational products, certain undergraduate courses), which became the institution's cash cows, to coexist alongside highly selective programs (master's, research) that maintained the institution's prestige and reputation.

Sciences Po's course offering was also deeply affected by its internationalization strategy. Contrary to the LSE, Sciences Po is not directly affected by the laws of the international higher education market. However, given its linguistic handicap, the French institution was forced to accommodate its offering in order to tackle international competition.

Thus, the revered architecture of the Sciences Po degree (traditionally organized across four years: a prep year, followed by two years of degree, then a year of specialization-professionalization or prep school for competitive entrance exams) was profoundly modified by the introduction of the compulsory third-year-abroad for undergraduate students in 1999. In anticipation of the European LMD education reform (bachelor's 3, master's 2, PhD 3), Sciences Po transformed its traditional course offering by instituting a three-year undergraduate cycle (including the compulsory year abroad), followed by a two-year master's (in partnership with foreign universities in some cases).

Another important transformation was the transition to English-language teaching. English-language electives aimed at French students that had been significantly increased during the 1990s were gradually replaced after 2005 by degree programs delivered entirely in English and aimed above all at non-Francophone foreign students. The development of joint degrees with Anglophone partner universities notably paved the way for English-language course offerings.

Double degrees and joint degrees were another innovation. The first were the result of simple collaborations between two associated yet independent institutions that would each grant their own degrees. These double degrees have gradually been replaced by joint degrees, characterized by close collaboration between partner institutions that define content and curriculum together and grant a single, common degree (Kuder and Obst 2009).

These structural transformations attest to the impact of internationalization, imperfect though it may be, on teaching. Further qualitative study is needed to address variations in the academic consequences of mobility and academic.

Conclusion

Statistical analysis of academic mobility is a necessary prerequisite to overcoming self-congratulatory and generic discourse on academic internationalization. It provides a timeline of the process, outlines its myth and reality, and explicates the need to qualify the meaning of "mobility" and "internationalization." At a national or institutional level, the study of the "general economy of flows" is thus fruitful, albeit insufficient to understand the underlying institutional strategies and accompanying academic consequences.

These two case studies attest to the considerable variety of paths to academic internationalization. The identity, institutional culture, and targets set by Sciences Po and the LSE—the relative insignificance of the latter and significance of the former in training the national elite—have dictated the terms of their openness on the world since the beginning of the twentieth century. National context, such as the transformation or upheaval of national university systems, has informed recent internationalization strategies. The anchoring of these institutions in State geopolitics—the centrality and dominance of Anglo-American institutions and the marginality of European continental institutions—explains the strengths and objective handicaps that have directed different forms of internationalization. These two examples attest to the fact that, beyond the apparent proximity of the two institutions at hand, internationalization is a complex process and it would be senseless to seek out an improbable European model of international university development.

NOTES

1. Statistics (LSE / Sciences Po, student body and faculty, 1870s to 2000s) were compiled by Marie Scot from archival materials.
2. The LSE sees itself as a research university and contributed to the development of emerging and then illegitimate social sciences (sociology, commercial studies, political science and public administration, and anthropology).
3. From 1920, support from the Rockefeller Foundation was conditional on the LSE's international openness.
4. LSE Director's Reports; LSE Court of Governors Minutes; LSE Archives retrieved by M. Scot.
5. With the unexpected success of the *Library Appeal* launched in 1971, the LSE's board understood the rare potential of foreign alumni in terms of financial support. From 1971 onwards, they would receive particularly careful attention.
6. LSE Archives, Central Filing after 1968, 20–89, Overseas, GOAL, External Diplomas.
7. Sciences Po Archives: DAIE Annual Reports.
8. Sciences Po is ranked 52nd in the 2010 QS social science world rankings.
9. As an example, the Le Havre campus provides French and foreign students with training in one of five Asian languages (Chinese, Japanese, Hindi, Korean, or Vietnamese), the promise of a third-year-abroad in Asia for Europeans and Europe for Asian students, and lastly a worthwhile specialty in Asia-specific social sciences.
10. Study conducted in January 2011 by Audrey Baneyx and Marie Scot for the Sciences Po Direction Scientifique.
11. Among the Europeans, Italy is best represented (13), followed by Greece (8), Germany (7), and finally France (5).
12. Nationalities in 2010: 7 Italians, 3 Germans, 1 Austrian, 2 Canadians, 2 Lebanese, 1 Swiss, 1 British, 1 Swede, and 1 Turk. Home university PhDs: 9

US, 1 UK, 1 Ireland, 4 Italy, 2 Spain, 2 Germany, 2 from the Florence IUE, 1 Switzerland, Sweden, Romanian, Belgium, Quebec.
13. The enrollment ratio jumped from four admissions for every ten candidates to seven for every ten in the 1980s. LSE Archives, Central Filing after 1968, Graduate School, Annual Report, 1980 to 1990.

References

Altbach, Philip. 1996. *The International Academic Profession: Portraits of Fourteen Countries*. Princeton, Carnegie Foundation for the Advancement of Teaching.
Ash, Mitchell G. and Alfons Söllner, eds. 1996. *Forced Migration and Scientific Change. Emigré German Speaking Scientists and Scholars after 1933*. Cambridge: Cambridge University Press.
Assayag, Jackie and Véronique Benei. 2003. *At Home in Diaspora. South Asian Scholars and the West*. Bloomington, Indiana: Indiana University Press.
Becker, Rosa. 2009. *International Branch Campuses: Markets and Strategies*. London: Observatory on Borderless Higher Education (OBHE).
Ben-David, Joseph and Randall Collins. 1966. "Social Factors in the Origins of a New Science: The Case of the Psychology." *American Sociological Review* 31(4): 441–465.
Byram, Michael and Fred Dervin (dir.). 2008. *Students, Staff and Academic Mobility in Higher Education*. Newcastle, UK: Cambridge Scholars Publishing.
Charle, Christophe. 1991. "Savoir durer: la nationalisation de l'ELSP 1936–1945." *Actes de la Recherche en Sciences sociales* 86–87: 99–105.
———. 1994. *La république des universitaires 1870–1940*. Paris: Seuil.
Charle, Christophe, Jurgen Shriewer, and Peter Wagner, eds. 2004. *Transnational Intellectual Networks. Forms of Academic Knowledge and the Search for Cultural Identities*. Frankfurt: Campus Verlag.
Clark, Burton. 1998. *Entrepreneurial Universities: Organizational Pathways of Transformation*. Oxford: Pergamon.
Clifford, James. 1997. *Routes. Travel and Translation in the Late Twentieth Century*. Cambridge: Harvard University Press.
Corbett, Anne. 2005. *Universities and the Europe of Ideas. Ideas, Institutions & Policy Entrepreneurship in European Union Higher Education Policy 1955–2000*. London: Palgrave-MacMillan.
Dahrendorf, Ralf. 1995. *LSE, A History 1895–1995*. Oxford: Oxford University Press.
Damamme, Dominique. 1987. "Genèse sociale d'une institution scolaire. L'École Libre des Sciences Politiques." *Actes de recherche en Sciences Sociale* 70(1): 31–46.
Descoings, Richard. 2007. *Sciences Po, De la Courneuve à Shanghai*. Paris: Presses de Sciences Po.
Favre, Pierre. 1981. "Les sciences d'État entre déterminisme et libéralisme. Émile Boutmy (1835–1906) et la création de l'École libre des sciences politiques." *Revue Française de Sociologie*. XXII: 429–465.

Huisman, Jeroen and Marijk van der Wende, eds. 2004. *On Cooperation and Competition: National and European Policies for the Internationalization of Higher Education*. Bonn: Lemmens.

———. 2005. *On Cooperation and Competition II: Institutional Responses to Internationalization, Europeanization and Globalization*. Bonn: Lemmens.

Jeanneney, Jean-Noel. 1997. "La FNSP de 1945 à nos jours." *Commentaire* 21(80): 957–961.

Jeanpierre, Laurent. 2004. "Une opposition structurante pour l'anthropologie structurale: Lévi-Strauss contre Gurvitch, la guerre de deux exiles français aux États-Unis." *Revue d'histoire des Sciences Humaines* 11: 13–43.

Karady, Victor. 2002. "La Migration Internationale d'étudiants en Europe, 1890–1940." *Actes de la Recherche en Sciences Sociales* 145: 47–60.

Kuder, Matthias and Daniel Obst (dir.). 2009. *Joint and Double Degree Programs in the Transatlantic Context: A Survey Report*. New York: Institute of International Education (IIE). 2009.

Larsen, Kurt and Stephan Vincent-Lancrin. 2002. "International Trade in Educational Services: Good or Bad?" *Higher Education Management and Policy* 14(3): 9–45.

Laurent, Sébastien. 1991. *L'École Libre des Sciences Politiques, 1871–1914*. Master Dissertation, IEP de Paris.

Mangset, Marthe. 2009. *The Discipline of Historians. A Comparative Study of Historians' Constructions of the Discipline of History in English, French and Norwegian Universities*. PhD Diss. Sciences Po-CNRS (Centre de Sociologie des Organisation) and Bergen University (Sociology Department).

Marginson, Simon and Erlenawati Sawir. 2005. "Interrogating Global Flows in Higher Education." *Globalization, Societies and Education* 3(3): 281–310.

McBurnie, Grant and Christopher Ziguras. 2007. *Transnational Education: Issues and Trends in Offshore Education*. London: Routledge.

Musselin, Christine and Stéphanie Mignot-Gérard. 2005. *Chacun cherche son LMD: L'adoption par les universités françaises du schéma européen des études supérieures en deux cycles*. Report CS0-ESN.

Osborne, Thomas Robert. 1983. *A Grande Ecole for the Grands Corps. The Recrutment and Training of the French Administrative Elite in the 19th C*. New York: Boulder.

Rain, Pierre and Jacques Chapsal. 1963. *l'École Libre des Sciences politiques*, suivi de *l'École, la guerre et la transformation de son statut, 1939–3945*. Paris: Fondation nationale des Sciences politiques.

Ravinet, Pauline. 2007. *La genèse et l'institutionnalisation du processus de Bologne Entre chemin de traverse et sentier de dépendance*. PhD Diss. CNRS-Sciences Po (Centre de Sociologie des Organisations).

Rivza, Baiba and Ulrich Teichler. 2007. "The Changing Role of Student Mobility." *Higher Education Policy* 20: 457–475.

Scot, Marie. 2011a. "La London School of Economics and Political Science 1895–2010." *Internationalisation Universitaire et Circulation des Savoirs 1895–2010*. Paris: PUF (Presses universitaires de France).

———. 2011b. "Faire école. Les *alumni* universitaires indiens de la *London School of Economics* 1900–1950." *Histoire@Politique. Politique, Culture, Société.* n°15, September-December 2011.
Welch, Anthony. 1997. "The Peripatetic Professor: The Internationalization of the Academic Profession." *Higher Education* 34: 323–345.
———. 2005. "From Peregrinatio Academica to the Global Academic: The Internationalization of the Academic Profession," in *The Professoriate. Profile of a Profession*, ed. Anthony Welch. Dordrecht: Springer, 71–96.

Chapter 9

International Student Mobility for East Asian Integration

Kazuo Kuroda

"The East-Asianization of East Asia" of Student Mobility

Underpinning the concept of East Asian regional integration is a situation in which the weight of this region in the world economy is expanding even while economic interdependence within the region is growing. Watanabe (2004, 9) demonstrated "the East Asianization of East Asia" based on his analysis of the amount of trade within and without the region, and concluded, "the most important issue now is whether this de facto economic integration can be transformed into a framework for institutionalized integration."

Can this trend observed in the economic sphere be confirmed in the sphere of international student mobility? UNESCO releases yearly statistics on the number of students studying abroad, but unfortunately there are many missing figures, making it difficult at the moment to conduct any comprehensive quantitative analysis such as those issued for economic exchanges. However, through the following data obtained for some countries, the situation of international student mobility in East Asia can be grasped with a certain degree of accuracy, as follows:

1. As can be seen in table 9.1, the number of students received by the United States, France, and United Kingdom, which traditionally

have accepted the largest numbers of foreign students, increased approximately two-fold between 1986 and 2008. In particular, the increase in the number of students accepted by the United Kingdom stands out. On the other hand, according to table 9.2, the number of foreign students studying in the three major host countries of East Asia increased almost twenty fold. The increase in the number of foreign students in China is especially striking. Although there is still a considerable gap in the number of students received by the major Western countries and East Asia, it can be assumed that the relative weight of the East Asian countries as host countries for international students has been rising.

2. Figure 9.1 shows the trends in the number of students from Asian countries studying in other Asian countries, revealing a sharp increase in international student mobility within the region. This tendency points to an increase in student exchanges within the region, suggesting that a tendency toward the "East Asianization of East Asia" in the field of the international education exchanges, as in other areas.

Table 9.1 Inbound Mobile Students to Three Western Countries

	1986*	1996**	2008***	2008/1986
US	349,610	453,787	624,474	1.786
France	126,762	170,574	243,436	1.920
UK	56,726	197,188	341,791	6.025
Total	**533,098**	**821,549**	**1,209,701**	**2.269**

Source: * UNESCO Statistical Yearbook (1988).
    ** UNESCO Statistical Yearbook (1998).
    *** UNESCO Global Education Digest (2010).

Table 9.2 Inbound Mobile Students to Three Asian Countries

	1986	1996	2008	2008/1986
China	6,174****	41,211****	238,184(2009)****	38.578
Korea	1,309*	2,143**	40,322***	30.803
Japan	14,960*	53,511**	126,568***	8.460
Total	**20,612**	**78,409**	**405,074**	**19.652**

Source: * UNESCO Statistical Yearbook (1988).
    ** UNESCO Statistical Yearbook (1998).
    *** UNESCO Global Education Digest (2010).
    ****Chinese Ministry of Education (2010).

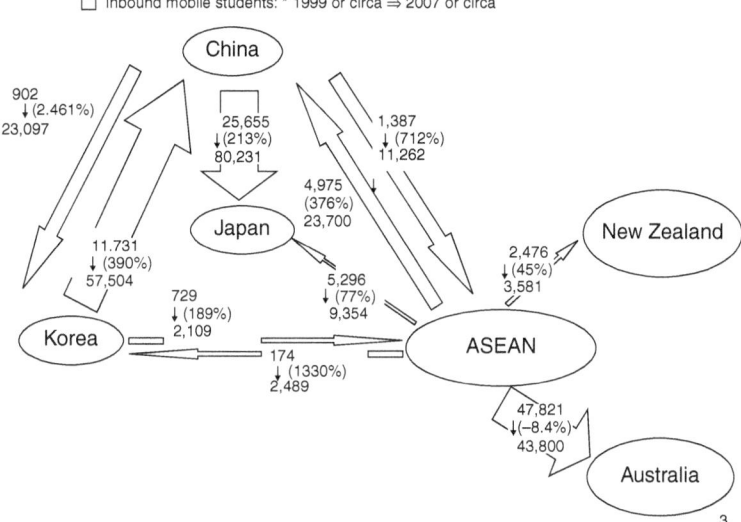

Figure 9.1 Growing Number of Students Move from Asia to Asia.
Note: Numbers in parenthesis indicate the percentage growth.
Source: UNESCO Statistical yearbook & UNESCO Global Education Digest.

Thus, although the situation differs from country to country, the "East Asianization of East Asia" could be confirmed to a certain extent in the field of the international education exchanges as well as in the economic field. It can also be observed that China has acquired a particularly major presence from 2000, both as recipient country and sender of students.

Changing Ideal of International Education Exchange

As international student mobility in the East Asia region grows rapidly, in order to examine their role in the scheme for future East Asian regional integration, we need to work out the framework in terms of philosophy and policy. Here, we will look back at the history of university models and the various ideas on international student mobility so far in order to obtain a basis for understanding the role of such mobility in the context of regional integration of East Asia.

Historical Development of University Models in Asia—"Cosmopolitan Model," "Nation-State University Model," and "Regional Integration Model"

The most traditional ideal for international student mobility is the view of universities based on universalism and internationalism, in which they were viewed as literally of the "universe," and perceived as communities of universal knowledge, not premised on states, that should be open to all regardless of cultural and political background. This view was based on the history of higher education at classical universities such as those of Bologna, Paris, and Oxford in the Middle Ages, which served students of various nationalities in a common language, Latin. In these universities, which were born before the advent of modern states, the international nature of both faculty members and students was quite peculiar, and at certain periods more than half of the faculty members and students of these institutions were foreigners (Kitamura 1984).

However, over time and with the strengthening of nation state features, universities no longer enjoyed their independent position without a sense of borders, and were gradually expected and then forced to play the role of promoting the integration of national populations and policy goals. As shown typically by universities in latecomer countries such as Berlin University in Germany and Tokyo Imperial University in Japan, universities with the tradition of universalism and internationalism were gradually transformed into those with a national nature coincident with the formation of nation states. Many universities that were established in Asia, Africa, and Latin America, mostly after World War II, were also built under the control and protection of the state, and with the idea of contributing to the state. Kerr (1990) calls these two models the "cosmopolitan model" and "nation-state university model," and states that today's universities are trying to find a way to contain both of these diametrically opposed, contradictory models.

International student mobility has been developed within this conflict between the model of universalism and nationalism. Under the former model, the nationality of the members of a university, who were seen as constituting a community of worldwide knowledge, did not matter, and the existence of foreign students was positively assessed as proof of its universal nature. This became the ground for promoting international student mobility. Under the latter model of universities based on nation states, the dispatch of students abroad and the invitation of foreign teachers were considered useful for the process of modernization, the integration of people, and state building; the need for receiving students from abroad, and cultivating an international outlook on the part of students were not considered.

However, as pointed out by Ebuchi (1997), as the modern states matured, even in the view of universities under the nation state there arose a recognition that the international nature of a university, represented by the presence of foreign students, was useful for the development of science and for raising the nation's political and cultural influence vis-à-vis foreign countries. This led to the pursuit of a third model, the "cosmopolitan nation-state university," with a strong sense of the need for internationalization.

During the process of regional economic and political integration in postwar Europe, a proper role of universities was sought for, and in 1987, the European Commission decided to establish the ERASMUS program to promote regional higher education exchanges and linkages. This led to a rapid expansion and development of international student mobility in the region—the beginning of the "regional integration model." In the context of East Asian Integration it is useful to ask, what significance the above mentioned historical development has when considering the ideal form of universities and international student mobility. Many universities in the East Asian region have developed in close linkage with their nation states. In this region, a situation emerged in international higher education that can be considered as a historical exception: the acceptance of students from other British colonies by the University of Malaya and University of Rangoon, and the common education of colonized peoples and Japanese at Taipei Imperial and Seoul Imperial Universities. These cases went beyond the model of the nation state and could be viewed as an imperialistic form of university and international student mobility. About 1905, near the end of the Qing period, Chinese students were dispatched to Japan on an unprecedented scale, said to be on the order of 8,000 people (a department for students from Qing China was established at Waseda University). It is undeniable that this had an aspect of nation-state construction for Qing China, and for Japan involved the imperialistic aspect of extending interests in China.

In the postwar period, East Asia was mostly a region that sent out students to the West, and international student mobility within the region was not necessarily active until the first half of the 1980s. However, the rapid economic development and extension and maturing of higher education in the region since the 1980s has influenced the shape of universities and international student mobility, leading to a strengthening of the idea of promoting exchanges based on the view of the "cosmopolitan nation-state university," with an eye to the acceptance of foreign students. While this is seen most clearly in Singapore and Malaysia, the formation of a knowledge economy centering around universities is clearly a part of national development strategies of most other East Asian countries, and they are actively engaged in moves to acquire excellent students and brains and, as a precondition, securing the international nature of universities as a central ideal of international education.

It should also be noted that in the 1990s, the Association of South East Asian Nations (ASEAN), founded in 1967, started to move in the direction of promoting regional integration following the end of the Cold War. It set up the ASEAN University Network (AUN) at its 1992 Singapore summit, leading to a gradual recognition of the role of universities and international student mobility within regional integration. In addition, in the framework of Asia-Pacific cooperation since the 1980s, the University Mobility in Asia and the Pacific (UMAP) program was established in 1993 to promote studying abroad within the region, and preparations began on institutional arrangements, such as credit transfer, to promote it. At the Fourth East Asian Summit in 2009, an agreement was made to promote regional cooperation in higher education. Thus efforts for university/international student mobility based on the "regional integration model" have come into existence.

Student Mobility for "International Understanding and Peace"

International student mobility has traditionally and historically entailed various ideals in addition to the significance of the above mentioned "cosmopolitan model" and "nation-state university model," and those that can be described as sublated models of them, namely the "cosmopolitan nation-state university model" and "regional integration model."

The most representative of the other ideals is the "international understanding / international peace model." The idea of linking international student mobility to international understanding and peace began to spread after World War I, becoming popular after World War II. For example, UNESCO was established based on the spirit that "since wars begin in the minds of men, it is in the minds of men that the defenses of peace must be constructed," as is stipulated in the preamble of its constitution adopted in 1945. It is this peace-oriented philosophy that has been at the basis of the ideal for UNESCO's international student mobility.

In contrast to this ideal of international student mobility to promote international understanding and peace, is a view that sees the acceptance of foreign students as a means to enhance the prestige of the culture and values of one's own country and to secure and increase its political influence. An example of this is the case of France, which has continued to accept students from its former colonies following its independence in order to maintain its influence, as well as in the case of the United States, whose peace-oriented Fulbright program contributed to the spread of U.S. style democracy around the world in an efficient and effective way.

In the case of Europe's regional integration, arousing the consciousness of people as European citizens and creating mutual understanding and confidence building among member states are important parts of the goal of the ERASMUS program. The promotion of regional student mobility is considered not as a simple return to the intellectual community of Middle Ages Europe, but as a process for consolidating "the concept of People's Europe" in order to promote conciliation toward the regional integration of countries that experienced various wars in the modern era (European Commission 1989). In other words, the "regional integration model" and this "student mobility for international understanding and peace" concept are inseparable.

When considering international student mobility within the region toward the East Asian Integration, it is essential to work based on the "student mobility for international understanding and peace" concept. In addition to the political frictions and differences in people's outlooks between Japan, on the one hand, and China and South Korea on the other, the East Asian region has greater diversity in terms of political regimes, culture, and religion compared to Europe, and international student mobility will be able to play a major role in the promotion and building of mutual understanding and confidence. However, we should not expect that international student mobility will automatically promote confidence building and international understanding. In fact, many foreign students end up returning home with strong ill feelings and mistrust toward the host country. In addition, the question of how international student mobility influences people's likes and dislikes toward a country should be discussed separately from the issue of their contribution toward building the fundamental infrastructure for mutual understanding.

Student Mobility as "Development Policy / Development Aid Policy"

Following independence, many developing countries adopted development and growth as imperatives, and developed countries strengthened their aid and cooperation for development partly due to Cold War competition. Developing countries, as part of their quest for modernization and development, sent students to developed countries, sometimes using scarce resources, to have them acquire technology and knowledge and thus contribute to their own country's development. There are in fact many countries that, like Japan in the Meiji period, have emphasized the sending of students abroad as part of their modernization and development policies and continued their efforts in terms of policies and finances.

The developed countries supported these efforts with aid and scholarships. In the United States, the Institute of International Education (IIE), which played an important role in establishing infrastructure during the period of the enlargement of postwar international student mobility, cites as goals of exchanges the promotion of international understanding and preparation of students so that they might serve their country by acquiring new knowledge and techniques (IIE 1955). In 1984, the "Recommendation on the foreign-students policy toward the twenty-first century" by the Council on Foreign Students Policy toward the twenty-first century of the Japanese Ministry of Education can be seen as the prototype for Japan's foreign-student policy, containing as its essence, "cooperation with developing countries for fostering capable people."

In recent years, the recognition has arisen that it is not only sending students abroad but also accepting foreign students that affects development, and some Asian countries have begun to adopt policies to actively accept foreign students. In Singapore, the Economic Development Board in collaboration with the Ministry of Education, in 1998 launched a World Class University Program, under which leading universities are invited to set up campuses in Singapore. So far, various universities including the Massachusetts Institute of Technology (MIT), the University of Chicago, INSEAD, and Waseda University have established graduate level education and research programs in Singapore, attracting excellent foreign students. Malaysia, for its part, long depended on foreign countries for higher education due to the Bumiputra policy and the lack of opportunities for domestic higher education, particularly among the Chinese population. However, in the latter half of the 1990s, the higher education policy was drastically revised, allowing the establishment of private universities and colleges and resulting in a liberalization and intensification of international cooperation of higher education and the promotion of the use of English in teaching. As a result, the number of students from Islamic countries such as Indonesia and Bangladesh, as well as from China, has increased sharply. Malaysia now has become a major host country for international students rather than merely a source country. For its part Japan renewed its 300,000 international student policy target and the recent government funded the "Global 30 program" to promote the internationalization of Japanese universities based more on the nation's new interest on brain gain. Thus, in East Asia and Southeast Asia, the acceptance of foreign students, along with the sending of students abroad, is becoming an important development strategy.

It should be noted, in relation to the "regional integration model," that under the ERASMUS program, as mentioned above, the purpose of international student mobility is on the one hand the building of the concept of a People's Europe and confidence, but is also considered to be a human resource strategy for securing competitiveness of the European region in the world market. In order to achieve regional integration in East Asia, international student mobility within the region should also be considered from the perspective of strengthening competitiveness vis-à-vis the human resources of the other regions. With regard to the effects of education on economic development, various empirical studies such as the rate of return analysis and growth accounting analysis on education from the perspective of human capital theory have often cited the educational systems of East Asia as examples of efficient and successful human resources development policies. However, few empirical studies have been conducted on the economic effects of international student mobility. In order to expand public resources for student mobility within the region, it is necessary to develop an analytical framework to evaluate the costs and benefits of international student mobility from an economic point of view.

Making a Healthy "International Higher Education Market"

The most salient trend in higher education throughout the world today is the rapid process of marketization. The trend of transforming national universities into incorporated administrative agencies or privatization is seen not only in Japan, but in many countries as well taking various forms. Partly because of the growth of private universities and the progress made in industry-academic cooperation, the diversification of higher education financing and the idea of self-cost recovery, including through the imposition of payments on the beneficiary, is becoming stronger. With the background of these changes in higher education lie the increase of students studying abroad at their own expense as well as dramatic changes in the characteristics of international student mobility as schools attempt to attract "customers" (known as students) through measures such as the provision of international remote instruction made possible by the information technology revolution, and progress in international cooperation among education institutions aimed at the acquisition of students in the international market. In the WTO, the liberalization of trade in education services and a policy framework concerning international education being readied have proceeded from the adoption of the General Agreement in Trade and Services. In addition, efforts to respond to the internationalization of the education market within regions have begun. For example, various Free Trade Agreements (FTAs) now contain provisions concerning higher education.

Such moves to promote the acceptance of foreign students, which see students as "customers," were not adopted in the past when higher education was part of the public sector and public funding was the main source of higher education income. Due to cuts in public funding for higher education by the Thatcher administration in the U.K. at the beginning of the 1980s, and in particular the introduction of the so-called full cost policy—under which foreign students who do not pay taxes are responsible for their full educational costs—the concept of the "acceptance of foreign students as a source of revenue" emerged.

In Australia as well, tight financial conditions within higher education during the 1990s induced universities to secure revenues independently, and the government to consider the acceptance of foreign students as an "export industry." It promoted a deregulation of policies related to foreign students, carried out public relations overseas, and worked to ensure the quality of educational services, and so on, all of which resulted in a drastic increase in foreign students.

Many countries in East Asia are also undergoing marketization of higher education / international student mobility, and major changes have been implemented in the higher education policies of various countries and the management of universities. For many the principle of cost-recovery by the beneficiary can be seen through the initiation of tuition fees and their increases, the transformation of national universities into incorporated administrative agencies, the authorization and establishment of private universities, and progress in industry-academic cooperation. Exchanges in higher education within the East Asian region are also directly influenced by marketization. In particular, the rapidly growing demand in China for higher education cannot be fully absorbed domestically and is overflowing overseas, forcing considerable changes in the acceptance of foreign students by neighboring countries. The increase in the numbers of foreign students, progress in international cooperation on higher education, and the transformation of higher education into a service industry in Japan, Malaysia, South Korea, the Philippines, and other countries, depend to a significant degree on the demand from China.

This rapid expansion in international student mobility in a market form has brought with it concerns and risks with regard to the quality of education. In some cases, private universities in East Asia have compensated for the drop in the higher education age population by expanding their acceptance of foreign students, without securing the quality of education. Diploma mills have become a cross-border issue in this region. In order to overcome quality problems related to international student mobility, there is a need to systematically develop, at the international and regional level, a mechanism to evaluate and guarantee the quality of higher education, akin to those already being implemented at a national level in various countries.

Reaction of Individual Universities—The Case of Waseda University

In this context of the "East Asianization of East Asia" in higher education, some individual universities in East Asia have started to play key roles. Waseda University, for example, has launched several initiatives to follow the direction of East Asian regionalization.

Waseda University was established in the late nineteenth century, at the dawn of Japan's modernization, to embody "Harmonization of Eastern and Western Civilizations," which is one of its principles. Today, under the slogan, "Co-creation of Academic Excellence in the Asia-Pacific Region," Waseda is promoting cooperation with major universities in Asia and carrying out proactive international development, with the aim of developing as a university that both competes and cooperates with universities in Asia and around the world. In order to achieve these objectives of internationalization and Asianization, Waseda has long accepted many international students and at present hosts more than 4,500, making Waseda the largest host institution for international students in Japan. The university has officially set a target to have 8,000 international students in the near future. More than 80 percent of these international students are expected to come from Asian countries. Waseda is a signatory to 611 interuniversity agreements with foreign institutions, of which 40 percent are with Asian universities. Currently, it has developed several international collaborative degree programs with mostly Asian leading universities such as Peking University, Fudan University, the National University of Singapore, and National Taiwan University. Waseda has established several English operated programs and schools over the past decade, including the Graduate School of Asia Pacific Studies (GSAPS), to attract competitive talents who wish to complete degree programs in English rather than in Japanese, the traditional instruction language in higher education in Japan. Currently, more than 70 percent of the GSAPS students are non-Japanese, coming from all over the world. In 2007, the university established a new "Global Institute of Asian Regional Integration" (GIARI) with large scale funding from the Japanese Ministry of Education's Global Center of Excellence (COE) grant. GSAPS and GIARI are now collaborating to nurture future leaders for Asian regional integration as well as conducting research on related topics to facilitate the direction.

Looking at Waseda's recent development of internationalization and Asianization from the perspectives of the three ideals of international education described above, the "international understanding and peace" oriented approach has had a significant impact on the university's decision-making process as the "Harmonization of Eastern and Western Civilizations" is still one of its living principles. At the same time, even more strongly, Waseda regards its historical ties with Asian leading universities as a great future potential and having more international students from Asia at Waseda as well as sending more of its students to Asia as a promising direction of the university to respond to social needs and global competition.

Connecting International Student Mobility in East Asia to Regional Integration

As the formation of an "East Asian Community" has become a full-fledged policy issue through the East Asian summits and the ASEAN+3 framework, international student mobility is discussed alongside political and economic issues such as trade and security. It will increasingly become necessary to plan an international cooperative scheme, perhaps an East Asian version of the ERASMUS program and a new East Asian framework of higher education in order to further promote regional student mobility and foster leaders in East Asia who can promote regional integration. For that purpose, there is a need for cooperation with existing frameworks for higher education exchanges and cooperation such as AUN, UMAP, and the South East Asia Ministers of Education Organization (SEAMEO), as well as the activities of international agencies in the region such as the Asia Development Bank and the UNESCO Asia and Pacific Regional Bureau for Education.

In doing so, Asian countries must share a vision concerning higher education and international student mobility that can foster a consciousness toward confidence building in East Asia and a concept of people's Asia, and strengthen the competitiveness of Asian human resources in the world. International student mobility in East Asia is carried out based on diverse models and ideals, as discussed in this chapter. By comprehensively discussing and internalizing diverse views, rather than relying on a single model or ideal, it will be possible to build international student mobility in East Asia that can be expected to contribute greatly to the formation of an East Asian Community, and thus, to the peace and prosperity of the region.

References

Ebuchi, Kazuhiro. 1997. *Daigaku Kokusaka no Kenkyu* (Study on the Internationalization of universities). Tokyo: Tamagawa Daigaku Shuppanbu.

European Commission. 1989. *ERASMUS Program. Annual Report 1988.* Brussels.

Heisei 15–16 Nendo Choso Hokokusho (Chukan Hokoku) (The policies of foreign students acceptance of Asia Pacific countries, Ministry of Education, Culture, Sports, Science and Technology Scientific Research Grant [Basic Research B] FY 2003–2004 Research Report [Interim Report]).

Kerr, Clark. 1990. "The Internationalization of Learning and the Nationalization of the Purposes of Higher Education: Two 'Laws of Motion' in Conflict?" *European Journal of Education* 25(1): 5–22.

Kitamura, Kazuyuki. 1984. *Daigaku Kyoiku No Kokusaika* (Internationalization of University Education). Tokyo: Tamagawa Daigaku Shuppanbu.

Ninnes, Peter and M. Hellstten, ed. 2005. *Internationalizing Higher Education, CERC Studies in Comparative Education 16.* Comparative Education Research Center, The University of Hong Kong.

Osato, Hiroaki and Son Ansuk, ed. 2002. *Chugokujin Nihon Ryugakushi Kenkyu no Gendankai* (Present Stage of the History of Chinese Students Studying in Japan). Tokyo: Ochanomizu Shobo.

Pan Pacific Research Center of Research Department, Japan Research Institute, Ltd. 2004. *Higashi Ajia Keizai Renkei no Jidai* (Partnership for Economic Development in East Asia), ed. Toshio Watanabe. Tokyo: Toyo Keizai Inc.

Tanguchi, Makoto. 2004. *Higashi Ajia Kyodotai* (The East Asia Community). Tokyo: Iwanami Shinsho.

Watanabe, Toshio, ed. 2004. *Higashi Ajia Shijo Togo Heno Michi* (The Path toward East Asia Market Integration). Tokyo: Keisoshobo.

Yokota, Masahiro, ed. 2005. *Ajia Taiheiyo Shokoku no Ryugakusei Ukeire Seisaku to Chugoku no Doko, Monbu Kagakusho Kagaku Kenkyuhi Hojokinn (Kisokenkyu B).*Tokyo: Hitotsubashi University.

Yonezawa, Akiyoshi and Kimura Tsutomu. 2004. *Koto Kyoiku Gurobaru Shijo no Hatten* (Development of Higher Education Global Market). JBICI Working Paper No. 18. Tokyo: Kokusai Kyoryoku Ginko Kaihatsu Kinyu Kenkyujo.

Chapter 10

Constructing a "Global University Centered in Asia": Globalizing Strategies and Experiences at the National University of Singapore

Francis Leo Collins and
Ho Kong Chong

National universities in Asia are now being reconceptualized as global universities, tasked with attracting talented students as well as building international research and teaching linkages. If in the past these universities could focus largely on building national capacity, today their reputations are increasingly determined by global positioning in rankings such as those produced by *The Times* and *Shanghai Jiao Tong*. Although several of East Asia's universities can be regarded as having well-developed national capacities, they vary in their ability to undertake global engagements. Unlike US universities that are "hegemonic exporters" of knowledge, East Asia's universities are more likely to import ideas, while exporting out students and scholars (Marginson 2004). This challenges the capacity to make significant contributions to knowledge-driven economic growth. This chapter addresses these developments through a discussion of the globalizing strategies of the National University of Singapore (NUS). We focus on the ways NUS has sought to chart a position for itself as a university that is at once "global" and "Asian." Building on the general focus of this volume on migration and mobility our discussion emphasizes the manner in which ideas about being global and Asian travel and are constituted within NUS, and the individual movement of students through the university's international student and student exchange programs and an emerging discourse around "student life."

Constituting the Global in Asian Universities

This chapter is based on reflections from early findings from a research project on "Globalising Universities and International Student Mobilities in East Asia." The project encompasses nine universities in China, Japan, Singapore, South Korea, and Taiwan that are currently engaging in efforts to "globalize" their institutional branding and structure and to attract international students. The aim of the project is to capture this unique moment in the migration-education nexus characterized by the transnational aspirations of East Asian students, and the ambitions of governments to use regional "talent" flows in nation building. Second, it captures changes in the function and governance of East Asia's universities in the face of a new world order that is being shaped by changes in geoeconomic and geopolitical positioning. We suggest that the broader politico-economic, urban, and social changes driving education and migration are also creating the conditions for significant epistemic struggles and renewals that hold possibilities for disturbing the existing Anglo-American locus of power and knowledge.

At the heart of such struggles appears to be a conflict between desires to global stature and the particularities of geographical positioning that might on the one hand limit the potential to be "global" yet also offer a route to reconfiguring this claim to universality. As Mok (2007, 269) notes, the push towards internationalization and ranking within the "Global University League" is often driven by "global standards" or "international benchmarks" dominated by "western academic paradigms." These standards and benchmarks have more than simply rhetorical significance, for as Massey (1999, 35) reminds us "the material and the discursive [always] interlock: the way we imagine globalization will affect the form that it takes." We also recognize, however, that "the global" in universities as both material and discursive is necessarily aspirational much more than it is a measurable achievement.

The question that concerns us then, is how universities in East Asia negotiate the tension between "global" and "Asian." Do they simply replicate Western knowledge and institutions and in the process submit to a "new imperialism" (Mok 2007) or do they seek to reconfigure the "global" in "Asian" terms? Certainly, if we recognize that "global imaginaries" are always in the making then it is clear that there remains the potential for new institutional forms that do not simply replicate the West or valorize its claims to universality. Indeed, as Larner and Le Heron (2002) note it is crucial to question the supposedly stable character of "global imaginaries" and to seek out the moments in which they are actively "stabilized," become rationalities, metadiscourses, and logics. Western institutions may well be established as hegemonic exporters of knowledge (Olds 2007) This is not fait accompli, but rather a position that must be actively achieved and is potentially unstable. The "global imaginaries" that are being produced in "Asian" universities need to be viewed in this context, as "discourses and practices that are, in turn, constitutive of new [global] spaces and subjects" (Larner and Le Heron 2002, 753).

National University of Singapore

NUS represents a useful example of the negotiations taking place to construct a "global" university through the geographical particularities of "Asia." As the leading university in Singapore it is at once the inheritor of a national and educational colonial legacy and yet also makes considerable contributions to connections between Asian and non-Asian knowledge and local engagements with the "global." Like the broader nation state of Singapore, NUS can be understood as part of the production of a discourse that Wee (2007, 2) describes as the "Asian modern," an "urban formation which, it has become almost predictable to say, East meets West, and in which center and periphery, old and new, are conjoined." NUS' self-description is indicative:

> A leading global university centered in Asia, the National University of Singapore offers a global approach to education and research, with a focus on Asian perspectives and expertise.

The aim of being a "global university centered in Asia" represents a new direction at NUS. It is a strategy that seeks to utilize NUS' position as an institution in Asia with a colonial heritage that provides important connections with non-Asian universities. Here, "Asia" meets "global," or to use Wee's cliché "East meets West." Indeed, the excerpt above suggests that NUS has constructed an imaginary of an already global university, able to bridge the universal with the particular—to offer a "global approach" that focuses on "Asian perspectives and expertise." The rationale for this approach is grounded in the reconfigurations culminating in "Asia Rising" and is usefully summarized by the current Provost, Tan Eng Chye (2008, 49):

> The shrinking, borderless world has flattened the global playing field, fueling the rise of Asian economies. China, the manufacturing powerhouse, and India, a growing IT powerhouse, have been forecast to join the United States as the world's largest economies by the middle of the twenty-first century.

NUS has explicitly sought to position itself between these two worlds. A superficial reading of this strategy would suggest that NUS is indeed subject to and agent of a "new imperialism" (Mok 2007)—acting as an interlocutor for engagements between East and West and a staging point for an increasingly "flat world." In the discussion below, we want to suggest that such a reading oversimplifies the manner in which "global imaginaries" (Larner and Le Heron 2002) can be transported between different locales. Indeed, we argue here that the interlocking of "global" and "Asian" that NUS seeks to achieve acts as a space-making device that constructs new versions of both these geographical imaginaries. In this respect, the "global Asian" is also indicative of an intrusion of difference into the supposedly stable metadiscourses of what constitutes the "global university." The achievement of a simultaneously "global" *and* "Asian" position is also not without problems and we note some of the tensions and contradictions that emerge in issues around "student life" and "student mobility."

NUS' approach to globalizing is characterized as a "deep engagement" that moves beyond simply "internationalizing" the university to achieve globalization through "educational innovation, research collaboration, and organizational culture" (Tan 2008, 51). There are multiple layers to this approach. On the one hand the university actively pursues a diverse student and faculty population through recruitment of international students and faculty and serious engagement in student mobility. These areas are central in the current president's emphasis on creating "globally effective citizens":

> For our students to develop into globally effective citizens, it is critical for them to be immersed in a very diverse environment which enables them to learn, live, work, and socialize with students and faculty from a wide range of cultural backgrounds. (President of NUS, Tan Chorh Chuan [Soman 2010])

There are two approaches employed for students in this regard: "bringing the world to NUS" and "tak[ing] NUS students to the world" (Soman

2010, 12). Currently, international students make up a quarter of undergraduate students and 70 percent of all graduate students; approximately 5 percent of students go on exchange each year. Other related strategies include joint programs with universities in Europe, North America, and Asia that range from short stints to full dual-degree programs. NUS has also established six overseas colleges in China, India, Sweden, and the Unites States where students intern in small start-ups while taking classes with partner universities (Tan 2008). More recently, the university has begun to link these diversity and mobility initiatives with a focus on "student life" centered on new campus facilities, interaction between students, and higher levels of attachment amongst graduates. In the remainder of this chapter we focus on assessing these student initiatives, beginning with the experience of international students through analysis of findings from our survey followed by discussion of approaches to student mobility and ideas around student life.

International Students

There are many reasons why international students choose to study at NUS but amongst these it appears that reputation is particularly significant. Of the 13 university attributes listed in table 10.1[1] an overwhelming 72.4 percent of students mentioned the university's reputation. It is possible that the high scores may arise from a tendency of students to buy into the label and not just consider the elements that go into making up quality. It is also possible that some of the students who cited this factor did so out of self-affirmation, that is: if the university is good, then I am good. These considerations aside, reputation does signal good quality. NUS offers an internationalized curriculum that draws on the global and regionalized networks of its faculty, and provides instruction in English, now regarded as a global language. These factors prompted 42.7 percent of our sample to choose to study at NUS because teaching is in English. The fact that NUS does not relegate undergraduate teaching to casual sessional staff as in many US and Australian universities also favors its academic reputation. It is also important to note that students in the sample surveyed were not selecting NUS because of failure to obtain a place in local universities, or because their preferred courses were not available. Only a small percentage of the sample we surveyed cited these factors—5 and 2.8 percent respectively—as reasons for choosing NUS. The majority interviewed wanted an overseas study experience and NUS figured highly because of its reputation and provision of financial support.

It is now well known that international students do not just select a good university but also consider attributes of the host country, particularly

Table 10.1 Reasons Given by NUS International Students for Studying in Singapore

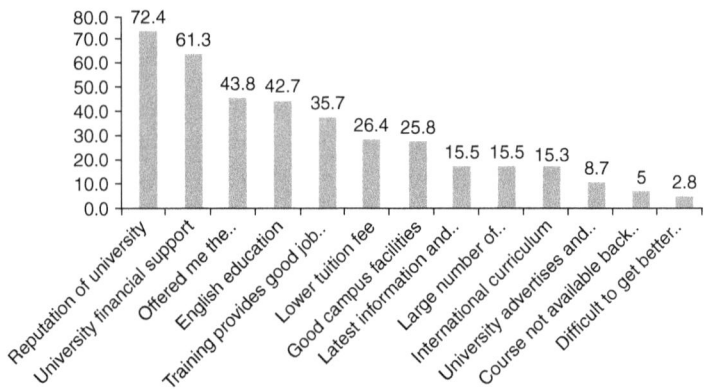

Source: Data compiled by authors from original survey—see statement of origin in endnote #1.

Table 10.2 Country Attributes and Its Influence on NUS International Students' Education Choice

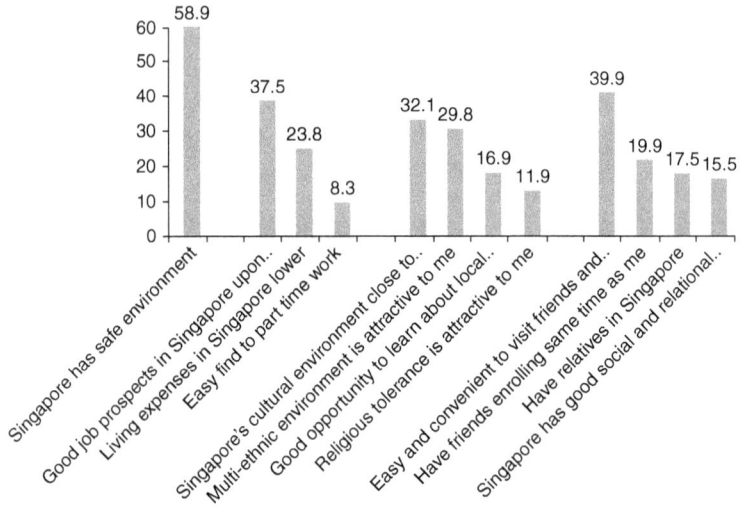

Source: Data compiled by authors from original survey.

safety, racism, and crime, along with cost of living issues (see Mazzarol and Soutar 2002; Pimpa 2003; Veloutsou, Lewis, and Paton 2004). Our survey confirmed these findings. Table 10.2 shows that safety is uppermost in the minds of international students, with 58.9 percent mentioning Singapore's safe environment as a reason for them studying here.

Given the focus on talent attraction, another indicator of the university's ability to recruit students is employment opportunities after graduation. That more than a third of those surveyed mentioned good job prospects as a reason for coming to Singapore suggests that the government's promotional message of an economically dynamic global city is being heard. Besides job prospects, the other significant economic factor is the relatively lower cost of living (compared to higher education markets in North America, Europe, and Australia), cited by 23.8 percent of the students.

One important feature of Singapore's attraction is its multiethnic environment and the fact that because the city-state is a migrant society, the cultures and ethnicities are similar to those in Southeast, East, and South Asia. The third cluster of variables captures this set of attributes. Here, we note that more than a quarter of the students surveyed mentioned the importance of Singapore's multicultural environment in their decision making, especially those in the immediate region. From biographical interviews with students, it is the family (see Pimpa 2003) that sees this as the more significant feature, the fact that Singapore offers an education that has good currency worldwide and yet is done in a familiar cultural environment. Given that China, India, and Malaysia are the top three sources of students it is also no surprise that 39.9 percent of the students surveyed mentioned proximity as an important factor. The proximity factor is also embedded in two other variables, namely the greater likelihood that they have friends applying to NUS and that they will have family members in Singapore.

The survey also provides some evidence of existing international student life. Student life may be enhanced by social amenities such as clubs and recreational facilities that provide opportunities for students to interact. Table 10.3 shows students' responses when they were asked to rate their satisfaction on 12 different facets of student life. Two particular items are relevant in understanding student bonding on campus: the satisfaction with social and recreational facilities, which received a mean score of 2.89, and interaction with students, where the score is 2.72. Overall, table 10.3 suggests that while amenities at NUS are good, mixing is more limited and workload adds to the constraints on a better social environment.

A more direct measure of student life may be in the actual friendships that international students form, the type of activities they do, and whether friendships and activities are on or outside campus. We see from table 10.4 that home country social networks are quite healthy, as students tap on their

Table 10.3 Satisfaction with Student Experience in NUS

Rank	Satisfaction with Student Experience (12 items)	Mean	Number of Responses (max 504)
1	Learning Resources	3.37	502
2	Health and Medical Services	2.90	496
3	Coping with Use of English	2.96	497
4	Social and Recreational Facilities	2.89	501
5	Opportunities for Further Learning	2.84	496
6	Curriculum Relevant to International Students	2.81	498
7	Services for International Students Like Me	2.77	496
8	Interaction with Students	2.72	503
9	Availability of Interesting Courses	2.70	496
10	Coping with Course Workload	2.66	497
11	Coping with Exams	2.63	498
12	Availability of Campus Student Housing	2.23	498

Note: 1=least satisfied, 2=less satisfied, 3=satisfied, 4=most satisfied.
Source: Data compiled by authors from original survey.

Table 10.4 Social Life On and Off Campus

	Within the University %	Outside the University %
Where friends are from		
Home Country Friends	11.71	5.72
Singapore Friends	7.01	3.90
Third Country Friends	7.7	2.85
Student Social Activity		
Clubs, Societies, Associations	46	11.5
Religious Organizations	8.1	16.9
Hobby, Interest, or Sports Groups	56.7	28.2

Source: Data compiled by authors from original survey.

compatriots for sociability. It is also telling that third country friends made on campus are scored higher than Singapore friends. The type of friendships formed outside of campus is less than half those on campus. This result should be seen with some ambivalence. On the one hand, one could say that campus life is rich, the amenities are plentiful, and a typical NUS international student will have most social needs met on campus. However, the danger is that the campus can have an enclave effect, with the result that international students may leave NUS without knowing much about the wider society they have come to study in.

In this respect, NUS and Singapore have had some difficulty converting their perceived positive attributes—a safe, multicultural environment located in Asia—into the experiences of international students once they arrive. International students do not always find it easy to make friends with local students even when supposed cultural proximity is less of an issue, and domestic students often perceive international students through a similarly distant frame:

> So they will tend to stick to their own groups rather than go out. So this is one of the things that I too see in terms of obstacles in integrating the local student and international students... international students and local students hardly really mix well is because of the assistance of these independent student groups... this actually promotes interaction within the group itself, rather than going out from the circles. There are very few that actually really go out from the circles. (NUS Student Union Representative)

This excerpt from a representative of the NUS Student Union seems to reinforce this, pointing to the common complaint that international students "stick to their own groups." There are of course two sides to this and as we discuss below the university is seeking to develop more "student life" that might promote interaction. Nevertheless, these kinds of gaps in perception and interaction between international and domestic students are a common theme in the literature on international student experiences in other major education destinations. They suggest that constructing a "global" university where students from different backgrounds interact freely is not a straightforward achievement, even for a country like Singapore that actively frames itself as a cultural crossroad.

Student Mobility

In addition to attracting international students as part of its effort to construct a global campus, NUS also engages in mobility initiatives that encourage students to travel overseas as part of their academic programs.

> Then the internationalization thing comes in especially for a place like Singapore where you realize that a global city state, every flight out of Singapore is an international flight as you said. So you need global sensitivity, you need to think beyond the country—which is a very small one, you need to be able to understand how different parts of the world function, and

be comfortable operating in those parts... So the curriculum is the formal part, and then the exchange, the travels, the overseas trips, the immersion trips. These are where they get to live and feel the internationalization of education. (Vice Provost (Student Life), Tan Tai Yong)

Here, "liv[ing] and feel[ling] the internationalization of education" clearly involves an explicit recognition of what it takes to be a global citizen, "to understand how different parts of the world function, and be comfortable operating in those parts."

The Student Exchange Program (SEP) has been a key part of NUS' internationalization strategies since the mid-1990s and the university sends and receives approximately 1,200–1,300 students annually. The SEP is viewed as a form of socialization, a means of self-cultivation and enrichment academically and personally. The stated aims are to "invigorate students' curiosity" and get fresh perspectives; develop individual characters; improve language and communication skills; challenge students to step outside of their normal routine; and to expose students to adventure experiences (Tan 2008). In this respect, the SEP fits within a rhetoric about student mobility that valorizes travel "as a vehicle for self-transformation," the engagement in "international experience" and a set of "moral discourses" about the benefits of "broader perspectives" (Amit and Dyck 2010, 1). A similar rhetoric is provided by the International Relations Office (IRO), the administrative unit with responsibility for student mobility:

> Few experiences challenge and reward you like living and studying in another country. Through the International Relations Office (IRO), you can learn about the excitement of living and studying in another country. The knowledge that the experiences you had acquired during your overseas studies will be valuable to your future employers makes it all the more rewarding. (Student Exchange Program, International Relations Office website: http://www.nus.edu.sg/iro//nus/students/prog/sep/index.html)

NUS' approach to student mobility has evolved significantly over time. Initially, the focus in developing the SEP was on increasing the number of exchange opportunities available to students with much less significance placed on the quality of the partners involved or on the outcomes. More recently the focus has shifted to an emphasis on qualitative aspects and a concern for the standing of exchange partners as well as the extent to which programs taken by students abroad will fit within the academic content at NUS:

> The targets have been reached. And we're now looking very much at how we can improve the quality of the student's experience. And for this we're looking at the partners themselves. Who are our partners? Where are we sending them

to? So, if possible to a good university where they can have a good, not just good experience, as in like a tourist, not from that aspects. But really to have a, to go to a university with strong academic programs. (Deputy Director, IRO)

The extension into joint educational programs, internships, and the development of NUS overseas colleges also reflects this qualitative shift in student mobility. The university now has established "66 joint- and double-degree programs with 34 top universities around the world" (Soman 2010), which involve students spending up to 50 percent of their degree program abroad. International internships and the development of NUS overseas colleges also illustrate an expansion outside of academically focused programs to an emphasis on cultivating globally transferrable entrepreneurial attitudes.

The SEP also illustrates some interesting examples of the challenges of integrating the global and the Asian in a university like NUS. Like the emphasis on "bringing the world to NUS" these mobility initiatives seek to enhance students' experience of different cultures and are often framed in a way that appears intangible or at least difficult to measure:

> Just having them go away for one semester, two semesters to experience a different educational system, to experience a different culture, a different environment. The larger cultural context, I think that itself is a worthwhile goal. Multiple experiences of the student. Sometimes it's not tangible. It's hard to measure the benefit. But certainly the impact on the student is not going to be short term. (Deputy Director, IRO)

In the current framing of NUS as a "global university centered in Asia" and the desire to produce graduates who reflect expertise on Asia there has been considerable emphasis on developing student mobility that will add to this emphasis. It is noted, for instance, that NUS "students should gain a strong appreciation of global issues, alongside perspectives from Asia" (Soman 2010). The emphasis on Asia is also reflected in an increasing number of partners in the region and the establishment of three of six overseas colleges in major Asian cities: Bangalore, Beijing, and Shanghai. Like NUS' overall focus on Asia as the key to geoeconomic and geopolitical transformations students are actively encouraged to go beyond "traditional destinations" in Europe and North America:

> Ride the Asia wave! Discover the modern cities of Asia by embarking on an affordable exchange to ASEAN, China, Japan, Korea, and India. Live it up in China and India—the new economic powerhouses—and experience for yourselves the vibrancy and changes happening everyday." ("Asia/Australasia," IRO website: http://www.nus.edu.sg/iro/partners/aa/news.html)

At the same time, however, like the interaction between international and local students, it is also apparent that there is a disjuncture between NUS' desire to promote greater knowledge of Asia through programs like SEP and the desires of students themselves:

> Destinations. If you talk about going, pushing them out to U.S., it's not a problem. It's always over subscription to the U.K. like-wise. It's more towards the Asian destinations particularly India, South East Asia. That's a big problem. (Deputy Director, IRO)

An orientation towards "Asia" and the skills required to engage the region are not already existing, even amongst the student body of "a global university centered in Asia," rather they must be actively cultivated and encouraged by the university both generally and with specific regard to destinations in the region:

> India, we haven't been very successful in sending students out on exchange...China is a challenge also in terms of the culture. I think that students, some of them have been quite adaptable. They find the conditions are not quite like Singapore but are we preparing them a mindset and the cultural differences that they will encounter. (Deputy Director, IRO)

These challenges then suggest that engaging student mobility through Asia requires specific effort on the part of the university to extend students' "global imaginaries" beyond North America and Europe. Like the presence of international students, also largely from the Asian region, it appears that an already existing notion of being "Asian" amongst students, or indeed the fact that NUS is in "Asia" is not enough to motivate an engagement with this regional imaginary. Rather, these tensions in the experiences of constructing a "global" university in "Asia" remind us that like the "global," there are multiple constructions of "Asia" and being "Asian."

Student Life

> So I guess the whole idea now is to bring the student experience right at the front. While we try to become a great university, you know, a great world class university, ultimately it's the kind of people that we produce that must matter, and if the people we produce are excellent in a number of ways but have no sense of feeling for the university, then I guess the work is not complete you see. So I think the whole idea of student life is not so much of management or facilitation but to think of ways to create that sense of vibrancy,

is a much often used word, in the sense where students feel that when they were studying in NUS, it was actually a very exciting and interesting experience that is part of their lives. (Vice Provost [Student Life])

This reflection illustrates some of the often unacknowledged challenges and tensions that exist around the achievement of world-class status. While strategies of "deep engagement" with international partners may foster a globalization of research and teaching and help NUS to achieve elevated ranking status, it is clear that this focus does not always translate well into the experiences of students. Indeed, during the same period that NUS has quite quickly become recognized as a leading university there has also been an increasing recognition of the difficulties of maintaining loyalty and a sense of connection amongst students after they graduate: "I think what the university has begun realizing, they must have realized it some time ago, is that students do not after they leave the university seem to have a special attachment to NUS." (Vice Provost [Student Life])

The current emphasis on improving student life is manifest in a number of specific initiatives. At the broadest level it is led by a more integrated approach through the creation of an office of Vice Provost (Student Life), which has responsibility for residential facilities, the development of the University Town project (see below), English language support, and student affairs. This new position explicitly seeks to draw together what are seen as disparate aspects of the university's approach to students' experiences inside *and* outside the classroom:

> [The focus on student life] tries to engage the students more intensely so that they have a good feeling and attachment to the university. But, at the same time also realization that what we want to do is to encourage the students to learn beyond the classroom because what you take from the classroom, what you take from the lecture theatres, will only give you that level of competency of knowledge, of ability to function professionally. (Vice Provost [Student Life])

One central aspect of this emerging focus on "student life" is developing the "experience beyond the classroom" by providing spaces for student-led activities, new residential facilities, developing iconic university events and traditions, as well as engaging students in leadership roles. The most significant example of these new initiatives is the "University Town" project—a large extension to the current Kent Ridge campus that incorporates new residential colleges with academic and curricular programs, a graduate residence, teaching spaces, student amenities and activity spaces, and the CREATE campus to host foreign research teams: "It offers a new dimension in living and learning in line with the university's mission to be a global university centered in Asia."

> As an expression of NUS' endeavour to enhance students' learning experience, UTown is part of NUS' long term plans to develop collaborative learning communities to engage young minds and maximise their potential. (University Town website: http://utown.nus.edu.sg)

These initiatives directly and indirectly reference an imaginary of what constitutes a global university and the place of student life within that. This includes a framing of these aspirations in terms of direct comparisons with institutions identified as the "best": "So we don't have that kind of residential experience to root people into the university unlike some of the best universities that we have encountered in the West." There is also an explicit effort to seek out "best practice" models and apply them to the Singaporean context:

> I think we just look at various models and we try to see what, we try to borrow what may work for Singapore...If you look at Harvard, Yale, and Princeton...they have quite interesting arrangement for small group learning so that within their halls, residence, or colleges, so we could borrow some of that...If you look at the Ox-bridge system, most of the teaching is done in the colleges, whereas ours is done in the faculty. So we can't sort of change that, but we can sort of introduce some elements of teaching in the colleges itself...So it's a little borrowing from the Ox-bridge system, a bit of borrowing from Harvard, Yale...(Vice Provost [Student Life])

The construction of a "global university in Asia" as it is described here clearly involves the incorporation of university models from elite Western institutions, a suggestion that the global university already exists in a particular locale and can be replicated elsewhere. But this is not an acknowledgment of a "flat world." Rather, geography matters significantly in the ways in which models can be incorporated into the Singaporean context. At times, as in the quote above, this relates to limits built into the institutional structure of NUS where there is an already existing infrastructure for teaching, learning, and residential life within the campus. Other limits apparently relate to environment, recognition that some of the campus life in elite universities may not even be physically possible in Singapore:

> We can't get people out, unless they are mad Englishmen, to run around in the field or to sit. The things you do in England, or North America, you can't do that here. So what do we do? Do we air-con more places, do we create shades or whatever? So these are things we are trying to look at holistically. (Vice Provost [Student Life])

In addition to these institutional and environmental limits, there also appear to be constraints in the siting of a "global university in *Asia*":

> The students grow up here within security. And that is very important as safety and security is part of Asian expectations especially amongst Asian parents... So we are still constrained in a sense, so we cannot go the whole hog, liberalizing in the American or European way. So there has to be some rules and regulations. But by and large, we want to take a more enlightened approach and say as long as students don't go overboard and not cross the lines, we are not going to run a very repressive sort of campus here and let students enjoy and grow up. (Vice Provost [Student Life])

From one perspective, these constraints—institutional, environmental, and geocultural—can be viewed as part of the geographical limits on the transferability of university models across borders. At the same time, they also illustrate the manner in which initiatives to become global in Asia actually constitute a space-making activity that has multiple dimensions. The application of supposedly "global" models of student life derived from the elite universities of North America and Europe illustrates the particularity of their origins. The fact that there is friction in the incorporation of these models reminds us that "global imaginaries" are also constructed from a specific locale and that these imaginaries can be disestablished in other places. The construction of the "global university in Asia" in these student life initiatives can also be viewed as constitutive of a new higher education spaces that are at once global *and* Asian. Indeed, as noted above, NUS' approach to student life and educational practices more generally does actively seek to produce "global citizens" but it is clear that graduates are also explicitly trained within an Asian context, with "Asian expectations."

Conclusion

The examples we have presented here around student life, student mobility, and the experiences of international students illustrate that the construction of a "global university in Asia" may not be a straightforward achievement. Ideas about "student life" on campus, for example, clearly refer to notions of what constitutes global/elite universities in terms of activities outside of the classroom and levels of attachment amongst students. Yet, these models cannot simply be transported into the NUS context but rather need also to be reconstituted in relation to cultural and environmental particularities of place. In a different way, our focus on student mobility in and out of NUS has also shown that the drive to be global and Asian must also be actively achieved, and cannot simply be the product of already existing institutional history and contemporary place. NUS is able to attract large numbers of international students because of its reputation for excellence and the result is a very diverse student body, especially from Asia. At the same time, inculcating a "global" outlook amongst both local and international students that would facilitate encounters between different "cultural backgrounds" is by no means guaranteed. Our initial findings suggest that, like the experience of many Western institutions, the presence of a diverse student body at NUS is reflected in high levels of nationality-based socializing. There is also evidence of a limited engagement amongst international students with society beyond the campus, a finding that perhaps questions the current drive towards increased emphasis on "student life" on campus. Finally, initial interviews with officials also suggest that there is difficulty in getting students to recognize "Asia" as a destination for student mobility with most of the flows from student exchange to traditional destinations like North America and Europe. At least one consequence of such tendencies is the possibility that younger generations of students lose a stronger identity with the region during their studies. That is, the implications of "being centered in Asia" may well be lost in the constant looking to the West amongst students and borrowing models from the West by the university.

There is certainly no doubt that the recent reduction in boundaries between different higher education systems has the potential to "change the global educational landscape from a 'center-periphery' pattern to a 'multi-centers' one" (Chan and Ng 2008) where emerging educational centers like Singapore can provide alternative locations for "world-class education." Achieving this more equal position in imaginaries of what constitutes the global in university is not straightforward however (Altbach 2004). Certainly it takes significant resources to build alternative reputations, particularly in the light of the continued hegemony of Western institutions. As our discussions here illustrate, however, the challenge of creating a global university is not simply about external perceptions but also involves the ways in which students and administrators view and relate to their own institutions. Both of these groups bring their own perceptions about what kind of institution is global and Asian and the importance that needs to be placed on issues like student life, student mobility, and interaction with a diverse student body. Initial findings here suggest that student practices and experiences do not necessarily map neatly onto the aspirations of university administrators, disjunctures that suggest constructing "a global university centered in Asia" requires ongoing negotiation and active construction of imaginaries of both the global and the Asian.

Note

1. The data comes from a survey of students conducted in mid 2008 supported by the Singapore Ministry of Education AcRF Grant R111-000-069-112. The nonrandom quota sample is designed to replicate the international student population in NUS: gender, science versus nonscience, undergraduate, and graduate. The sample contained 20 percent from the highest sending country; 20 percent from second highest, 10 percent from the third highest, 30 percent from all other East, South, and Southeast Asian countries; and 20 percent non-Asians. Respondents completed a 15-minute questionnaire on how they selected NUS, their adjustment process, and their future plans.

References

Altbach, Philip G. 2004. "Globalization and the University: Myths and Reality in an Unequal World." *Tertiary Education and Management* 10(1): 3–25

Amit, Vered and Noel Dyck. 2010. "Unsystematic Systems." *Anthropology in Action* 17(1):1–5.

Chan, David and Pak Tee Ng. 2008. "Similar Agendas, Diverse Strategies: The Quest for a Regional Hub of Higher Education in Hong Kong and Singapore." *Higher Education Policy* 21: 487–503.

Larner, Wendy and Richard Le Heron. 2002. "The Spaces and Subjects of a Globalizing Economy: A Situated Exploration of Method." *Environment and Planning D* 20(6): 753–774.

Marginson, Simon. 2004. "National and Global Competition in Higher Education." *Australian Education Researcher* 31(4): 1–34.

Massey, Doreen. 1999. "Imagining Globalization: Power-Geometries of Time-Space," in *Global Futures: Migration, Environment and Globalization*, ed. Avtar Brah, Mary Hickman, and Martin MacanGhaill. Basingstoke, United Kingdom: St. Martins Press.

Mazzarol, Tim and Geoffrey N. Soutar, 2002. "Push, Pull Factors Influencing International Students Destination Choice." *International Journal of Educational Management* 16(2): 82–90.

Mok, Ka Ho. 2007. "Questing for Internationalization of Universities in East Asia: Critical Reflections." *Journal of Studies in International Education* 11(3–4): 433–454.

Olds, Kris. 2007. "Global Assemblage: Singapore, Foreign Universities, and the Construction of a 'Global Education Hub.'" *World Development* 35(6): 959–975.

Pimpa, Nattavud. 2003 "The Influence of Family on Thai Students' Choices of International Education." *The International Journal of Education Management* 7(5): 211–219.

Soman, Leena. 2010. "Interview Series: Professor Tan Chorh Chuan, President, National University of Singapore." *IIE Networker* Spring: 12–13.

Soutar, Geoffrey N. and Julia P. Turner. 2002. "Students' Preferences for University: A Conjoint Analysis." *International Journal of Educational Management* 16(1): 40–45.
Tan, Eng Chye. 2008. "Globalization of Education: The Experience of the National University of Singapore." *Asian Journal of University Education* 4(1): 49–56.
Veloutsou, Cleopatra, John W. Lewis, and Robert A. Paton. 2004. "University Selection: Information Requirements and Importance." *International Journal of Education Management* 18(3): 160–171.
Wee, Wan-ling C. J. 2007. *The Asian Modern:Culture, Capitalist Development, Singapore*. Singapore: NUS Press.

Chapter 11

Contributions of Foreign Experts to Chinese Academic Development: A Case Study of Peking University[1]

Ma Wanhua

Introduction

Inviting foreign experts to work for education and economic development has been a policy for many years in China, but only recently, two of my graduate students began to study their contributions (Hu 2010; Ma 2011). Two different processes are key to the internationalization of Chinese higher education: faculty circulation and student mobility. In this chapter, faculty circulation refers to foreign experts coming to work, teach, and carry out research in Chinese universities, and student mobility refers to Chinese students and scholars going out to other countries for education and study, as well as international or foreign students coming to China for short-term or long-term study.

Since the adoption of the open door policy in 1978, China has experienced both of these forms of higher education mobility. While sending students out has caused a serious brain-drain problem over the past two decades, a growing number of foreign experts and students are coming to China to work in its universities. Statistics show that in 2005 alone, 97,471 scholars and researchers were invited to China, and in 2009, 238,184 foreign students attended 610 Chinese universities, research institutes, and other related education institutions (Ministry of Education (MOE) 2010, www.gov.cn). This chapter focuses on the contributions both groups have made to Chinese academic development. I first provide some background information for the development of faculty circulation and student mobility, and then pursue this subject employing Peking University as a case study for the analysis.

Background of the Study

To promote faculty circulation and student mobility, China adopted different policies and strategies in different developmental periods. For instance, at the beginning of the 1950s, the national policy was greatly in favor of the Soviet model and many experts from the former Soviet Union were invited to work in China while many Chinese students were sent to study in the Soviet Union, which was the major country that supported the newly established People's Republic. After a difficult negotiation, China and the Soviet Union signed an agreement to send Soviet experts and teachers to work in Chinese enterprises and universities for economic recovery, and for China to send engineers, technicians, and students to study or to be trained in the Soviet Union. Statistics show that from 1952 to the early 1960s, around 5,000 Soviet experts and teachers worked in China, and in the same period, 8,000 Chinese technicians accepted training in Soviet enterprises, 11,000 students studied in different Soviet universities, and 1,500 engineers was sent to the Soviet Union for on-job training. In the early 1960s, disputes between China and the Soviet Union stopped the exchanges. All Soviet experts and teachers were withdrawn, and China stopped sending students to the Soviet Union (Zhang, Jiang, and Yao 2008). Statistics also indicate that 90 percent of Chinese who studied in the former Soviet Union returned to China, where many started their careers in higher education. Together with many returnees from the United States and other European countries in the 1950s, those students trained abroad made great contributions to "Chinese socialist construction." The most well-known scientists were Xuesen Qian, Sanqiang Qian, and Jiaxian Deng. Those scientists were foreign educated Chinese scholars, and are not considered as foreign experts in this chapter.

The Concept of Foreign Experts

In this chapter, foreign experts refer to those non-Chinese nationals who came to work in China as specialists. In the 1950s, China sought Soviet Union experts to assist with economic recovery, so most foreign experts came to work in the development areas and national defense and seemed not to make direct contributions to education, except for a few Russian language teachers in universities. Most students studying in the Soviet Union returned without an academic degree. After the withdrawal of Soviet experts in the early 1960s, the country basically closed itself to the outside world.

During the Cultural Revolution, or specifically between 1966 and 1972, no student had the opportunity to study abroad and no foreigner was invited to China for academic purposes. In 1972, the normalization of relationships with the United States and Japan brought new opportunities for Chinese education. Young scholars and students began to have opportunities to visit and study in foreign countries. Statistics show that between 1972 and 1978, 1,977 students and scholars were sent to 57 countries, and among them 963 came back to China after their studies (Ma 2011). Most traveled with a government scholarship for studying languages, for China then had a great demand for interpreters and translators.

With the open door policy in 1978, China began to experience an internationalization in universities. First, many universities were given permission to establish foreign language programs, and many foreign language teachers were needed to operate those programs. Under these circumstances, to invite foreign language teachers to teach on Chinese campuses became such an urgent issue that the national government put forward a special effort to recruit those scholars worldwide.

To show respect to those foreign language teachers, whoever came to China were called "foreign experts." They received relatively high pay with coverage of accommodation and international traveling expenses. In the later 1970s, a full professor in China was paid less than 100 RMB monthly (then 3.7 RMB=1 USD), but foreign experts were paid from 800 to 1000 RMB monthly. From the latter 1970s to the 1990s, thousands of foreign language teachers were invited to teach English, Japanese, and other languages in Chinese universities.

Meanwhile, an increasing number of Chinese scholars and students went abroad for education. According to the *People's Daily* (Overseas Edition, October 24, 2008) in 1978, only 860 students went abroad, but by 2007, 144,500 students and scholars were traveling abroad, a number 168 times greater than in 1978. The total number of Chinese students and scholars who went abroad between 1978 and 2007 was 1.212 million, traveling to more than 100 countries.

Most students and scholars studied in foreign universities for PhD degrees, but in an unanticipated result, the majority of them remained in the countries in which they studied or moved to a third country or region for better employment, with only about one third returning permanently to China. Overwhelmingly the countries they choose to study or for a long-term employment were the United States, United Kingdom, Canada, Australia, and New Zealand, the English speaking countries.

Even now, the situation is not much changed. Just in 2009, the author conducted a survey of 2,500 Chinese students, who planned to study abroad for further education. The unidirectional mobility is obvious: all of the students plan to study in the United States, United Kingdom, Canada, and so on. Brain drain has been an issue for China in the past two decades. But recently, either due to the international financial crisis, or rapid economic growth in China, there is a developmental tendency that more overseas students choose to return after they get the degrees. Gradually, the country is witnessing a brain circulation.

Although there is the brain-drain problem and the majority of "foreign experts" who came to China were mainly language teachers in the 1970s, policies supporting students and scholars to study abroad and to invite more foreign scholars to China have not changed since the beginning of the open door era. In order to attract more foreigners to China, the State Administration of Foreign Experts Affairs established the "National Friendship Award" in 1991 for those foreign experts who made significant contributions to China's social development, education reforms, technology innovation, and culture exchange. Since then, 800 foreign scholars and scientists from 55 countries have received these awards. Now in addition to the "National Friendship Awards," "Provincial Friendship Awards" have also been established. Earlier this year, a new program was established to increase financial support for foreign experts to teach and conduct research. This program is called the "Well-known Scholar Plan," which provides full traveling coverage for eminent international scholars to visit Chinese universities for short terms.

From the beginning of 2005, the Chinese government has provided lump-sum awards to those Chinese self-financed students abroad, a symbolic show of governmental concern for them. In recent years, the number of students studying abroad has steadily increased. According to the information published by the Ministry of Education through Xinhua Network on March 25, 2009, in 2008 alone, 179,800 students and scholars went abroad, and among them, 161,600 students were self-financed—fully 90 percent of the total Chinese students and scholars that went abroad that year.

Foreign Experts and International Students in China

Recently, the numbers of foreign students and scholars in China has increased. As indicated above in 2009, 238,184 foreign students were studying on 610 Chinese campuses. Among them, Asian students make up 67.84 percent, Europe 15.05 percent, North America 10.73 percent, and Africa 5.22 percent. According to the "Mid and Long Term Education Development Plan (2010 to 2020)" published by the MOE, Chinese universities, and the Plan estimates that by 2020, the number will increase to 5 million. But it should be pointed out that currently many foreign students come to Chinese universities for short-term study, while most Chinese students and scholars study abroad for degrees. The author thinks by 2020, there should be some kind of change in this aspect, with more international students coming to Chinese universities for academic degrees.

Research on faculty circulation is something new. There does not seem to be much international data to show how many faculty members become mobile each year, and even national data is limited. It is clear, however, that it is always hard for developing countries to attract top-level scientists or professors even though different strategies have been tried. In an effort to attract more foreign experts and international students to China, two governmental institutions were established in the 1980s, the China Scholarship Council and the State Administration of Foreign Experts Affairs. The former is in charge of governmental scholarships to international students studying in China as well as governmental scholarships for Chinese scholars studying abroad, with the latter also in charge of policy and finance of foreign scholars and experts and coordination of related activities and affairs. In China, not all institutions are authorized to host foreign experts, and any institution that wants to invite foreign experts needs to file for authorization through the State Administration of Foreign Experts Affairs, which is the only organization responsible for granting authorization. Information on the organization's website indicates that in 1994, only 1,130 institutions were authorized to have foreign experts, and by 2009 this number had grown to 5,751, including universities, research institutes, and related organizations.

In 1978, when the country restored its higher education system, two strategies were adopted to meet the urgent need for qualified university teachers: sending students out to study in foreign universities and inviting foreign experts to teach on Chinese campuses, as mentioned above. In the latter 1970s, the Chinese government first initiated a program to invite foreign experts to teach in China, but because few understood the program, not many foreigners came; of the few who did, most were language teachers. The statistical composition of foreign experts in the late 1970s and early 1980s reveal that language teachers made up 85 percent of all of foreign experts. Only in the mid-1980s did the situation begin to change with the percentage of language teachers dropping to 70 percent. Between

2000 and 2005, the percentage of language teachers was about 20 percent in comparison with 28 percent between 1990 and 1995.

Between 1979 and 1997, China attracted only 70,677 foreign teachers and researchers, but in the last decade, the number of foreign experts in China has increased dramatically. In 1998, 13,538 teachers and researchers were invited, a number that increased in 2001 to 50,122, and in 2005, to 97,471. This number has continued to increase. According to Zhang (2009), in 2007, 320,000 foreign experts/time came to China, and, in 2008, the total number recruited reached 480,000. However, one major difference must be noted: in the 1980s and 1990s, these foreign experts were mainly longer stay teachers; whereas, the number for the last decade includes many short-term visitors who come to lecture for a week or a month, or simply to attend international conferences, so in effect the base element of these data has shifted.

For faculty circulation in China, intergovernmental agreements play an important role. In 1979, the Fulbright program on exchange scholars and students agreement was signed, which was the first intergovernmental agreement between the United States for scholarly exchange. Now many programs, both intergovernmental and nongovernmental, exist and the DAAD program (Deutscher Akademischer Austausch Dienst, or the German Academic Exchange Program) between Germany and China is another one that facilitates a regular scholarly exchange between the two countries. More recently, the EU-Erasmus-Asia program was established to enhance scholarly exchange between Europe and Asian countries.

The New National Strategies

China has become one of the world's major economic powers with the greatest potential, and the overall living standard has reached that of a fairly well-off society. In the past 30 years, China's economy developed at an unprecedented rate. Now, the national government has further strengthened and improved its macro control, and the economy has entered its best ever development period. Optimizing and upgrading the economic structure to sharpen China's competitive edge requires the introduction of high-level and urgently needed personnel from abroad. Consequently, a range of high-level and urgently needed overseas professionals were brought in through projects such as Programs Supporting Major Scientific Research Institutions to Expand International Cooperation, the International Partnership Program for Creative Research Teams (the Changjiang scholar project), the Expertise-Introduction Project for Disciplinary Innovation in Universities (the 111 plan), and the Project for

Introducing Eminent Teachers from Overseas. These plans have received a positive international reaction, and the number of foreign experts to China has increased every year.

Besides these strategies, in the 1990s, when many Chinese undergraduates and young scholars went abroad, there was a great need of teachers in most universities. Then the Chinese government began to adopt different strategies to attract overseas Chinese young faculty or fresh PhDs to return back to work in Chinese universities. The "Chunhui Plan" is one of the programs that provide short-term grants to Chinese scholars who study and work abroad.

"The Chunhui Plan"

In the early 1990s the "Chunhui Plan" was created to attract Chinese students who had gone abroad for their PhD degrees, including those who had already become residents, back to China. Its goal is to have overseas Chinese scholars and professors understand how the country has changed, and to encourage them to be part of the country's economic development. This program is focused on science, so only PhD holders in science could file for the three-month governmental supported program. As a result many Chinese PhD students returned for a three-month visit. However, for various reasons, most students still choose to stay in the country where they have found better employments with good pay. Since this plan did not seem to work well, another program was launched in 1998 supported by the donation of a wealthy businessman from Hong Kong.

"The Changjiang Scholar Program"

Originally called the "International Partnership Program for Creative Research Teams," the "Changjiang Scholar Plan" aims to attract experts abroad to work in Chinese universities for longer terms. It is sponsored by the Chinese government with the donation mentioned above. This is intended to be the most prestigious government scholarly program, intending to attract world-known professors to teach and carry out research on Chinese campuses. In 2006, the name was changed to the "Changjiang Scholars and Creative Research Team Development Plan."

At the earlier stage of the program, humanities and social sciences were excluded, leading to the selection of 100 professors in sciences and engineering each year. In 2004, under the idea of "developing the country with science and technology and strengthening the country with talents," the humanities and social sciences were included in the awards. Currently, Peking University has about 100 Changjiang professors, with the humanities and social sciences accounting for about 20 percent of the total.

Changjiang professors can accept a three-year or lifelong appointment. The option exists to be a special appointed professor, or to hold a professorial chair.

Specially appointed professor are required to work full time on campus, while a chair professor need not be full time but should spend at least 3 months on campus annually. The age requirement for a Changjiang science professor requires the recipient not to be older than 45, and in humanities and social sciences, the professor should be under 50. The special appointed professor annual award would be 100,000 RMB on the top of basic salary and bonus, plus a 2,000,000 RMB annual research grant. A chair professor's monthly salary would be 15,000 RMB on top of basic salaries and bonus. In the social sciences, there should also be 500,000 RMB research grants annually (the current exchange rate is 1 US dollar=6.5RMB).

"The 111 plan"

In 2006, another plan was launched for top scientists to work at the top-level research universities. Organized jointly by the Ministry of Education and the State Administration of Foreign Experts Affairs, it aims to upgrade scientific research and peer competition in Chinese universities by establishing innovation centers and gathering groups of first-class minds from around the world. Its goal is to bring in about 1,000 overseas "talents" from the top 100 universities and research institutes worldwide. These experts will team up with domestic research infrastructures to create 100 subject innovation centers within universities. Only universities from the "985 Project," which aimed at developing a number of world-class universities, and the "211 Project," which aimed at strengthening about 100 institutions of higher learning and key disciplinary areas in the twenty-first century, are authorized to recruit overseas Chinese under "the 111 Plan." It states that under one "111 plan" professor, at least 10 overseas talents should be employed to organize a team. In each of these teams, at least one should be an overseas academic master while the foreign representatives can only emanate from the top 100 universities and research institutes. Generally, the academic masters should not be older than 70, with the exception of Nobel Prize winners, with other representatives under 50. Subjects should include basic sciences, technology, and project management among others.

The full name of this project is the "Expertise-Introduction Project for Disciplinary Innovation in Universities." Both universities and the central government would jointly sponsor the plan. Those professors and top scientists will mainly work in "985 Program" universities. Under this plan, those scientists would have a financial reward of 1 million RMB annually on the top of their basic salary, and school and departmental bonus, plus a 500 million RMB research grant.

These three plans demonstrate the national government's determination to attract the best talents for the service of the country. The offered incentives are significant: for example, if a 1 million RMB award is converted into local employment equivalents, it would equal the value of ten years annual income for a full regular English professor. While the "Changjiang Scholars Program" and the "111 Project" target overseas Chinese scholars and scientists, four regular national projects attract foreign scholars. They are the "Project for Inviting Language Teachers," "Plan for Foreign Lecturers" (in different disciplines other than language teaching), "Key Project on Foreign Experts under MOE" (research), and the "Center for Excellence in Disciplinary Development Plan," in addition to those intergovernmental exchange programs. Besides the programs and plans discussed above, different small projects also exist for those Chinese students back from abroad, such as the Scientific Research Fund for the Returned Overseas Chinese Scholars administered by the Ministry of Education.

Contributions of Foreign Experts in Peking University

Since there are so many programs to attract foreign experts to China, we would like to know what contributions they have made to Chinese universities. Since the beginning of foreign expert programs in the latter 1970s, foreign experts have made significant contributions to Chinese higher education, especially for research universities. Statistics from the Ministry of Education show that in the 1980s, 600,000 undergraduate students benefited from foreign experts in teaching, 60,000 graduate students, and 80,000 teachers had worked with those foreign professors either in teaching or in advising. In the 1990s, many more foreign experts were involved in supervising masters and PhD students, developing new curricula, and helping to establish research labs. According to MOE statistics, in the 1990s foreign experts participated in supervising 12,197 PhD students, and 64,384 master students. 480,771 students took classes taught by foreign experts (Bai 2009).

Peking University has the most foreign experts and international students of any institution in China. In 2010, the university received 7,200 international full-time students from 140 countries, and currently 150 foreign scholars teach and do research annually on campus. In addition, the university also received more than 500 short-term lecturers and researchers in 2006 (recorded by the international offices for visas). There are also school sponsored visitors whose traveling data is not collected by the university; they come to specific schools for a week or two, offering one or two lectures or conducting some cooperative research. For the composition of foreign experts in the university, of those invited by the university, 60 percent are in natural sciences, and 40 percent are in humanities and social sciences. One of the important things to point out is that many of them are overseas Chinese, especially for those experts who hold long-term appointments. For instance, in the College of Software and Computer Science, six department heads are overseas Chinese, and in the College of Engineering, all the deans are overseas Chinese.

It is not surprising to see that most foreign experts are from North America and Europe, with only a few from Asia and other regions. This is especially the case in the natural sciences. In her research, Hu Jing (2010) found that since 2008, among those professors on campus for three months or longer, 44 percent were from the United States in the colleges of mathematics, life sciences, information sciences, history, English, law, management, and governmental administration. 7 percent were from Japan, concentrating on law, languages, international relation, history, philosophy, and archeology. There are also foreign experts from Russia, Canada, Australia, France, United Kingdom, Sweden, Germany, Spain, and many other countries.

Facilitating Multiculture Understanding

In order to have a better understanding of the contributions of foreign experts, the author conducted a survey in 2009. The research first distributed questionnaires to students, staff in charge of foreign affairs, and then interviewed staff who were in charge of foreign affairs in the colleges, students who took the foreign experts' classes and faculty members who worked with foreign professors or researchers. The contributions the foreign experts made are multiple and complicated, and here I only provide five key findings.

The first contribution foreign experts make to students is multicultural understanding. In the latter 1970s, when the first foreigners presented on a Chinese campus, they were treated like "Animals in the Zoo." Wherever they went, they were always crowded with people who were full of curiosity on what the foreigners looked like, how they lived, and what they ate. Then they were all given a nickname called "Lao Wai," which simply means "foreigners." Students always crowded the classrooms trying to know more, or they might attend just for the sake of seeing foreigners. Many foreigners did not understand why they were being crowded and felt uneasy as a result. Thirty years later, with the campus full of foreigners running to and from classes, working in university labs, or participating in conferences, this kind of curiosity is no longer observed. Instead, students, faculty, and foreign experts get together and discuss common concerns, and the campus is a site of international culture. This increases students' multiculture understanding.

Internationalization of the University Curriculum

The second contribution is the internationalization of the university curriculum. Foreign experts offered many new courses that local professors may not have been able to provide, especially at the master's level. According to my survey of the 13 schools, 21 new courses are offered by foreign experts, and most of them are graduate courses. Their length could be intensive one-week lectures, or three-month classes, ranging from one credit to three credits. What is more important for the internationalization of the curriculum is that the contents of courses offered by foreign experts are mostly at the frontiers of their researches.

The new ideas foreign experts bring to such classes are always stimulating to the students. For example, Professor Thomas Rendell from Canada in the English Department is a professor specializing in ancient and medieval Western culture and literature. In his classes, he does cover not only the classics of European literature, but also the epics of ancient Rome, and medieval English literature. Both graduate students and undergraduate students benefit from those courses by understanding more of the history of Europe. Another professor, Donald Stone from the City University of New York, specializes in nineteenth-century English literature, and every fall he would come to the campus to teach classes from English novels in Western culture.

He enjoyed teaching his students and was very proud of them. By teaching on the campus, he developed a close relationship with the university and donated his collection of paintings to the university. Both Thomas Rendall and Donald Stone are well-known professors from North America.

Contributing New Approaches to Teaching

Together with the new curriculum is the new approach of teaching. In the survey, many students reported that foreign experts brought in new approaches. Whether it is in the language courses or in science courses, foreign experts always use seminars or class discussion other than merely lectures to teach. In the interviews, many students said that foreign experts in foreign language courses have gone far beyond traditional language teaching, as it was 20 years ago. Now foreign experts offer language courses with specific literary topics, bringing cultural elements and historical events into language learning. By taking those classes, students not only learn languages, but also learn specific knowledge subjects.

There are plenty examples of such new approaches. A professor from the English Department, Joe Graves, specializes in performing arts. He teaches English by combining performing arts with language teaching, asking students to perform plays in English, and has also helped the department to establish a research institute of opera and recommended many students to the United States for further study. There are also other courses such as English writing in the sciences that help science students to write science papers for publication.

Another example is a three credit course taught in the Law School with the title "Law English," and each year, a different foreign professor is invited to teach it. The Philosophy Department offers a course called "Introduction of Religions," cotaught by a Chinese and an American professor. Because the two have very different intellectual training and different approaches to teaching, the students welcomed those differences. Besides, English as the media of teaching increases students' English competence.

Promoting International Cooperation in Research

Peking University has many national key research labs. To promote knowledge production with international cooperation has been a key area for national policy in mobilizing foreign experts, as it is for Peking University. Every year, the MOE creates a special fund for international research cooperation. Based on the survey, 43 such projects at Peking University received 1.44 million RMB for support in 2006; 51 projects were financed with 1.53 million RMB in 2008. The total size of the fund may not be large, but when professors get regular projects sponsored by the national government or MOE, he or she can file for a special grant to invite foreign experts to join their research projects.

In 2009, within the School of Physics alone, there were at least five cooperative projects completed with foreign experts from America, Germany, Russia, and the United Kingdom. The survey report indicates that in scientific research, foreign experts' academic contributions could be translated into different forms, such as joint publications, joint field researches, joint reports, and joint international academic conferences. In the author's own experiences, faculties at Peking University through those foreign experts programs have developed long-term research cooperation, and help faculties and the university go global.

A good example comes from a world-known higher education researcher, Philip Altbach. The author came to know him in person when he was invited to visit the graduate school of education at Peking University in the 1990s. Since then the school developed a close tie with his center at Boston where he received visiting scholars and students from the school, and in 2000, he became a guest professor of the school. With his academic leadership, the author has got many opportunities to participate in international cooperative research projects. There are plenty of cases, such as Professor John Hawkins from University of California, Los Angeles (UCLA) and the editors of this book, Deane Neubauer from the East West Center of the United States and Kazuo Kuroda from Waseda University, Japan. What they have done directly increases Peking University faculty's global experience and international cooperative competence.

Challenges for Foreign Experts

Foreign experts' contribution to Chinese higher education could be noted from many different aspects, though it is difficult to provide a full description in this chapter. However, working on Chinese campuses is not without its challenges for foreign experts.

The first challenge relates to the country's immigration policy. In China, it is difficult for a foreigner to obtain a green card, so many foreign experts find it correspondingly difficult to work permanently on a Chinese campus. That is one of the reasons why Chinese universities, including Peking University, receive so many short-term visitors but not long-term professors. Second, financial constraints are another consideration. The survey found this to be a bottleneck issue for regular foreign scholars to stay longer, as they lack financial support. Though Peking University gets significantly more government funds for its overseas scholars programs, these funds cover only 40 percent of the total spending on foreign experts, the rest coming from different sources, including 32 percent from school or department development funds, and 14 percent from "Key Research Projects" administrated by various faculties. This means that if an expert or scholar is invited, the school or inviting faculty has to provide funding for the visit. This will definitely reduce the faculty's motivation to invite more foreign scholars. In the long run, it will hurt the university in becoming internationalized.

Third, salary provided for foreign experts is an issue except for those under the "Changjiang Scholar Project" and the "111 Plan." In reviewing the salary paid to regular foreign experts, one may find that it is quite low. It is true in the latter 1970s, that foreign experts were considered well paid because Chinese faculty salaries were very low. But now that Chinese faculty salaries have risen, the following situation arises. According to the state regulations, currently foreign experts are paid monthly from the day of starting work to the expiration of the contract. In case it is not enough for a whole month, the payment shall be counted by the day. Based on the regulation by the State Administration of Foreign Expert Affairs, the starting amount of taxation is 1001 RMB. Government suggested salaries for foreign experts are based on their education experiences. If the invited expert held a bachelor's degree with more than two years working experience, the monthly salary shall be no less than 2,500 RMB. For those who held a master's degree and the working experience is more than three years, the monthly salary shall be around 3,500 RMB. For those who have a doctor's degree and the working experience is over five years, the monthly salary shall be about RMB 4,000 (about USD 620). Though there are indirect payments, as the host institution will always guarantee lodging and international airfare, with current exchange rates, even with foreign experts being paid 4,000 RMB, these are very modest amounts given prevailing international standards. And this suggested salary regulation was issued in 1997, which makes it dated. In 2000, an adjustment to increase the salary to 6,000 RMB for full professors was made, but still it is still not competitive.

In order to attract top foreign experts, many institutions, including Peking University, have already allocated additional funding to provide extra honoraria. Statistics show that in some universities, the annual payment for foreign expert has increased to 80,000 RMB (USD 12,418) or

120,000 RMB (USD 18,618). Besides salary increases, many institutions have improved working conditions for foreign experts by providing office space and more research facilities, including staff support to make such positions more attractive.

Conclusion

To conclude the discussion, several things can be observed. First, China experienced a serious brain-drain problem at the end of twentieth century, but following China's recent economic development, the situation has already begun to change with the development of different strategies to attract foreign experts and overseas Chinese to return. Second, the level of "foreign experts" has been improved, from mainly language teachers to specialists and higher-level researchers, and this change is very important for Chinese universities to improve their research and knowledge structure. Foreign experts on Chinese campuses are very important to enhance their internationalization. Third, there is an increase of foreign students to study in Chinese universities, and these come from all over the world and bring many different cultural values. It would be mutually beneficial to have them work with Chinese students and faculties, but so far there does not seem to be much consideration on how to use this resource. Fourth, the policies in attracting foreign experts are coming to favor overseas Chinese with ties to China, but not foreign nationals. Whether it is in Peking University or other Chinese universities, one can find that most Changjiang scholars and 111 plan professors are overseas Chinese. There is nothing wrong with those overseas Chinese scholars and scientists to return since by being trained in foreign countries and working many years outside of the country, they return with new ideas and knowledge. But for the academic development of the university, the diversity or internationalization of the faculty should be taken into consideration. Academic inbreeding in Chinese universities has been a serious problem, and if more foreign experts come to work, even for short periods, they can constantly introduce new ideas and knowledge.

Note

1. This research is supported by the funding of Social Science Research, Department of Education, PR. China, Project no. 09YJA880007.

REFERENCES

Bai, Yan. 2009. *Academic Performances of Foreign Experts and Effect on International Cooperation at Peking University: Faculty's Perspective of Host Institutions.* Unpublished report, Peking University.

Chen, Huabei. 2006. "To be Creative in the Service of Attract Talents and to Enforce Higher Learning Institution's Internationalization," in *International Human Resources Exchange*, No.11.

Hu, Jing. 2010. *An Analysis of Academic Performances and Related Efforts for Foreign Scholars in Chinese Research University.* Unpublished Master Thesis, Peking University.

Ma, Xueni. 2011. *Overseas Chinese Scholars Return to Work in China: Reasons and Their Contributions—Take Peking University as an Example.* Unpublished Master Thesis, Peking University.

Zhang, Jianguo. 2009. "Important Components on Attracting Foreign Talents Since the Open Door Policy," in *Internationaltalent* (1): 35–37.

Zhang, Jiuchun, Long Jiang, and Fang Yao. 2008. "Sending Students to Study in Former Soviet Union at the Beginning of the PR. China," in *Hundred Years Tide* (11): 56–59.

Chapter 12

International Accreditation and Its Impact on Student Mobility in Taiwan Universities—A Case Study of School of Management of Fu Jen Catholic University

Yung-chi Hou (Angela)

Introduction

Over the past ten years higher education in Taiwan has expanded impressively both with respect to increases in the number of institutions and the number of enrolled students. As of 2008, the number of higher education institutions had increased to 163, largely due to the upgrade of junior colleges into four-year universities. Student enrollment increased 65 percent to a total of 1.3 millions. The University Entrance Exam admission rate is currently close to 97 percent. According to estimates by the Ministry of Education (MOE), Taiwan's universities and colleges will fall 15,000 freshmen short in 2012, leading to the closure of over 10 universities or colleges in the following years resulting from the dramatically declining numbers of the 18 to 24 year-old enrolled cohort (MOE 2010).

Since 1990 globalization has accelerated Taiwan's higher education move into a new era of quality education (Mok 2003). Over the past decades Taiwan's rapid expansion of higher education has witnessed public concern over quality assurance, which is expected by the public to achieve international standards. In response to the regional-global competitiveness in higher education, Taiwan's government has reformed its higher education system, with a particular focus on provision, regulation, and financing (Mok 2000). In addition to several key initiatives for internationalizing Taiwanese universities launched by the MOE, such as recruiting international students and faculty, a strong demand for seeking international recognition for quality has started to pressure universities and colleges in Taiwan to sharpen their global competitive edge. The purposes of this chapter are to examine Taiwan government policy over the internationalization of higher education, review the current situation of student mobility in higher education, and analyze the impact of international accreditation on the Management School of Fu Jen Catholic University in terms of organizational change, curriculum reform, faculty evaluation, and innovative teaching methods.

Internationalization in Asian Higher Education

Throughout the world the internationalization of higher education has dramatically expanded in volume, scope, and complexity over the past two decades. Universities started to develop international academic activities designed to attract students at home and abroad successfully. Some may upgrade the international perspectives and skills of students, increase foreign language programs, and provide students cross-cultural understanding. Others may set up branch campuses in countries where local institutions lack sufficient educational resources (Altbach and Knight 2007). Most universities make great efforts to establish partnerships with foreign universities to bring global vision into classes and teaching.

However, the motivations behind internationalization may be quite different. For most English speaking countries, such as Australia, Canada, the United Kingdom, and the United States, internationalization is a financial and economic issue. The major reason for recruiting international students is to gain income by charging high fees. In return, international graduate students can also provide research and teaching services for modest compensation. Indeed, international students help boost the local economy by spending significant amounts of money in the host countries.

In contrast, in East Asia, including Japan, Korean, and China, "internationalization" specifically tends to be regarded as an issue of "global competitiveness" in research and human resource development (Yonezawa et al. 2009). Asian universities internationalize themselves, mainly for improving the quality and cultural composition of the student body, gaining prestige and enhancing strategic alliances of higher education institutions (HEIs) rather than earning profits. Altbach identified this as "traditional" internationalization (Altbach and Knight 2007).

Much evidence, such as the "21 COE project" and "Global 30" in Japan, "Brain 21" in Korea, and the "985 Excellence Program" in China demonstrates that achieving academic excellence to build world-class universities is becoming the primary goal for internationalizing higher education in many Asian countries. Unwilling to be left out of the evolving trend, the Taiwanese government in 2005 launched the "Five-year Fifty Billion Program" for developing first-class universities and top research centers. The program aims to propel at least one university into the ranks of the world's top 100 universities in five years and at least 15 key departments or cross-campus research centers to the top in Asia in ten years (Hou 2010).

In fact, those nonnative English speaking institutions at the top 100 of global rankings indeed provide attractive international learning and teaching environments, such as offering English taught graduate programs. The Tertiary Education coordinator at the World Bank, Jamil Salmi (2009, 60) emphasized that "one way of accelerating the transformation into a world-class is to use the internationalization strategies effectively." The internationalization polices in the above Asian nations have the following common features: (1) the main purpose of internationalization is to enhance national competitiveness; (2) these countries are aggressively seeking to attract global talents to study or teach at schools; (3) universities are encouraged to offer English taught courses at both undergraduate and graduate levels; (4) flows of students and faculty are frequent; (5) universities are working hard on alliances of foreign partners in terms of research and curriculum (Hou 2011a).

The development of knowledge-based economies and the enhancement of global competitiveness has accounted for growing efforts by national policymakers to attract international students and to retain them as proficient workers after their study completion. When "international outlook" as one of the popular indicators in global rankings is accepted, the influence of student mobility on the higher education market is strengthened as well. Hence, it is believed that international students can have both a short-term and long-term impact on skilled labor markets and economies in their countries of origin and destination. Inevitably, student mobility is considered to be part of global brain circulation (Salt 1997).

In summary, Asian countries work hard to expand and increase higher education internationalization, while at the same time expecting to be able to inform local trends with a global context. Driven by globalization, countries need to encourage the local student to study aboard, which can lead to significant inputs to innovation and knowledge production in the multidimensional academic and enterprise development. However, Asian nations have also to maintain their cultural identity and characteristics in the process of curriculum reform in order to attract excellent international students.

Internationalization of Taiwan's Higher Education Profile of International Students in Taiwan

The MOE has developed four key programs to support the internationalization of Taiwan universities and colleges. First, in 2002, the MOE launched the "Enhancing Global Competitiveness Plan" aimed at fostering international exchange activities to improve the international competitiveness of institutions. Second, increasing the number of foreign students studying in Taiwan has been made a priority of the MOE since August 2003. Higher education institutions offer scholarships and English taught courses in both undergraduate and postgraduate programs to achieve this objective. Third, the MOE encourages Taiwanese students to study abroad through the "Study Abroad Loan Program" launched in 2004. In addition, the MOE expanded the Taiwan Culture Research Program in scale with foreign academic institutes to attract attention to the global academic stage (Hou 2011a).

Based on these policies and strategies, and to facilitate various types of cross-campus academic collaborative activities with foreign universities, Taiwanese universities are encouraged to promote their international outlook. One initiative seeks to attract more international students studying in Taiwan. In August 2003, under the guidance of the Executive Yuan, the expansion of overseas student recruitment was incorporated into Taiwan's National Development Plan, prompting all universities to make inroads into international education markets and recruit international students. As of 2009, the total number of international students, including degree-level, exchange, and language study students, and overseas Chinese students had reached 33,948. The number of degree-seeking international students in Taiwanese higher education institutions increased by three times from 2,853 in 2005 to 7,764 in 2009, accounting for 34.7 percent of all international enrollment (see figure 12.1).

Generally speaking, public universities have more international students than private universities. Eleven research universities accounted for 30 percent of such students, in comparison with 61 percent in comprehensive universities. National Chi Nan University ranked at the top with a rate

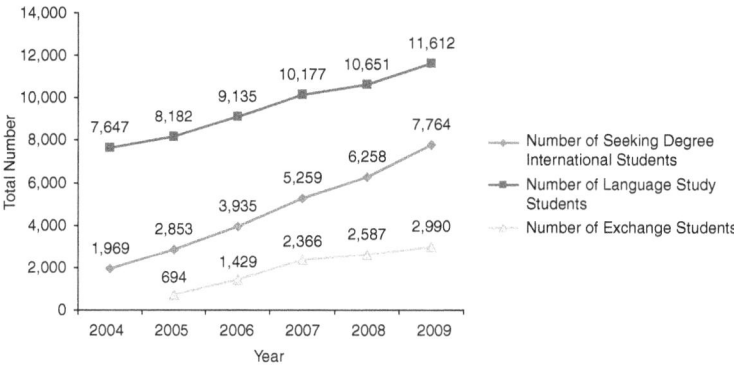

Figure 12.1 International Students in Taiwan Universities.

Table 12.1 Proportion and Number of International Students in Top 5 Universities in Taiwan

Institutions	Proportion of International Student (%)	Number of International Students	Total Enrollment	Rank
National Chi Nan University	6.42	340	5,295	1
National Taiwan University	5.81	1,940	33,416	2
National Chengchi University	5.73	893	15,588	3
Kaohsiung Medical University	4.29	351	7,417	4
Ming Chuan University	4.73	882	18,641	5

Source: Ministry of Education. 2010. *International Comparison of Education Statistical Indicators 2010*. Available online at: http://english.moe.gov.tw/ct.asp?xItem=12261&ctNode=815&mp=2 (accessed March 20, 2010).

of 6.42 percent, and National Taiwan University followed with a rate of 5.81 percent, but its enrollment totals more than 1,900 (see table 12.1).

Along with increases in the total number of students, there is a slight change in international student demographics. During the 2005 to 2009 period, the percentage of degree-seeking students has seen a huge increase from one-fifth to one-third. While the numbers of exchange students grow at a steady pace, the number of language study students grows slowly.

The data show that more than half of international students come from Asia, at 61.2 percent, while 22.7 percent are from the United States, and 12 percent from European countries. The top 5 countries are Vietnam with 20 percent, Malaysia, Indonesia, Korea, and the United States, respectively, which accounted for nearly 50 percent of the overall international students in Taiwan.

Student Mobility Across the Strait

Three years ago top ranked universities in the Asia-Pacific region, such as Hong Kong City University, Hong Kong University, Waseda University, Ritsumeikan Asia Pacific University, and New York University (NYU) Abu Dhabi, aggressively began seeking to recruit the brightest students in Taiwan. However the outward academic flow didn't become an emerging concern in Taiwan society until Beijing announced that Taiwanese high school graduates who score within the top 12 percent in Taiwan's General Scholastic Ability Test would be able to apply directly to 123 universities in China without having to take China's college-entry exam. In the face of increased efforts by foreign and Chinese universities to woo Taiwan students by offering attractive scholarships, good quality programs, and flexible policies for entry, the Taiwan government is expected to take actions not only to keep elite students at home but also to lure foreign and Chinese youths to study in Taiwan.

According to the Chinese MOE, 14,907 Taiwanese students have studied in China over the last two decades. Each year, an average of 900 Taiwanese students seek advanced degrees from Chinese universities. On the contrary, up to the present, only hundreds of students from Mainland China study in Taiwan for just brief periods of time, usually a semester. The major cause for the unbalanced status is that Taiwan's laws still ban Chinese students from obtaining degrees from Taiwan universities and Chinese degrees and diplomas are not recognized by Taiwan's MOE.

Currently, as a result of great pressure from global competition in higher education, Taiwanese society is having a serious debate over whether the MOE should admit Chinese degrees and diplomas and allow Mainland students to study and obtain Taiwanese degrees. In fact, the presidents of a vast majority of universities in Taiwan are strongly in favor of allowing more mainland students to study in Taiwan and believe that Chinese students can increase the competitive edge of local students as well. On the one hand, Taiwan's government was being forced to adopt a more open policy toward Chinese students seeking to study in Taiwan; on the other hand, the government has had to ease anxieties over how to assure the quality of Chinese universities if the degrees and diplomas are to be recognized. After the MOE held 20 seminars and hearings to collect opinions from the public in mid December 2009, it finally announced the policy of "Three Limits and Six No's" publicly to reflect the effect of international and local demands. Three Limits include the limitation of volume on recognized Chinese universities, Chinese students studying in Taiwan, and the exclusion of professional medical license recognition. In the initial stage, the degrees of only 38 of the 985 project universities (exclusive of National University of Defense Technology) and four academies from agriculture, sports, and fine arts including the China Agricultural University, the Central Conservatory of Music, and the Central Academy of Fine Arts are recognized by the MOE. Degrees or diplomats in medicine or related fields would not currently be recognized by the MOE. Each year, the proportion of Chinese students should not exceed 1 percent of the total freshman enrollment. In other words, there would be only around 2,000 Chinese students admitted to study in Taiwan each year. More strictly, Chinese students will not be allowed to apply for scholarships, join work-study programs, or internship programs, to work in Taiwan after they complete study, or take national governmental officials' exams, and so on (MOE 2009).

The MOE immediately received much criticism from the Taiwanese academic community with its new policy announcement. Many private universities were not satisfied with the unfavorable policy, and wondered aloud if it would lead to an even more uneven situation given that only public universities could be the beneficiaries of the new policy. Dr. Ting-Ming Lai, president of Shih Hsin University, criticized the policy harshly arguing "admitting Chinese students to study in Taiwan is an evolving trend, and it should be dealt with as an educational issue instead of regarding it as a political concern" (Chaiwan Ben Post 2010). Some Chinese exchange students also felt discriminated in Taiwan; and others thought it might definitely hurt Taiwan's global competitive edge in the long term.

In the face of global competition, the key to success lies in creativity and the quality of higher education. The trend is that educational markets tend to be more open, which leads to fiercer competition across campuses. Accordingly, the beginning consensus between the government and universities has emerged to develop more practical internationalization strategies to attract excellent Chinese students. In the global higher education market, "if you attract them, it confirms the high value of your universities and degrees" (Salmi 2010).

International Accreditation in Taiwan

The accreditation process is becoming internationalized and commercialized as a result of market forces. To increase their reputations and safeguard enrollment, some institutions prefer to seek international recognition rather than local accreditation, which causes "a commercial dimension to accreditation practices and the desire for institutions or providers to have as many accreditation labels or stars as possible" (Knight 2005, 2). As demands grow, more professional accrediting agencies such as ABET (engineering) from the United States and European Quality Improvement System (EQUIS) (business) from Europe expand their services internationally.

With more than 80 institutional and programmatic accreditation agencies that recognize postsecondary education in developing nations, the United States has become a substantial exporter of quality assurance (CHEA 2008). According to the Council on Higher Education Accreditation (CHEA), 40 accrediting agencies were active in 52 countries from 2006 to 2007, accrediting 385 non-US institutions and programs compared with the lower number of 364 in the United States. Ewell (2008) pointed out, "U.S. accreditation may provide an additional cachet in a competitive local market especially for private institutions" (153). Hayward (2001) also states, "Some foreign colleges and universities want U.S. accreditation because it is, at least at the moment, 'the gold standard' in many areas of higher education." Obviously, American accreditation, which offers a "nongovernmental, mission-oriented model, with trained and impartial evaluators and applied to both public and private institutions," is sought by more institutions abroad as higher education globalizes (Morse 2008). The fact that institutions in South America, Asia, Eastern Europe, are encouraged by governments to seek international accreditation, particularly from the United States, has indeed contributed to the standing of US accreditation worldwide.

In order to "oversee current assessment mechanisms, enhance teaching assessments, maintain teaching quality, and periodically conduct administrative assessment," the Higher Education Evaluation and Accreditation Council of Taiwan (HEEACT) was established jointly by the MOE, and 153 colleges and universities in 2005. Since then, HEEACT has undertaken a five-year, program-based, nationwide, modified accreditation of over 76 four-year comprehensive institutions, including military and police academies. Participation is mandatory. At the same time, HEEACT announced the exemption policy over these internationally accredited programs of Taiwanese institutions, including the programs accredited internationally by the Association to Advanced Collegiate Schools of Business (AACSB international). In other words, if the programs have been accredited internationally, the accreditation outcomes would be automatically recognized by HEEACT.

In the late 1990s, US accrediting organizations approached Taiwan higher education institutions for non-US program accreditation. Presently, five business schools in Taiwan have gained AACSB's international accreditation. Fu Jen Catholic University and National Sun Yat Shen University were reaccredited in 2010. Seventeen public and private institutions have become members of AACSB international and are committed to the accreditation process (AACSB International 2009). Currently, some Taiwanese universities have also started to pursue US institutional accreditation. The Middle States Commission on Higher Education (MSCHE), an American regional institutional accreditor, which began a pilot project accrediting non-US institutions in 2002, accredited Ming Chuan University in 2010. However, MSCHE's accreditation granted to Ming Chuan University aroused severe discussions over the issue of whether international institutional accreditation could exempt an institution HEEACT accreditation (Hou 2011a).

Generally speaking, these Taiwanese institutions accredited by US accreditors all agreed that international accreditation made it easier to attract students and faculty, to develop joint-degree programs, and to compete with local institutions (AACSB International accreditation Forum 2010). In other words, internationalization is the greatest benefit brought by international accreditation. According to my survey of Taiwan higher education institutions accredited internationally, most staff and faculty admitted that the positive impact includes increasing international reputations domestically, being recognized internationally, strengthening their global competitive edge,

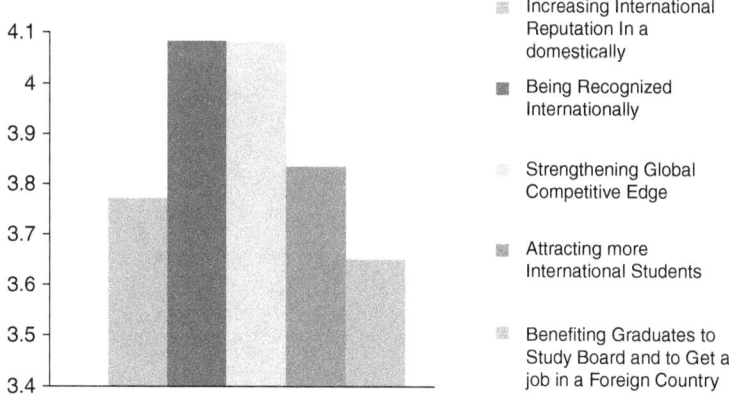

Figure 12.2 Rate by Different Elements of Internationalization.

attracting more international students, and benefiting graduates who study abroad and have better opportunities to get a job in a foreign country (Hou 2011b). However, there is a different level of agreement among top administrators, faculty members, and staff on these issues. The study showed that department heads thought that the impact on "strengthening global competitive edge" is greater than for other elements, such as compared with "being recognized internationally" by faculty and staff. As to the less influential elements, department heads agreed on "attracting more international students, benefiting graduates to study abroad, and to get a job in a foreign country," in the professorial sample and "increasing international reputation domestically" by staff. In sum, most respondents expressed the opinion that international accreditation will benefit the universities on two main areas: being recognized internationally and strengthening their global competitiveness. To our surprise, top ranks were not given to attracting international students (see table 12.2).

Table 12.2 Different Type of Respondents 'Attitude Toward Level of Impact on International Accreditation

Impact of International Accreditation	Dean		Department Heads		Professors		Staff	
	M	SD	M	SD	M	SD	M	SD
Increasing International Reputation Domestically	5	–	3.58	1.084	3.75	1.065	3.73	.786
Being Recognized Internationally	5	–	3.67	1.073	4.06	.854	4.09	.701
Strengthening Global Competitive Edge	5	–	3.77	1.013	4.06	.772	4.00	.632
Attracting More International Students	5	–	3.08	.900	3.81	.911	3.82	.751
Benefiting Graduates to Study Board and to Get a Job in a Foreign Country	5	–	3.62	1.121	3.63	1.088	3.91	.701

Source: Hou, Yung Chi. 2011. International Quality Review and the impact on Taiwan Higher Education—Assessing the Outcomes of AACSB and IEET' accredited Programs. 2011 National Science Council Research Report. Taipei: National Science Council.

In addition to internationalization, the study also showed that the focus on self-enhancement has helped these programs and institutions to develop a continuous self-evaluation mechanism, and to implement outcomes-based and mission-oriented goals set internally. Their strengths and weaknesses can also be determined easily through the process of internal and external quality assurance (Hou 2011b).

Impact of International Accreditation on Taiwan Higher Education: A Case Study of the Management School of Fu Jen

Established in 1961, Fu Jen Catholic University was the first Catholic higher education institution in Taiwan. Affiliated with three religious orders, Fu Jen has been growing into a comprehensive doctoral-type university with an approximate enrollment of 26,000 and 760 full-time faculty members organized into 12 colleges, including a business school. Fu Jen emphasizes a diversified, holistic, interdisciplinary, and international learning environment. Aided by scientific research, Fu Jen has stated that it is committed to "the pursuit of truth and the integration of Western and Chinese cultural values so as to promote the well being of the human family and strengthen world solidarity" (Fu Jen Catholic University 2009).

Founded by the Society of Jesus, the Management School of Fu Jen has become the most international college at Fu Jen since it gained AACSB International accreditation in 2005. It is composed of five undergraduate programs, six master's programs, seven executive master's programs, and one PhD program. About 2,755 students are enrolled at the undergraduate level, 252 for master's programs, 518 for executive master's programs, and 41 PhD students. Currently, 90 percent of the 85 full-time faculty members have a PhD degree. The college's goal is to cultivate talents in the business-related fields in line with Taiwan's economic development (Management School of Fu Jen Catholic University 2010). Based on its Jesuit mission and academic tradition, the School has been committed to the search for the meaning of life, helping the disadvantaged in a society, and the pursuit of justice and professional ethics over the past decades. It seeks to develop a spirit of compassion and service as well as an active commitment to social justice with a view to international solidarity. It aggressively encourages faculty members to embed service learning in their pedagogies through humanistic values and hopes that students not only pursue business profits but also show sympathy to disadvantaged minorities and actively provide them help (Lee 2010).

As a Jesuit business college, the Management School has gained full membership in the International Association of Jesuit Business Schools (JAJBS), in which most members are accredited by AACSB international. Hence, two major motives for the college to apply for AASCB international accreditation are: (1) to strengthen its global competitiveness and facilitate its international engagements, and (2) to improve the overall quality of teaching, research, and services of the institution (Lee 2010).

Following the learning outcomes orientation and continuous improvement philosophy of the AACSB international standards, the Management School developed several strategic plans to improve its student learning assessments, overall academic quality, and international outlook through organizational change, curriculum reform, faculty evaluation, and innovative teaching methods. First, it established an office of international accreditation to integrate resources of the college and to assist departments and graduate institutes to prepare the necessary materials for accreditation. In order to meet the standard faculty/student ratio, however, all evening programs were forced to close. After the reorganization and structural changes were completed, the process of curriculum review and integration began, and support to teachers for developing the learning goals of their courses at the undergraduate and graduate levels respectively proceeded. Along with curriculum reforms, selected core courses such as Business Ethics were redesigned to be co-taught by a group of teachers collaboratively. All faculty members were invited to join teaching workshops, pedagogical seminars, and educational conferences. Several student-based pedagogical models, such as those focused on competency, problem solving, and case studies, were often practiced in class. In addition, faculty members were inspired to embed service learning in class.

To firmly assure academic quality, all faulty members are also obligated to be evaluated regularly in terms of their academic performance, teaching quality, and administrative support. Those who fail the evaluation are fully reviewed again by the Faculty Committee to determine if the subject faculty member is sufficiently academically qualified to be retained as a teacher.

As mentioned above, one of the major impacts of international accreditation for most accredited institutions is enhancing their international reputation and global competitiveness. The Management School of Fu Jen is no exception. To enhance international connectivity and outlook, the Management School has developed academic exchanges and cooperative programs with more than 28 schools from nine countries, offered dual-degree programs to provide local students with international experience, and planned service learning activities abroad. In addition, it has expected faculty members to lecture in English, publish papers in prestigious international journals, attend international conferences, and so on.

Indeed, AACSB accreditation has had a positive impact on the school, particularly in its international outlook. The number of visiting scholars and international students has steadily increased. The joint business master's program has developed into a triple program, where students can study in three different universities respectively in Taiwan, the United States, and Spain. According to the former dean of the Management School, Dr. Ming-Hsien Yang, "AACSB international's accreditation did help the school successfully develop the academic cooperation with foreign universities and to benefit its graduates in the international job market greatly" (Yang 2009). The new dean, Dr. Lee Tan Xing, also has spoken positively about the benefits of international accreditation, " Fu Jen indeed gained more international recognition and had [a better] reputation after being granted the maintenance accreditation in 2010" (Lee 2011).

Challenges for the Future

However, institutions still face several challenges both during and after being accredited. The success of accreditation is very much tied to presidential leadership and presidential engagement, particularly when international accreditation is being sought. For the college, the internal problem comes from the absence of full support from the university, particularly on the part of the president and vice presidents. Though Fu Jen's president has promised to increase the human and financial resources for the college while facing several questions from the on-site maintenance team, the dilemma of how to allocate resources equally to each faculty makes it difficult to keep the promise of contributing additional resources. This explains the concerns of the associate dean of the Management School as well as the director of the office of AACSB international accreditation, Professor Pei-Gi, who has suggested "though we have passed renewal accreditation successfully this time, I felt discouraged at not being able to get sufficient physical and psychological support from the University continuously, which will likely become a big obstacle for the second renewal accreditation" (Su 2010). The underlying reason for this support level could be an emerging political struggle in university leadership between the president and the dean. Many cases indicated that once the institute was accredited successfully, the dean immediately would become a very tough competitor to the incumbent president. On the other hand, the failure of accreditation may often result in the resignation of the dean instead.

With independent governing boards, however, private institutions may have difficulties in obtaining sufficient resources to reduce faculty-teaching loads and to increase student-support services to meet the standards of international accrediting agencies. The recommendation by the accreditation renewal team suggesting increasing the publications of academic staff per capita has also caused anxiety and resistance from all faculty members. English language usage is also a challenge for the faculty, staff, and students of the college. Communicating in fluent English with visiting team members is a challenge for all senior administrators, faculty, staff, and students. The translation of materials into English required for accreditation also causes problems and requires significant additional work, both in the process of application and in preparation for accreditation renewal. In fact, the external forces that focus on creating and maintaining good quality for all aspects of international education is driving the college toward continuous self-improvement efforts.

On the other hand, how to integrate an international accreditation system into a local context still challenges the college immensely, including such issues as finding a balance between transparency and confidentiality, integration of international and local accreditation standards, recruiting more international or Chinese students, and so on. In a manner quite different from HEEACT compulsory accreditation that publishes all information on the website, AACSB international does not disclose all information publicly, a practice meant to protect the voluntary nature of its accreditation process. Therefore, finding the right balance between confidentially and disclosure of public information has become a key issue for international accreditation in Taiwan higher education.

In addition, HEEACT is still at the developmental stage in transforming the new cycle of program accreditation into a student learning outcomes-based model, so *compliance* with international standards of quality in the current national framework could be difficult. Importantly, when many Western and Asian universities are making great efforts to enhance academic exchanges with foreign institutions in every part of the world, particularly turning to the Chinese higher education market, Taiwan's universities are still constrained by governmental policies and strict regulations regarding student mobility, credit transfer, and degree recognition (Tang 2010). This is consistent with the result of the study on *"The Impact of International Accreditation on Taiwan Higher Education Accredited Internationally,"* which indicated that faculty and staff alike believed that international recognition was enhanced to a greater extent, but that the goal of attracting international students was not achieved as expected (Hou 2011b). To some extent, such policies not only obstruct student mobility and faculty exchanges across the Strait, but also damage the college's global competitive edge and collaborative opportunities with other foreign AACSB accredited programs and institutions around the world.

Conclusion

International accreditation is being pursued concurrently by many Asian nations such as Mainland China, South Korea, Hong Kong, and Japan, as it is in Taiwan, mainly for enhancement of global competitiveness and as a vehicle to attract more international students. However, this process has begun to challenge their national quality assurance systems, particularly the rationale for and nature of compulsory accreditation. Still, most of these nations do not have clear policies or standards that correspond to the quality measures set by international accreditors. Many institutions have little sense of the kinds of impact that international accreditation can have on them. Yet, Fu Jen's case has definitely inspired the government to think deeply about this issue and make its own ways according to local/global concerns and their potential impact on higher education development. Thus, based on a national consensus and learning from the experience of Europe and the United States, the Taiwanese government has published regulations and provisions supporting the legitimacy of the MOE in giving recognition to local and international accreditors. Currently, two local accreditors are under review, but still none of the international accreditors have applied for recognition voluntarily.

International accreditation, in recent years, has become a discernible trend, both with accrediting bodies and academic institutions. There are many motives for institutions and programs to seek international accreditations, including wooing good students, and enhancing academic flows. Most important of all, for those accredited and preparing for accreditation, the main priority should be to assure that international accreditation would benefit students and teachers, and not simply be a response to a trendy practice.

References

AACSB International. 2009. Available online at: http://www.aacsb.edu/ (accessed February 2, 2009).
AACSB International accreditation Forum. 2010. Taipei.
Altbach, Philip G. and Jane Knight. 2007. "The Internationalization of Higher Education: Motivation and Realities." *Journal of Studies in International*

Education. Available online at: http://jsi.sagepub.com/cgi/content/abstract/11/3-4/290
Chaiwan Ben Post. 2010. *Establishing Friendly Learning Environment in Taiwan Higher Education Institutions.* Available online at: http://chaiwanbenpost.blogspot.com/2010/07/blog-post_22.html (accessed July 22, 2010).
Council for Higher Education Accreditation (CHEA). 2008. *Quality Review 2007.* Washington D.C.: CHEA.
Department of Higher Education. 2007. *Higher Education.* Available online at: http://english.moe.gov.tw/public/Attachment/81141982471.pdf (accessed February 2, 2009).
Ewell, Peter. 2008. *U.S. Accreditation and the Future of Quality Assurance.* Washington D.C.: CHEA.
Fu Jen Catholic University. 2009. *History.* Available online at: http://140.136.240.107/english_fju/ (accessed October 3, 2009).
Hayward, Fred M. 2001. *Finding a Common Voice for Accreditation Internationally.* Available online at: http://www.chea.org/international/common-voice.html (accessed February 2, 2009).
Hou, Yung-Chi. 2010. "The Role of Accrediting Agencies as Quality Assurance Gatekeepers and College Rankers in Building World Class Universities." Paper Presented at the 2009 HEEACT International Conference. Taipei, June 4, 2010.
———. 2011a. "Quality Assurance at a Distance: International Accreditation in Taiwan Higher Education." *Higher Education* 61(2):179–191.
———. 2011b. *The Impact of International Accreditation on Taiwan Higher Education Accredited Internationally.* Working Paper. National Science Council.
Knight, Jane. 2005. "The International Race for Accreditation." *IHE,* No 40. Available online at: http://www.bc.edu/bc_org/avp/soe/cihe/newsletter/Number40/p2_Knight.htm (accessed November 13, 2008).
Lee, Michael Tian-Shyug. 2010. Personal Interview. June 25, 2010.
Management School of Fu Jen Catholic University. 2010. *Introduction.* Available online at: http://www.management.fju.edu.tw/english/introduction.asp (accessed February 2, 2010).
Ministry of Education. 2009. Meeting Minutes of Seminars for Admitting Chinese Students Studying in Taiwan.
———. 2010a. *Number of International Students.* Available online at: http://www.edu.tw/files/site_content/b0013/98_ab98.xls (accessed March 20, 2010).
———. 2010b. *International Comparison of Education Statistical Indicators 2010.* Available online at: http://english.moe.gov.tw/ct.asp?xItem=12261&ctNode=815&mp=2 (accessed March 20, 2010).
Mok, Ko Ho. 2000. "Reflecting Globalization Effects on Local Policy: Higher Education Reform in Taiwan." *Journal of Education Policy* 15(6): 637–660.
———. 2003. "Globalization and Higher Education Restructuring in Hong Kong, Taiwan and Mainland China." *Higher Education Research & Development* 22(2): 117–129.
Morse, J. A. 2008. "US Regional Accreditation Abroad: Lessons Learned. International Higher Education." Available online at: http://www.bc.edu/bc

_org/avp/soe/cihe/newsletter/Number53/p21_Morse.htm. (accessed February 27, 2009).
Salmi, Jamil. 2009. *The Challenges of Establishing World Class Universities.* Washington D.C.: The World Bank.
———. 2010. Personal Communication. June 22. 2010.
Salt, John. 1997. *International Movements of the Highly Skilled.* Paris: OECD
Su, Pei-Gi. 2010. Personal Interview. June 25. 2010.
Tang, Wei Min. 2010. Personal Interview. June 24, 2010.
Yang, Ming-Hsien. 2009. Personal Interview. February 9, 2009.
Yonezawa, Akiyoshi, Hiroko Akiba, and Daisuke Hirouchi. 2009. "Japanese University Leaders' Perceptions of Internationalization: The Role of Government in Review and Support." *Journal of Studies in International Education* 13(2):125–142.

Part 3

Conclusion

Chapter 13

Conclusion: Ways Forward for Migration and Mobility in Asia-Pacific Higher Education

*Deane E. Neubauer and
Kazuo Kuroda*

As the chapters of this volume detail, both the pace and nature of migration and mobility within higher education have changed over the past few decades. As global interdependence continues to grow, and as the world of higher education is itself transformed by various global processes, not the least of which is its role in the emergent knowledge society, the traditional functions performed within these historic and storied institutions is coming to be performed at least in part by a multitude of social institutions (Neubauer 2011b). Perhaps accordingly, the very nature of the roles performed within traditional higher education are also changing, perhaps in no way more than that of students who are moving throughout the world with an unprecedented pace and variety.

Variations of Student Mobility

This increasing variety of student mobility represents a distinct historic transformation from past eras and more recent decades of students who are internationally mobile. As Marie Scot points out in her case study of

Science Po and the London School of Economics and Political Science (LSE) (chapter 8 of this volume), the international mobility of students *per se* is hardly novel, but when one examines these historical cases (and the implication is: many others as well), it is clear that past patterns of mobility were coincident with the social structures that gave rise to and supported them. For these two famous and notable institutions, their purpose lay primarily with the desire to educate social elites for governance and social position, including those of empire in both the case of France and Britain. This pattern could be found not only among dominant empire countries seeking closer social and governmental ties to their imperial countries, but also among aspirant economically developed nations such as post-Meiji Japan that supported active policies of sending students "out" to gain the talents and predispositions so essential to a science and technology based economic development aspiration.

Two important variants on this model would emerge in the post–World War II period in what came to be commonly viewed and accepted as the "education" approach to economic development. In a clearly increasingly technologizing world, especially one in which capital mobility itself was becoming the leading edge of what would emerge as this era of contemporary globalization, the "sending out" of students to create capacities for economic development became commonplace as a basic strategy for knowledge capital development, even when large numbers of such students chose to remain outside the sending country. In more recent years quite different and targeted patterns of student mobility can be observed. One such is that reviewed by J. C. Shin in his chapter on differentiating native and foreign trained PhDs within Korea's higher education system (chapter 5 of this volume). In this instance, Korea, which like so many other countries, based much of its economic development strategy on externally educated faculty has come to the point in its own knowledge capital development where structural attributes of higher education can be traced back to the influences of domestic or foreign trained faculty. In this case (and one can hypothesize in many others within Asia as well, for example Thailand and Taiwan), the research proclivities of foreign trained faculty become an issue as they have brought with them orientations toward knowledge productivity within higher education that are novel when compared with domestic trained faculty. Even greater tension can be observed within teaching modalities as foreign trained faculty are more likely to impart this orientation to their own students, who in turn may develop "outward seeking" views of education, engendering a cascade effect that over time operated intergenerationally. To the degree that the knowledge explosion itself "quickens" these processes, one can see that the initial economic development strategy that promoted the wholesale sending out of students to seek advance degrees comes in turn to create a dynamic within the higher education structure that was both unpredicted and is unpredictable. At the very least, the dominant predispositions of these two groups as detailed by Shin result in a structural cleavage that imparts its dynamics to the whole of higher education.

An entirely different mobility pattern has resulted from the overall increases in student mobility, as characterized by Ziguras review of Australia (chapter 3 of this volume). Caught in the crossover between higher education capacity and student availability and compounded by increased governmental reluctance to further fund higher education under what had been the traditional model, Australia was ahead of the curve, as it were, in transposing the student mobility flow both to meet existing capacity availability and as a significant source of higher education funding—a model that has come in for increasing emulation in other Asian societies, especially those themselves having developed surplus higher education capacity, in the cases of Japan, Taiwan, and Korea largely as a result of declining birth rates. As Australia aggressively began to seek international students as a source of income for higher education, significant changes began to occur in where students were recruited, in who was recruited to what kinds of higher education, and indeed in much of the overall structure of higher education itself. As Ziguras makes clear, the pattern of sending out students to gain a value-added increment of knowledge capital that could be returned to the overall economy and society, the Australian model developed as de facto immigration policy with that vector employed as a primary means to both supplement population and enhance the country's overall knowledge capital. It was only a matter of time, it seems, until other global players, for example, Malaysia, Singapore, and Hong Kong began to advertise themselves as education hubs of one kind or another, institutionalizing these patterns of directly induced migration.

It can be argued, nevertheless, that these student mobility patterns, structured as they are by practice, are essentially representative of market-type flows—especially those described by Shin and Ziguras. Morshidi Sirat identifies quite a different notion of student mobility with his proposal of a "shared space" in Southeast higher education (chapter 4 of this volume). In this notion the actual exchanges and mobility of students are much more characteristic of the circuits of exchanged discussed in chapter 1, in which a structure of expectations and arrangements of input, throughput, and output are arranged based on the common interests shared by the participants, ergo the notion of a shared space. Sirat emphasizes that this concept moves beyond the models that focus on the acts of mobility themselves to be alert to the longer run effects that emerge and result from the structured and continued participation within the shared space. Effects flow both ways within such circuits of exchange and as he makes clear, the movement of people is always attended by a movement of ideas as well, and within these shared spaces their impact on all participating institutions is likely to be highly dynamic and to some degree unpredictable. In fact, in the end his argument turns more to the impacts wrought by the exchange of ideas within these shared spaces than that of the mobility of students themselves.

Student Mobility for What?

When we ask the question of what provokes the kinds of mobility that have come to characterize contemporary higher education, especially cross-border higher education, the various roles being played by higher education in the everchanging global economy become apparent. To economize on the explanation, one can suggest that the specific purposes of student mobility depend on the context at hand, differing to some degree in each country; on the other hand one can see that the dynamics of increasing global interdependence frame those contexts in specific and important ways.

Again, the chapters of this volume provide a variety of different answers and examples. Collins and Chong (chapter 10 of this volume), writing about the National University of Singapore (NUS) have before them perhaps *the* paradigmatic example of a complex research university that has self-consciously embraced one model of being a *globalized* entity. The context is controlling: Singapore as a small city-state lacks many of the resources (some would say: most) possessed by countries with which it is in economic competition. For it to participate at that level of global competition, it is clear that it must expand the frame of its knowledge resources and capital. The NUS is at the core of this strategy with its notion of becoming a regional educational hub by simultaneously pursuing a variety of goals: to strategically target research fields in which it can gain competitive advance and move to successful technology transfer; to recruit top flight research and teaching faculty from throughout the world (in no small measure by offering globally competitive salaries); by developing and recruiting administrative personnel able to produce "a management edge" in institutional effectiveness; and by recruiting highly competitive students primarily from the region, but ultimately from throughout the world. Assisting in all these strategies has been its very ambitious and largely successful goal of partnering with other "top ranked" universities throughout the world, for example, Yale and New York University (NYU). This combined package is melded together with a university commitment that all graduates will exit the university possessed of "globally competitive" skills (Tan 2011). Much like Australia, a major portion of this overall strategy is to promote in-migration of knowledge capital—the case of Singapore may be seen to differ from that of Australia by the degree to which the numbers involved are significantly smaller, thereby placing a much higher premium on issues of initial selection of migrants in all of the above categories—a highly focused strategy and set of policies targeted at brain gain.

Kuroda's chapter suggests a quite different set of motivations for the promotion of migration, one based on a complex melding of the goal of regional integration, the promotion of mutual understanding, and the gain of political peace, even while seeking to become more economically and educationally competitive. Unlike the Singapore strategy that gains viability in part through the cohesive social, political, and economic structures of a compact city-state, Kuroda sees these more general and complex motivations for mobility as arising out of the intersect between the particular and highly focused endeavors of given societies, including those with very different national, social, and religious traditions embedded in their individual higher education development experiences. In practice these complex values exist in a constant state of flux, waxing and waning as they are interacted on by broad forces circulating through society. Universities both in the past and in the present distinguish themselves in part by focusing these values and employing them as signals to the rest of the higher education community and to the society at large as to what makes them distinctive and "worthy" in the overall exchange networks that lead students to seek an institution that meets their needs, for faculty who wish to align with these particular set of values, and often to funders (governmental and private) who also wish to support this particular value set.

For certain higher education institutions (HEIs), as Scot argues, this has long been the way signals are generated through circuits of exchange, a process that in more contemporary parlance we might link to the capacity of a university or other form of HEIs (e.g., a research institute) to brand itself through careful and repeated association with a given set of values, constituency, processes, or other characteristic. (In the United States it would be naïve to ignore the linkages to athletic activities as part of this endeavor.) In this way, Scot's focus on Science Po and LSE as "elite recruitment" institutions has its parallel in most other countries, as a small set of institutions has both the historic tradition of such recruitment, and in contemporary periods has organized its external recruitment and marketing around this characteristic. In a recent article, Simon Marginson argues that one way to interpret the current fascination with the ranking of "globally competitive universities" is that such rankings provide a symbolic currency for the global circuits of exchange, allowing "consumers" of such messages to make complex decisions on issues as mobility and investment. Without such a system, he argues, something else that could perform the same kinds of functions would be required given the nature of the global exchange system that higher education has become (Marginson 2010).

Mobility, especially student mobility, can be viewed as an end result of a variety of other forces as well. As Angela Yung-chi Hou argues (chapter 12 of this volume) student mobility often has multiple benefits to a society and country. In the case of Taiwan, seeking to create a globally competitive society and economy after the migration of nationalist forces from China, the creation of universities of quality was an important instrumental ingredient of both legitimacy and status, thereby serving important globally symbolic functions, even as it also performs the critical instrumental goal of promoting brain gain, in a manner not unlike that of Singapore. Similarly, mobility at both the student and faculty level is a direct means for societies to engage academic excellence and quality. As Shin points out, this function operates at both the sending and receiving level of mobility, and countries need to be mindful that in the promotion of mobility as a means for obtaining excellence (at both the student and institutional level), facilitating such mobility does not inadvertently create an unwanted exodus of talented students unwilling to return to their country of origin.

Increasingly, however, the case made by Ziguras for student mobility in Australia may account for the answer of why students become mobile. In a world in which population growth continues at a rapid pace, moving toward a global population in the neighborhood of 10 billion by 2050, and with most of this population growth continuing to take place within developing societies and economies, outward movement through student mobility probably has more to do with changing one's life-situation calculation including permanent relocation than it does with the more transient patterns of knowledge and skill acquisition. In this sense, the steady and progressive increases observable in cross-border higher education probably contain a larger proportion of migrational populations than merely mobile ones.

Mobility and Migration in the Future

Some of the possible prospects for student mobility are presented in the foregoing chapters. One of the more intriguing of these is Sirat's notion of shared spaces. As Sirat explicates this notion of shared space as both a policy and idea space, it serves to articulate and bridge affinities of institutions and countries in ways that differentiate them from those "outside the space." From this complex construction and interaction, novel identities are created for HEIs that can both supplement and displace more familiar and traditional identities. Such is the emergent role of Universiti Sains Malaysia (USM) as Malaysia's first Accelerated Program for Excellence (APEX) university and its role in mobilizing ideas and programs for the "Bottom Billions" within the world community. Operating first within the shared space framed by the Association of South Eastern Nations (ASEAN), this project operates to create new discourses outside traditional higher education frames that can come to be conjoined to these more familiar academic disciplines and practices. The result for students drawn into such shared spaces is a particular and delineated role that both distinguishes them from others within similar circuits of exchange and empowers them with a set of particularized discursive practice tools. As such, the entire system can serve as a powerful recruitment tool or perspective, operating to draw students to this space from other competing but more conventional spaces. Building on Sirat's work, it may be useful to allow this analytical frame of reference to migrate itself from other more conventional geographic shared spaces, such as North or South America, East Asia, or Europe to begin the process of identifying discourses unique to them that either do operate to frame student identities and motivate mobility or could come to perform this role.

Collins and Chong provide another illustration of the kinds of inducements and expectations that may propel students into both more intense and diversified patterns of mobility in the future, as well as to alert us to how the migration of higher education forms, ideas, and structures is taking place. The NUS is modelling several elements currently that may indeed come to be exemplars that other institutions seek to emulate within the circuits of global exchange. One is to be able to actually function as an educational hub by partnering with other attractive and quality universities throughout the world in such a way that a NUS student by the act of choice of becoming one, is entered into a set of relationships that provide effective and highly "lubricated" pathways of exchange and development with other HEIs within the hub.

It is useful to note the innovative difference here with many other patterns of "student linkage" that have characterized international education over the past couple of decades. Even while opportunities for student "exchange" and "joint programs," and even joint-degree programs have been relatively common over these decades, what appears different about the NUS approach is a higher level of conceptualization, commitment, and implementation in effectuating the content and level of integration of these exchanges. Whereas, for example, many such exchange programs seek to "implicate" the student in the cultural, political, and economic milieu of the receiving university and find various ways to value these additions to the student's curriculum and experience, NUS seeks to engage such "encounters" with its partner institutions in ways that maximize the extent to which these experiences also prepare such students for the acquisition of perspectives, tools, and competences that prepare students on graduation for success in the increasingly competitive global market place (Tan 2011). In this sense, we suggest that the efforts being undertaken differentiate themselves from others by being *strategic* in ways that provide a distinctive value-added benefit to the student. To repeat: our suggestion is that this technique is likely to find many imitators in the near future, coming to transform global student mobility in a distinctive and important way. In this sense, it can become an emergent higher education structure that may migrate across multiple national and regional settings.

Following this line of demonstration as provided by the foregoing chapters, we wish to suggest that increasingly efforts to promote student mobility will borrow more specifically from the plentitude of institutional forms that currently exist. Efforts to recruit to one's institution as well as to promote it internationally will be marked not only by efforts to gain status through such mechanisms as rankings, as discussed above in Marginson's comment, but by increasingly differentiating and branding the particularities of such quality achievements. Hou, for example, in the chapter referred to above, emphasizes the distinctive role that quality assurance entities can play in providing the kinds of information that students may increasingly seek within the broader context of global rankings, a point also made by Federkeil in his suggestions that what may be evolving out of the first wave of global rankings is a set of measurements that frame "quality" far more in the direction of institutional characteristics of interest to students (and parents) that focus increasingly on the *relationship* between research quality and teaching, and such differentiations of the latter as learning opportunities, teaching and learning styles and opportunities, and learning outcomes (Federkeil, 2009). Hou suggests that this latter value, difficult to define and measure, but nevertheless becoming increasingly important in the "commerce" of globalized education, may come to have a new currency that will figure importantly in the kinds of decisions that students will make when embarking on cross-border education—especially in the context of the overall increasing costs of higher education throughout the world, and especially for cross-border students. Increasingly it would seem, creating and being able to transmit an effective currency for student learning outcomes will constitute an important mobility channel in global higher education.

If one seeks to view the near future from the perspective of the prospective student contemplating movement within these growing and transforming circuits of global exchange, it seems clear that in the way Kuroda has drawn the distinctions between the nation-state and cosmopolitan models of higher education, that they are merging—giving up their distinctiveness to the impress of the forces of global interdependence that have been documented in various ways throughout these chapters. As this takes place, we want to ask: to what effect? The nation-state model for example had as one of its intrinsic elements the centrality of the nation as the provider of higher education and as its primary recipient: first of elites, later of the functionaries of the administrative state and industrial society. The cosmopolitan model for its part privileged a set of values that were held to be "universal" with a presumption that at some level "all educated" people might come to subscribe to such values.

We need to ask whether the forces that are promoting a merging of these models—which for convenience we have called the dynamics of contemporary globalization—will eventually rise to the status of "universal values" held in common by the "cosmopolitan" community, or whether other forces are at work that will influence what this "merged" or "synthetic" view of the world proffered by these global dynamics may come to represent. Will, for example, this quickening of mobility and the migration of ideas through these circuits of exchange create in some near future a greater awareness of and respect for "global public goods" such as the environment in general, global water supplies, food security, and so on—elements that could certainly be conceived under the framework of a new cosmopolitanism—or, from another point of view, will they result in a recalibration of a supranational higher education / university model in which the benefit of "winning" the quality "battle" (represented by the global rankings phenomenon) be the *projection* of a kind of national-focused consciousness through the articulation of those national values as the de facto values of the new cosmopolitanism (which is, in the end, what much of the critique of the early stages of this era of globalization as de facto Americanism amounts to). It may be useful, as we collectively pursue research into the continued development of mobility and migration through global higher education circuits to frame at least part of our research on this issue of how the "new global" is being constituted by these forces.

An important caveat is also due with respect to both the dimensions of higher education migration and mobility given that our methods for assessing each are still in their early stages. As Hawkins' argument in this volume (chapter 7) holds, we are very much collectively caught between the rhetoric of both migration and mobility but have done little to measure and assess either in systematic ways. The UCLA case that Hawkins presents seeks to differentiate *instance*, which, for example, is capable of demonstration through various levels of evidence, and the reality of *institutional* transformation, which he suggests has tended to be modest for a leading, globally ranked research institution such as UCLA. Indeed, even as we seek to discern the nature and degree of changes that take place within the dual frameworks of migration and mobility, it would seem as if we can begin to develop much more finely gauged concepts of change and transformation to make these assessments. Simply at the level of concept clarification, for example, it would seem as argued in chapter 1, that we might differentiate between four kinds of change: that which is genuinely innovative—bringing something new into the contents, processes, or structures of higher education; change that is profound and enduring, such that once introduced a content or structural change persists (e.g., as in the development of new "synthetic" disciplines); change that is gradual, but cumulative and ultimately transformational (which may be what we are seeing in student learning patterns, or in problem-based learning, or in research across the curriculum, or in the growth of multiuniversity consortia); and change that is more "apparent than real"—change that tends to represent a fashion that spreads quickly across HEIs, but in the end does fail to be transformative.

And, as we seek to sharpen our conceptual and measurement tools to gain greater understanding of both migration and mobility, we may have real success in moving away from our current concentration with student movement per se and develop a richer catalogue of subjects for study—to populate as it were the circuits of exchange with varieties of content. In this regard, I summarize briefly the more extensive project outlined in chapter 1. We may seek a research net that conjoins the movement of students with those of faculty, administrators, and other staff for a variety of purposes, such as degree study; movements of lesser duration than degree study; of both funded and unfunded research, with or without external appointments, or academic meetings that range in output from presenting research results to being exposed to new models of some aspect of higher education through training or cooperative engagements. With respect to the migration of "ideas" we can review such things as the growth and diversification of faculty participation in scholarly publication; the growth and spread of outlets for scholarly publication; the development, growth, and spread of new pedagogies and their consequences; the development, growth, and spread of "institutional standards" that could include (but not be limited to) quality matters, governance issues (e.g., public and private), financial modalities, ideas of "accountability"; and the development and growth of regional public policy "discourses," for example alignment, autonomy, and so on. From such endeavors might emerge a kind of academic geography in which nodes of innovation are linked through diffusion networks to their emulators.

And just to extend this exercise one step further, it may be useful to study the circulation of higher education *structures*. These may be usefully separated as a distinct subclass of ideas that focuses on: the growth of new discourses and suggestions about how HEIs should be organized (traditional faculties, departments, etc.); the emergence of new internal governance structures (e.g., transformation of the presidential role from symbolic to acting CEO); internal mechanisms of audit; and aggregation of institutional units into systems (e.g., such as the diffusion of the California master plan).

These endeavors are intimately related, of course, and some of this work of review, aggregation, and dissemination is taking place through the various versions of university rankings. To date, however, it would seem as most of the work of ranking has been done at the level of developing indicators and publishing rankings. The task envisioned in the preceding paragraphs would focus far more on the question of what rankings mean both in terms of what they purport to measure and in terms of what their effects are likely to be in the near and more distant future (Neubauer 2011a). It would seem in this regard, for example, that to the extent that the policy space of *globally competitive university* is occupied almost exclusively by those successful in meeting the specific criteria for limited outlets of research publication (Liu 2011) that the induced competition produced by such rankings leads aspiring universities to move inexorably toward the particularized research model(s) of those that occupy the highest rankings on such lists. In this way rankings act as both a structural "framer" for institutional development and as its reinforcement mechanism.

Conclusion

It seems clear to us that this moment in higher education throughout the world is one of historic and fundamental transformation. The forces that are operating to reforge the world as one of increasing interdependence assure that willingly or not, important innovations in one part of this complex system are experienced throughout—often as Hershock (chapter 2) underscores, with surprising and unexpected consequences. As these dynamics come to be represented within national systems of higher education and as practices and purposes are similarly transformed, feed-forward and feedback loops of information, communication, and practice are triggered with the result that even institutions that purposefully seek to "remain in place" and pursue traditional values and practices are likely to be incrementally moved to new positions within their belief and behavior frames that in the end culminate in substantive change—the famous and seemingly invariant rule that a sequence of incremental changes will eventuate in a qualitative change.

We see both of these dynamics in the chapters of this volume. Some detail efforts to "catch the wave" of change that is surging through global higher education, and that we have sought to frame within the metaphor of circuits of exchange. Others detail efforts on the part of specific national systems to deal with what they experience as "problems" of local origin and meaning, such as those that attend to changes in demographics and the resulting "over capacity" of higher education provision in some countries that impels efforts to import students to justify that capacity. Our interest is in the range of constructions that can arise from this confluence of forces that simultaneously create dynamics that move toward patterns of cohesion and differentiation. These kinds of inherent conflicts appear to be part and parcel of the pattern of globalization/interdependence emerging in the world.

As a parallel expression of these contradictory dynamics we can observe efforts, especially within regional associations and networks, to develop what are intended as cohesional frameworks to accommodate all of this diversity. We see this in quality endeavors (e.g., ASEAN, APQN), in the long-standing efforts of education ministries to work in concert (e.g., SEAMEO), in transnational regional endeavors (e.g., UNESCO), and in targeted efforts at cooperation among countries in the region with complicated past histories of conflict (e.g., Third Japan-China-Korea Committee for Promoting Exchange and Cooperation among Universities). All of these efforts signify in some way a strong intentionality to provide cohesional frameworks to accommodate the diversities that are represented in current patterns of migration and mobility in the Asia-Pacific region.

REFERENCES

Federkeil, Gero. 2009. "Rankings and Quality—a European Perspective," in *Higher Education in Asia Pacific: Quality and the Public Good*, ed. Bigalke, T. and Neubauer, D. New York: Palgrave Macmillan.

Liu, Nian Cai. 2011. "The Phenomenon of Academic Ranking of World Universities Model: Future Directions." Paper Presented to the Conference on Quality in Higher Education: Identifying, Developing, and Sustaining Best Practices in the APEC Region. Honolulu, Hawaii, August 4–6, 2011.

Marginson, Simon. 2010. "The Global Knowledge Economy and Culture of Comparison in Higher Education," in *Quality Assurance and University Rankings in Higher Education in the Asia Pacific: Challenges for Universities and Nations*, ed. Kaur, Sarjit, Morshidi Sirat, and William G. Tierney. Pulau Pinang: Penerbit Universiti Sains Malaysia.

Neubauer, Deane. 2011a. "*How Might University Rankings Contribute to Quality Assurance Endeavors?*" Paper Presented to the Conference on Quality in Higher Education: Identifying, Developing, and Sustaining Best Practices in the APEC Region. Honolulu, Hawaii, August 4–6, 2011.

―――. 2011b. "The Changing Social Ecology of Higher Education," in *The Emergent Knowledge Society and the Future of Higher Education: Asian Perspectives,* ed. Neubauer. London: Routledge.

Tan, Eng Chye. 2011. "The National University of Singapore's (NUS) Mission to be a Leading Global University." Paper Presented to the Conference on Quality in Higher Education: Identifying, Developing, and Sustaining Best Practices in the APEC Region. Honolulu, Hawaii, August 4–6, 2011.

Contributors

Francis Leo Collins is a postdoctoral fellow in the Asia Research Institute at the National University of Singapore. His research interests revolve around the relationship between different forms of migration and changing urban spaces. His recently completed PhD thesis focussed on the lives of South Korean international students in Auckland, New Zealand, as a route to interrogating the role of increasing international student mobilities in the changing spaces and functions of that city. More recently, Francis has started to develop a new project that looks at the influence of increasing levels of labour migration (at a range of socioeconomic levels) into Seoul and South Korean cities more generally. He is also involved in the development of a large collaborative research project on international student mobilities and globalising universities in East Asia. He has published or has forthcoming articles on these subjects in *Global Networks, Social and Cultural Geography, Journal of Ethnic and Migration Studies, Asia Pacific Viewpoint* and *Population, Space and Place*.

John N. Hawkins is professor emeritus and director of the Center for International and Development Studies at the Graduate School of Education and Information Studies at the University of California, Los Angeles. He is also a consultant at the East West Center in Honolulu, Hawaii for the International Forum on Education 2020 project. He was dean of International Studies at UCLA, and has served as a director of the UCLA Foundation Board, director of the East-West Center Foundation Board, and director of the J. F. Oberlin Foundation Board. He is chief editor of the new Comparative Education Series of Palgrave MacMillan Press. He is a specialist on higher education reform in the US and Asia and the author of several books and research articles on education and development in Asia. He has conducted research throughout Asia since 1966 when he first visited the People's Republic of China and Japan.

Peter Hershock is coordinator of the Asian Studies Development Program at the East-West Center in Honolulu, Hawai'i, and was trained in both

Western and Asian philosophy at Yale University and the University of Hawai'i, respectively. Alongside his work envisioning and implementing faculty development programs aimed at globalizing higher education humanities and social science curricula, he has sustained research interests in using Asian philosophical perspectives to address such contemporary issues as the relational impacts of technology, human rights, and the role of values in cultural and social change. His recent books include: *Technology and Cultural Values* (edited, 2003); *Chan Buddhism* (2005); *Buddhism in the Public Sphere: Reorienting Global Interdependence* (2006); *Changing Education: Leadership, Innovation and Development in a Globalizing Asia Pacific* (edited, 2007); and *Educations and their Purposes: A Conversation among Cultures* (edited, 2008).

Kong Chong Ho is associate professor of Sociology and vice dean (Research) at the Faculty of Arts and Social Sciences, National University of Singapore. Trained as an urban sociologist at the University of Chicago, his research interests are in the political economy of cities, migration, higher education, and youth. Dr Ho is board member of Research Committee 21 (Sociology of Urban and Regional, International Sociological Association) and an editorial board member of *Pacific Affairs*. He is currently the lead researcher in the project "Globalizing Universities and International Student Mobilities in East Asia" that examines leading universities in China, Japan, Korea, Taiwan, and Singapore.

Yung-Chi Hou (Angela) is professor of Higher Education and Director of Faculty Development and Instructional Resources Center, Fu Jen Catholic University, and dean of the Office of Research & Development of Higher Education Evaluation & Accreditation Council of Taiwan (HEEACT). She specializes in higher education quality management, internationalization of higher education, faculty development, and quality assurance of cross-border higher education. Over the past four years, she has worked on international exchange affairs for HEEACT and engaged in many international activities of quality assurance of higher education of HEEACT. She currently serves as an APQN board member and consultant. Author of over 100 Chinese and English papers, articles, books, and reports in the areas of higher education evaluation and rankings in local and international referred journals, she is also subeditor of "Evaluation in Higher Education" published by HEEACT and IREG.

Deane E. Neubauer is emeritus professor of Political Science at the University of Hawaii, Manoa (UHM), senior research scholar at the Globalization Research Center and senior advisor to the International Forum for Education 2020 of the East-West Center. He has long been interested in the conduct of policy within and between democratic national states, an interest that has over time focused on comparative democratic institutions, policy processes, health care, food security, education, and more recently the development and conduct of globalization. He has served as chancellor of UHM and as the vice president for Academic Affairs for the ten-campus University of Hawaii system. His current work examines the varieties of national policy expressions in health care, food security, and education within the contemporary dynamics of globalization with particular attention to nations in the Asia-Pacific region.

Marie Scot is research fellow at Sciences Po Paris (France). Trained at the ENS (Ecole normale supérieure), Marie Scot holds the agrégation and a PhD in modern History. Her research interests deal with the history of the social sciences as well as with higher education and research in a comparative and transnational perspective (europeanization of higher education).

Jung Cheol Shin is associate professor at Seoul National University. He served for the Korea Ministry of Education about 18 years. His research interests are higher education policy, knowledge production and social development, academic profession, quality assurance, and higher education finance. His researches have been published in international journals *Higher Education, Review of Higher Education, Studies in Higher Education, Scientometrics, Education Policy Analysis Archive,* and *Asia Pacific Education Review.* He is the executive editor of *Asia Pacific Education Review,* the review editor of *Higher Education,* and a board member of *Tertiary Education and Management.* He has been invited as guest speakers by leading research universities in many countries. Currently, he is leading a ten year research project on knowledge production and social development with Prof. Loet Leydesdorff of University of Amsterdam funded by the National Research Foundation of Korea.

Morshidi Sirat is professor and deputy director-general (Public Sector), Department of Higher Education, Ministry of Higher Education, Malaysia. Between April 2002 and February 2011, he was the director of the National Higher Education Research Institute Malaysia (IPPTN) and during this period he specialised in higher education policy research. Secondment to the Ministry of Higher Education has given him the opportunity to implement IPPTN's research findings accumulated since 2002. He was instrumental in launching *Malaysia's Global Reach* initiative in June 2011. In the early eighties, he decided to study regional economics and on his return to Malaysia in 1982 he started his academic career at Universiti Sains Malaysia, Penang. In late eighties, he made another disciplinary change, opting to pursue further studies in economic geography at the University of Southampton, England. Three years later he was back at Universiti Sains Malaysia to continue his academic career. But with the passing of the Private Higher Education Act in 1996, he saw a "blue ocean" and took up higher education policy research.

Reiko Yamada is professor of Faculty of Social Studies and director of Center for Higher Education and Student Research at Doshisha University, Kyoto, Japan. She has long been interested in comparative higher education policy in OECD countries. More recently, she has conducted a quantitative study for student development and is engaged in the comparative student research between Japan, Korea and the United States. Ms. Yamada served as the director of the Center for the Faculty of Development at Doshisha University between 2006 and 2009. She serves on the committee of the Central Education Council in Japan. She is the president of Japanese Association of the First-year Experience. She is a single author of six books in Japanese. Her current work examines the comparative quality assurance of higher education in United States, Eurpean Union, and Asia. Ms. Yamada holds a BA from Doshisha University and an MA and PhD from the University of California, Los Angeles.

Kazuo Kuroda is professor of International Education at the Graduate School of Asia Pacific Studies of Waseda University and dean of the Center for International Education of Waseda University. He has long been interested in educational development and policies in developing countries, international cooperation in education and internationalization of higher education. Mr. Kuroda is also visiting professor at the University of Tokyo, visiting professor at the Institute of Developing Economies Advanced School (IDEAS), visiting fellow at the Japan International Cooperation Agency (JICA) Research Institute, member of the Japanese National Commission for UNESCO, managing director of the Global Institute for Asian Regional Integration at Waseda University, board member of the Japan Society for International Development and Japan Comparative Education Society, and editorial board member of several academic journals including *International Journal of Educational Development, Peabody Journal of Education, African Education Research Forum*. His current work examines regionalization and globalization of education and tries to create a prospective regional and global governance framework of education. He holds a BA from Waseda University, an MA from Stanford University and a PhD from Cornell University.

Ma Wanhua is professor of Education at the Graduate School of Education, Peking University. She received her PhD from Cornell University in 1997, specializing in educational psychology and higher education administration.

In November 1997, she joined the faculty of education at Peking University and has carried out research projects funded by UNDP, UNESCO, and Ford Foundation concerning issues of girls' education, vocational education in China and the development of higher education in Asia and the Pacific Rim. In conjunction with her research, she served as a visiting professor at the School of Education, UC Berkeley, as affiliate faculty at the Center for International and Development Education, UCLA in 2003, and as education consultant to the East-West Center. Her special contribution to higher education research in China earned her the Fulbright New Century Scholar in 2005/2006. Her recent book *From Berkeley to Beida and Tsinghua: The development and governance of public research universities in the US and China* was awarded second prize by the Association of Education in China. Her current research focuses on internationalization of higher education and the development of research universities in China.

Christopher Ziguras is associate professor in the School of Global Studies, Social Science, and Planning, and program director, BA International Studies at RMIT University in Melbourne, Australia and associate dean . His research explores various aspects of the political economy of international education, and he has written widely on the growth and the cross-border delivery of tertiary education, international education policy, and the impact of trade agreements on education services. A recent book is *Transnational Education: Current Issues and Future Trends in Offshore Higher Education* with Grant McBurnie (Routledge 2007). Previous appointments include: Research fellow at the Monash Centre for Research in International Education (1999–2001); deputy director of the Globalism Research Centre, RMIT (2002–04); acting head of the School of International and Community Studies, RMIT (2004–05); and director of research in the School of Global Studies, Social Science, and Planning, RMIT (2007–08) and deputy dean of the School of Global Studies, Social Science, and Planning.

Index

2008 Recession, 28, 31, 46, 121
Academic Scholarship Reconsidered, 70, 72
Accelerated Program for Excellence (APEX), 55–56, 60–61, 63, 217
Accountability, 14, 60, 84–86, 96, 100, 220
Accreditation, 1, 50, 130, 132, 191–205
Admissions, 11, 15, 83, 88, 96, 112, 116, 120, 139, 191
Advisory Committee for Asia-Europe Foundation (ASEF), 62
Africa, 128, 134, 146, 179
Alignment issue, 8, 14, 220
Altbach, Philip, 61, 187, 193
American Council on Education (ACE), 110–112, 118–119
   Mapping Internationalization in U.S. Campuses, 110
Articulation Model, 99
Asia Development Bank, 154
Asia Pacific Professional Leaders in Education (APPLE), 61
Asia-Pacific region, 5, 8, 10, 16, 57, 59, 61–62, 105–109, 111–113, 116, 119, 148, 153, 196, 211, 222
Asianization, 143–145, 153–154
Assessment tools, 88–91
   college-impact theory, 90, 92, 100
   College Student Survey (CSS), 90

Cooperative Institutional Research Program (CIRP), 90
   input-environment-output (I-E-O) model, 90
   theory of involvement, 90
Association of Commonwealth Universities (ACU), 61
Association of International Education, 62
Association of Pacific Rim Universities (APRU), 106
Association of South East Asian nations (ASEAN), 54–55, 61–62, 145, 148, 154, 167, 217, 222
   ASEAN University Network (AUN), 61, 148, 154
Association of Southeast Asian Institutions of Higher Learning (ASAIHIL), 60–61
Association of Universities of Asia Pacific (ACAP), 61
Association to Advanced Collegiate Schools of Business (AACSB international), 198–205
Australia, 39–51, 66, 107–109, 112, 121, 145, 152, 161, 163, 178, 184, 213, 215–216
   Federation of Western India Cine Employees, 47
   Indian student assaults, 45–50
   Melbourne, 45–47, 87
   migration pathway, 40, 42–44, 49
   permanent residence, 39, 41, 43, 50

Australia—*Continued*
  points system, 39, 41–42, 50
  Professional Hairdressers
    Association, 44
  Queensland University of
    Technology, 47
  skilled migration, 39–42, 46, 50
  Sydney, 46–48
  University of Melbourne, 87
Australia-Korea Teacher Exchange
  Program, 9
Australian Council for Private
  Education and Training, 44
Austria, 138

Balkans, 128
Bangladesh, 42, 150
Belgium, 139
Blue Ocean Strategy (BOS), 60, 62
Bologna process, 10, 14, 21
Boston, 187
Brain drain, 107, 126, 175, 178, 189
Branch campuses, 6, 15, 24, 31, 110,
  119, 192
Brazil, 67, 86
Buddhist University at Nalanda, 23
Bulgaria, 128

Cab Drivers Association, 46
California master plan, 221
Cambodia, 62
Canada, 42, 112, 121, 178,
  184–185, 192
Carnegie Foundation, 68, 86
Changing Academic Profession (CAP),
  68–70, 72–73, 75–78, 80
Chile, 86
China, 11, 13–14, 25, 42–43, 67,
  107, 115–117, 120–121, 127,
  144–145, 147, 149–150, 152,
  158, 160–161, 163, 167–168,
  175–181, 183–184, 187,
  189, 192–193, 196, 197,
  205, 216, 222

Beijing, 167, 196
Center for Excellence in
  Disciplinary Development
  Plan, 183
Central Academy of Fine Arts, 197
Central Conservatory of Music, 197
Changjiang Scholars and Creative
  Research Team Development
  Plan, 181–183, 188–189
China Agricultural University, 197
China Scholarship Council, 179
Chunhui Plan, 181
college-entry exam, 196
College of Engineering, 184
College of Software and Computer
  Science, 184
Cultural Revolution, 177
economic liberalization, 25
Expertise-Introduction Project for
  Disciplinary Innovation in
  Universities (the 111 plan),
  180, 182–183, 188–189
Faculty salary, 177, 187–189
Fudan University, 153
Hong Kong, 13, 42, 115, 181,
  196, 205, 213
  Hong Kong City University, 196
  Hong Kong University, 196
International Partnership Program
  for Creative Research Teams
  (the Changjiang scholar
  project), 180–182
Key Project on Foreign Experts
  under MOE, 183
Ministry of Education (MOE), 175,
  178–179, 182–184, 187
  Mid and Long Term Education
    Development Plan (2010 to
    2020), 179
National Friendship Award, 178
National University of Defense
  Technology, 197
open door policy, 175, 177
Peking University, 153, 175–189

Law School, 186
Philosophy Department, 186
School of Physics, 187
People's Daily, 177
People's Republic of China, 176
Plan for Foreign Lecturers, 183
Programs Supporting Major Scientific Research Institutions to Expand International Cooperation, 180
Project 211, 11, 182–183
Project 985, 11, 182–183, 193
Project for Introducing Eminent Teachers from Overseas, 180–181
Project for Inviting Language Teachers, 183
Provincial Friendship Awards, 178
Qing, 147
Scientific Research Fund for the Returned Overseas Chinese Scholars, 183
Shanghai, 167
Soviet Union exchange, 176–177
State Administration of Foreign Experts Affairs, 178–179, 182, 188
Well-known Scholar Plan, 178
Chinese, 7, 25, 41, 109, 138, 144, 147, 150, 175–179, 181–189, 194, 196–197, 201, 204
Chinese socialist construction, 176
Chong, Ho Kong, 214, 217, 226
Circuits of exchange, 1, 4–6, 8–11, 14, 16, 25, 29, 53–56, 59–62, 112, 119, 121, 213–215, 217, 219–220, 222
City University of New York, 185
Cold War, 23, 27, 148–149
Collins, Francis Leo, 214, 217, 225
Columbia University, 132
Commodification, 21, 32
Commonwealth Universities Study Abroad Consortium, 62

Cosmopolitan model, 146–148, 219
Cosmopolitan nation-state university, 146, 148
Council of Graduate Schools, 112
Council on Higher Education Accreditation (CHEA), 198
Crossborder exchange, 4, 6, 7, 22
Cuba, 62

Digital revolution, 2
Diploma mills, 153
Dual degrees, 31, 132, 161, 167

East Asia, 143–155
 human capital theory, 151
 movement of students, 144–145
 new imperialism, 158, 160
East meets West, 159
East West Center, 187
Egypt, 127
Elite recruitment institutions, 215
Emergent knowledge society, 211
English, 41, 43, 48, 66, 75, 85, 89, 94–95, 99, 114–116, 127–128, 130–135, 137, 150, 153, 161–162, 164, 169, 177–178, 183–186, 192–194, 203–204
Erasmus program, 131, 147, 149, 151, 154, 180
Eurasia, 23
Europe, 10, 23–24, 53, 59, 62, 68, 70–71, 73, 77–78, 107, 116–117, 120, 125–138, 147, 149, 151, 161, 163, 167–168, 171–172, 176, 179–180, 184–185, 196, 198, 205, 217
European Commission, 147
European LMD education reform, 137
European model of higher education internationalization, 126
European Quality Improvement System (EQUIS), 198
European Union, 24, 53

Faculty research, 7–8, 12–13, 65–78, 86, 118, 175, 212, 214
Faculty types, 86
  Anglo-American, 86
  German, 86
  Latin American, 86
Financial aid, 11
Flat world, 16, 160, 170
Flying geese model of economic development, 30
Fourth East Asian Summit, 148
France, 23, 66, 68, 70, 107, 116–117, 121, 126–129, 132–133, 138, 143–144, 148, 184, 212
  Declaration of the Third Republic, 127
  Paris, 60, 127–129, 131–133, 146
  Université de Paris, 128, 146
Free Trade Agreements (FTAs), 152
Fundamental change, 3

General Agreement on Trade in Services (GATS), 106, 152
Germany, 23, 66–68, 86, 107, 117, 121, 127–128, 130, 138, 146, 180, 184, 187
  Berlin University, 146
  Berlin Wall, 23
  German Academic Exchange Program, 180
Global citizen, 160, 166, 171
Global informational capitalism, 27, 31, 34
Global University League, 158
Global University Network for Innovation Asia and the Asia Pacific (GUNI-AP), 61
Globalization, 2, 3–5, 9, 11, 15, 22, 24–25, 28–30, 32, 34–35, 61, 63, 83–85, 99–100, 106, 109–113, 117, 120, 129, 134, 158, 160, 169, 191, 193, 212, 219, 222

Globalizing Universities and International Student Mobilities in East Asia project, 158
Graves, Joe, 186
Great Britain, 23, 212
The Great Brain Race, 107, 120
Greece, 128

Hard disciplines, 77
Harvard University, 87, 135, 170
  Task Force on General Education at the Faculty of Arts and Sciences, 87
Hawkins, John, 3–4, 11, 187, 219, 225
Hershock, Peter, 221, 225
Higher education institutions (HEIs)
  center-periphery pattern, 172
  doctoral institutions, 3, 7, 67, 72, 201
  graduate institutions, 1, 3, 12, 67, 74, 109, 111–112, 115, 120, 130, 132, 175, 185, 192–194, 199, 202
  multi-center pattern, 172
  postdoctoral, 7–8, 67, 133
  undergraduate, 7–1, 12, 67, 74, 84, 87–88, 100, 109, 111–113, 115, 119–120, 130–131, 137, 185, 193–194, 201, 202
Hou, Angela Yung-chi, 216, 218, 226

Immigration authorities, 40–41, 43, 46, 49–50
India, 42, 44–50, 109, 115–117, 121, 128, 160–161, 163, 167–168
  Bangalore, 167
Indian Overseas Affairs minister, 47
Indonesia, 13, 42, 150, 196
Information and Computing Technology (ICT), 55
Interdependence, 4, 22, 24, 28, 32, 34–35, 143, 211, 219, 221–222
International Association of Jesuit Business Schools (JAJBS), 202

International Association of
 Universities (IAU), 61
International understanding /
 international peace model,
 148–149
Internationalization, 3–5, 21, 34, 57,
 60–62, 65, 69, 71, 74, 83,
 85, 100, 105–106, 109–113,
 117–120, 125–138, 147, 150,
 154, 158, 165–166, 175,
 177, 185–186, 189,
 192–194, 199, 201
Internet, 2, 92
Ireland, 139
Israel, 86
Italy, 67, 116, 138–139

Japan, 7, 11, 13–14, 42, 66–68, 70, 75,
 83–101, 108–109, 112, 115, 117,
 121, 138, 144–146, 149–154,
 158, 167, 177, 184, 187, 192–193,
 205, 212–213, 222
 21 COE program, 11, 193
 accountability, 86–87
 Central Council for Education in
  Japan, 84–85, 87–88, 99
  For Restructuring Undergraduate
   Education, 84
  Future of Japanese Higher
   Education, 85
 Council on Foreign Students
  Policy, 150
 declining birth rate, 83–84, 213
 First Year Experience (FYE)
  programs, 88, 95–100
  types of, 98
 graduate attributes, 87
 grass eaters, 109
 honors programs, 99
 learning-centered programs, 84
 Meiji period, 150, 212
 Ministry of Education, Culture,
  Sports, Science, and
  Technology [MEXT], 83–84,
  86, 98, 100
 300,000 International Students
  Plan, 85
 Global 30 program, 85, 100,
  150, 193
 Remedial Classes, 95
 taishuka, 83
 Tokyo Imperial University, 146
 universalization, 83
 Waseda University, 147, 150,
  153–154, 187, 196
  Global Institute of Asian
   Regional Integration (GIARI),
   153–153
  Graduate School of Asia Pacific
   Studies (GSAPS), 153–154
Japanese, 7, 68, 70, 83–89, 91–95,
 97–100, 109, 138, 147, 150,
 153–154, 177
Japanese College Student Survey
 (JCSS), 91–94
Japanese Freshman Survey (JFS), 91,
 94–95
Japanese Ministry of Education, 150
Joint degree, 31, 85, 106, 119, 132,
 137, 167, 199, 217

Knowledge-based society, 83–85, 87, 100
Korea, 7, 9, 11, 13–14, 65–80, 109,
 144–145, 167, 192–193, 196,
 212–213, 222
 academic career paths, 67
 academic freedom, 78
 Brain Korea (BK), 21, 11, 76, 193
 campus-wide decision-making, 69
 course materials, 75
 Humanity Korea (HK), 76
 Social Science Korea (SSK), 76
Korean Center for Education, 65–66
Korean Research Foundation
 (KRF), 68
Kuroda, Kazuo, 187, 215, 219, 228

Lao PDR, 62
Latin America, 87, 113–114, 132, 135, 146
League tables, 12–13
Lebanese, 48, 138
London School of Economics (LSE), 125–139, 212, 215
 client-consumer satisfaction, 135
 Faculty composition, 135
 Graduate School, 136
 international development model, 132
 international recruitment strategy, 129–130
 language barrier, 133
 Malthusian education policies, 129
 nationalist education policies, 129
 system of External Degrees, 130
Loops of information, 221

Malaysia, 42, 54–63, 107–108, 147, 150, 152, 163, 196, 213, 217
 Bumiputra policy, 150
 Kuala Lumpur, 59
 National Higher Education Action Plan 2007–2010, 57
 National Higher Education Strategic Plan Approaching 2020, 57
 Penang, 60
 research collaboration, 57–59
  Memorandum of Agreement (MoA), 58
  Memorandum of Understanding (MoU), 58
 Universiti Kebangsaan Malaysia (UKM), 57, 59
 Universiti Malaya (UM), 57, 59
 Universiti Putra Malaysia (UPM), 57
 Universiti Sains Malaysia (USM), 55–57, 59–62, 217
  A'la Carte University, 60
  Corporate University, 60
  Invisible University, 60
  State University, 60
  University in the Garden, 60
 Universiti Teknologi Malaysia (UTM), 57
 University and University Colleges Act (UUCA), 59
Marginson, Simon, 215, 218
marketization, 26, 29, 31–32, 151–152
Massachusetts Institute of Technology (MIT), 150
Massification, 83–84, 88, 97, 100, 108
Mexico, 86
Middle East, 48, 59, 129, 132, 135
Middle States Commission on Higher Education (MSCHE), 199
Migration-education nexus, 40, 44, 49, 158
Millennium Development Goals, 32
Minds on the Move, 107
Modernization, 22, 26, 28–29, 34, 146, 149–150, 153
 reflexive modernization, 28–29, 34

Nation-state, 21, 23, 25, 146–148, 219
Nation-state university model, 146–148, 219
National Science Board, 76
Nationalization, 26, 129
Neoliberalism, 13–14, 16, 23, 31, 34, 85
Netherlands, 86
Network society, 27–28, 132
Neubauer, Deane, 187, 226–227
The New York Times, 157
New York University (NYU), 214
 New York University (NYU) Abu Dhabi, 196
New Zealand, 42, 50, 112, 145, 178
Nobel Prize, 183
Non-Articulation Model, 99
North America, 134, 161, 163, 167–168, 170–172, 179, 184, 186, 217
Norway, 67

Organization for Economic Co-operation and Development (OECD), 66–67, 76

Pacific Economic Cooperation Council (PECC), 106
Pacific Rim, 116, 118–119
Philippines, 10, 152
   De La Salle, 10
Poland, 128
Princeton University, 170
Privatization, 21, 151
Protectionist policies, 34
Publications, 13, 57–58, 67, 71, 75–77, 186–187, 203–204, 220–221
Purchasing Power Parity, 25

Quality assurance, 8–9, 50, 72, 84, 87, 100, 192, 198, 201, 205, 218
Quebec, 139

Rankings, 12, 24, 56–57, 132–133, 157–158, 169, 193, 215, 218–219, 221
Regional Centre of Expertise (RCE), 61
Regional integration model, 146–149, 154
Regionalization, 21, 107, 153
Rendell, Thomas, 185–186
Ritsumeikan Asia Pacific University, 196
Romania, 128, 139
Russia, 86, 128, 177, 184, 187

Salmi, Jamil, 193
Scandinavia, 128
Science Citation Indexed (SCI), 67, 75
Sciences Po, 125–139, 212, 215
   American detour, 132
   compulsory third-year-abroad, 131, 136–137
   faculty composition, 135
   international development model, 132–133
   international policy, 131
   language barrier, 133, 136–137
   satellite campuses, 132
Scot, Marie, 212, 215, 227
SEAMEO-RIHED, 62, 222
Seoul Imperial University, 147
Shanghai Jiao Tong (China), 157
Shared space, 53–63, 213–214, 216–217
Shin, J.C., 212–213, 216, 227
Singapore, 42, 108, 147–148, 150, 153, 157–172, 213–216, 225
   Asian modern discourse, 159
   Economic Development Board, 150
   Ministry of Education, 150, 172
   National University of Singapore (NUS), 153, 157–173, 214, 217
      CREATE campus, 169
      International Relations Office (IRO), 166
      Kent Ridge campus, 169
      nationality-based socializing, 172
      NUS Student Union, 165
      Office of Vice Provost (Student Life), 160, 165, 168, 169, 170–171
      reputation, 161–166
      Student Exchange Program (SEP), 166–167
      student experience, 163–165, 168–171
      University Town project, 169
   World Class University Program, 150
Sirat, Morshidi, 213, 216–217, 227
Soft disciplines, 67, 77
South America, 198, 217
South Korea, 42, 65, 115–117, 149, 152, 158, 205
Southeast Asia, 49, 53–63, 150, 163, 173, 213

Southeast Asian Ministers of Education, 53, 154
  Regional Centre for Higher Education and Development (SEAMEO-RIHED), 53
Soviet Union, 25, 176–177
Space-time compression, 28
Spain, 116, 139, 184, 203
Spellings' Commission on the Future of Higher Education, 89, 100
Sri Lanka, 42
Stone, Donald, 185–186
Study-abroad programs, 108, 110–111, 116
Sweden, 86, 139, 161, 184
Switzerland, 128, 138

Taipei Imperial University, 147
Taiwan, 11, 13, 42, 107–109, 115–116, 153, 158, 191–205, 212–213, 216
  Executive Yuan, 194
  five-year Fifty Billion program, 11, 193
  Fu Jen Catholic University, 191–205
    Management School, 192, 201–203
    Society of Jesus, 201
  General Scholastic Ability Test, 196
  Higher Education Evaluation and Accreditation Council of Taiwan (HEEACT), 198–199, 204
  The Impact of International Accreditation on Taiwan Higher Education Accredited Internationally, 204
  junior colleges, 191
  Ming Chuan University, 199
  Ministry of Education (MOE), 175, 179, 183, 187, 191–192, 194–198, 205
    Enhancing Global Competitiveness Plan, 194
    Study Abroad Loan Program, 194
    Taiwan Culture Research Program, 194
  National Chi Nan University, 195
  National Development Plan, 194
  National Sun Yat Shen University, 199
  number of international students, 195–196
  Shih Hsin University, 197
  Three Limits and Six No's, 197
  University Entrance Exam, 191
Test of English as a Foreign Language (TOEFL), 89
Test of English for International Communication (TOEIC), 89
Thailand, 13, 42, 116, 212
  Bangkok, 53, 62
Third Japan-China-Korea Committee for Promoting Exchange and Cooperation among Universities, 14, 222
Tiananmen Square protests, 41
Transborder exchange, 6–7
Trow, Martin, 24, 183
Turkey, 138

UN Declaration of Universal Human Rights, 32
UNESCO, 17, 60, 62, 143–145, 148, 154, 222
  Asia and Pacific Regional Bureau for Education, 154
United Kingdom, 42, 50, 66–68, 86, 107, 116–117, 121, 126, 143–144, 178, 184, 187, 192
  Thatcher administration, 152
United States, 10, 23–24, 28, 67–71, 73, 75, 77, 78, 86, 88–89, 91, 96, 99, 105, 107–108, 110–115, 118–119, 121, 135, 143, 149–150, 160, 176–178, 180, 184, 186–187, 192, 196, 198, 203, 205, 215

Accreditation Board for
    Engineering and Technology
    (ABET), 198
advance placement system, 99
Fulbright program, 121, 149, 180
Institute of International Education
    (IIE), 150
Universities of Cambridge, 128, 170
Universities of Oxford, 128, 146, 170
University Cooperation for
    Internationalization
    (UNICOFIN), 61
University Mobility in Asia and the
    Pacific (UMAP), 61, 148, 154
University of Bologna, 23, 146
University of California, 113,
    115, 118
University of California, Los Angeles
    (UCLA), 91, 112–121, 187,
    219–220
  College of Letters and Sciences, 113
  Dashew Center for International
    Students and Scholars,
    113–114, 116
  Education Abroad Program,
    114–117
  Extension Program, 115
  The Global Environment: a
    Multidisciplinary
    Perspective, 119
  Graduate Division, 118
  Higher Education Research
    Institute (HERI), 91
  International Education Office
    (IEO), 115
  International Student and Scholar
    Office, 117–118
  Politics, Society, and Urban Culture
    in East Asia, 119
  UCLA International Institute,
    113–114, 116
University of Chicago, 150
University of Malaya, 147
University of Rangoon, 147
University of South Carolina, 96
  First-Year Experience & Students in
    Transition, 96

Vietnam, 42–43, 62, 107, 196
Visa requirements, 11–12, 24, 41–42,
    46, 48–50, 54, 115, 184
Vocational education, 8–9, 44–45,
    48, 50

Wanhua, Ma, 228
Woodrow Wilson National Fellowship
    Foundation, 108
World Bank, 193
World-class universities, 9, 56, 76,
    121, 125, 182, 193
World risk society, 29, 31
World Trade Organization (TWO),
    151–152
World War I, 148
World War II, 23–24, 127–128,
    130, 146, 148, 212

Xing, Dr. Lee Tan, 203

Yale University, 135, 170, 214
Yamada, Reiko, 228
Yang, Dr. Ming-Hsien, 203

Ziguras, Christopher, 213, 216, 229

GPSR Compliance

The European Union's (EU) General Product Safety Regulation (GPSR) is a set of rules that requires consumer products to be safe and our obligations to ensure this.

If you have any concerns about our products, you can contact us on

ProductSafety@springernature.com

In case Publisher is established outside the EU, the EU authorized representative is:

Springer Nature Customer Service Center GmbH
Europaplatz 3
69115 Heidelberg, Germany

www.ingramcontent.com/pod-product-compliance
Lightning Source LLC
LaVergne TN
LVHW011814060526
838200LV00053B/3770